The Agile Innovation Playbook

How to Develop Products Better, Faster & Cheaper in the Modern Marketplace

Bill Harte & Ben Davies

The Agile Innovation Playbook

How to Develop Products Better, Faster & Cheaper in the Modern Marketplace

Bill Harte & Ben Davies

Dedication

To my steadfast parents, my uplifting wife, Karen, and my patient children, all of whom without their support this book would never be completed, never mind started. I hope this book inspires you to achieve things you never thought possible.

Bill Harte

To my wife Jeanie - without your unconditional love and support over the past 20 years nothing of any significance would have been possible, least of all this book. You are my rock. To my amazing children Stanley & Eleanor - it may be quite some time before you read this book, if you read it at all (!), but suffice to say you do and always will be a source of joy and inspiration to me.

Ben Davies

Acknowledgments

We would like to acknowledge a number of people in their support over the years.

Bill Harte:

Thanks to Paul Cornell, a colleague from Diageo, who back in 2006, showed the first example of a more agile innovation process where we successfully tested MVP in bars in Southwest London.

Also, thanks to Graeme Tulloch for pushing the initial ideas for Agile Innovation into more practical steps and helped form the foundations of Agile Innovation in their infancy.

Thanks to Jake Trubridge, Gareth Budd, Darren Foley, Sam Matthewson, and Matt Woodhams for helping refine the Agile Innovation process over countless coffees, chats, and zoom calls.

Special thanks to Ian McCabe for his support in challenging times in championing the Agile Innovation process.

A massive thank you to both Laura Sheard and Hugh Pile for their editing, helping in taking meandering words and turning into more considered and more coherent writing.

Ben Davies:

Massive thanks to Mark Fielding at Vypr for being a constant advocate of Agile over all the years we've worked together. And to Tasmin Sibbald at Vypr for really professionalising and driving forwards the Agile Innovation vision in her uniquely determined & energised way.

A huge thanks to April Preston - without the belief of someone of her standing in the industry I'm not sure we would have had the confidence to get to where we've got to today. She's become a great friend as well as a sounding board, advisor and advocate over the years.

And thank you to Neil Nugent for the being the first person in the industry of significant reputation to really believe in what I was trying to do in those early days of Vypr.

Contents

Foreword from April Preston
Food Product Director Marks & Spencer PLC

I first met Ben when I was Director of Insight & Innovation at 2 Sisters Food Group back in 2014, and was immediately impressed by his vision and drive to effect change in this field. I knew nothing about Agile Innovation at that time nor was I very savvy about the accelerating digital world, but I was curious to learn. Ben's background, rooted in retail, meant that he was able to not only explain in words I understood, but also provide an extremely practical and grounded approach in an area that to me previously had felt overly theoretical. I met Bill some years later and was struck by what a brilliant team they made together, with fantastically complimentary but diverse experience and personalities that just worked. Privately, I also loved the fact that they were 'Bill and Ben', but couldn't be more different from the originals if they tried!

When Ben told me he was publishing this book it hit me that it was a brilliant time for this. In my thirty-year career I have never seen customer attitudes, needs and behaviours change so rapidly as they have through Covid-19 and lockdown. Never before have we needed to innovate with more pace and keep our fingers more firmly on the pulse of what customers are doing and thinking. There are more new opportunities for problem-solving with great innovation than ever before. Combined with the fact that we are all tightly controlling our costs, none of us can afford to launch products that fail to provide a good return.

I've spent many years in the food world and always in the fields of insight and innovation. The success rate of new product launches has barely budged in this time, both within the industry and as regards my own personal track record. Does that mean I am no good at my job? Surely I must have picked up some experience along the way? No I think it is more because of the way we do innovation. The old adage that if you do what you have always done you will get what you have always had has never rung truer. Even before Covid-19 there was a need to change the way we work, and for me Agile Innovation offers a great new direction.

When Ben asked me to write this foreword, I was a little hesitant. Did I really want to share the knowledge I had of this when it was giving me a competitive advantage? But I feel passionately that the industry needs to change to ensure less waste in terms of time, costs and resources. Agile innovation can massively help with this, but you will always need good people who have great gut feel and business nous; that, combined with Agile Innovation thinking, can help transform our industry.

Ben and Bill can take you through what Agile Innovation is and what it has the power to achieve much more eloquently than I ever could, and I truly encourage you to read this book. For me, we need greater pace, objectivity, data and the customer deeply ingrained in the process if we are to become more successful in the innovation world. This will save time and money, and it is precisely this that Agile Innovation will help you to achieve.

Retailers, manufacturers, brands agencies and even the hospitality industry, which we know more than anyone needs to reinvent itself in this challenging time, will benefit from all this book has to offer, and I would recommend it to anyone in the food world who wants to drive growth through new products, concepts, propositions and inventions!

Be curious, be open and seek to drive change for the better of our whole industry … This book is not the silver bullet, but could well be the best gun you ever buy. Just don't forget that you will always need great people to fire it!

INTRODUCTION

From the authors

Bill on Ben

When I first heard of Ben from a friend, Sam Matthewson, I was furious. He had independently taken one of my amazing ideas that I had only ever dreamt of and never told anyone about and made it happen with VYPR. We met over a coffee in Manchester for possibly the easiest sales pitch of Ben's life. From that moment on, we've been applying the principles of The Lean Startup and pushing ourselves to find out more about innovation and how to make innovation work better in consumer packaged goods (CPG). We've partnered together on working with clients and large multiple grocers, as well as sparking off each other to come up with simple and elegant solutions to previously complex and expensive research methodologies. For me, Ben has been the biggest supporter of the Agile Innovation mindset, of moving away from 'make then sell' to 'sell then make'. He has encouraged me to challenge the norms of innovation and of myself, and continually developed his own proposition to fit the needs of his clients.

Bill on Bill

Innovation has been in my blood working in consumer goods manufacturers since 1995. I've found innovation to be a rollercoaster, with lots of highs and a fair few lows. My first true innovation job was in 2003, and subsequently I've generated millions of pounds in new products for large multinationals such as Diageo and Muller, as well as a multitude of startups. Throughout my working life in innovation, I have an innovation failure rate that is well below the fast-moving consumer goods (FMCG) average, and in the last five years, my innovation failure rate has been zero percent. In 2010, after working in innovation in Japan for Diageo, I realised that innovation in CPG as a process was failing – irrespective of the size of the company or the budget available, innovation was always more likely to fail. Thus, I started on a journey to find a better way to innovate, researching and copying various different elements from other industries, culminating in a unique Agile Innovation approach that has the consumer absolutely at the heart of innovation. Based on my experience over the last 17 years, I want to demonstrate how our approach can work whether you have an innovation budget of millions or literally a few hundred pounds. I want to show you how innovation can still have all of the thrills of the rollercoaster with none of the current ills.

Ben on Bill

Bill and I first encountered each other back in 2014, Bill as a prospective customer of my technology company, and we played 'Agile' and 'Lean' bingo in our first conversation over hipster coffee in the Northern Quarter in Manchester. It was the first time I'd met anyone else who had the same levels of enthusiasm and optimism about changing the world of product development within consumer goods through technology and data. Bill began to use our technology platform in genuinely leading-edge ways, helping to test and refine many of the principles that you will encounter in this book. Over the years we have continued to develop our thinking around Agile Innovation and its application within Consumer Packaged Goods (CPG), working together on numerous projects culminating in the co-creation of this book you are reading now. Trying to build a movement within what can be quite a traditional sector is so much more achievable when you have a co-conspirator, and Bill is firmly that guy. His unwavering belief in what we are doing continues to inspire and energise me to carry on spreading the word alongside him.

Ben on Ben

Prior to meeting Bill, my corporate career was a history of retail buying littered with making unreasonable, untested demands of suppliers to invest in new production kit or packaging formats that ended up in sizeable losses when the products hit the shelf. I began to see the light when I got interested in the technology sector, exploring how the application of technology and crowdsourcing could help validate all these massive assumptions being made every day by the whole CPG sector. Seven years ago I founded a technology company called Vypr as a way to generate the consumer testing data required, wanting to build a company that allowed the CPG sector to innovate in the same way as the technology sector does. Bill and I continue to bang the drum for Agile Innovation, rock solid in our belief that it will change the way that our industry develops and launches new products.

Why we needed to write an innovation book

We both joked with each other for years that we should write a book, baulking at the idea of becoming such a thing as a 'Thought Leader'. We had calls from companies asking us to explain what we were doing. We had 'round table' discussions with those in the industry to highlight the inefficiencies of the current innovation process and on the need for a new innovation solution. We presented to industry peers on our case studies and our thoughts, with more and more requests to come and talk to senior teams about the need to change the innovation process. The joke about writing a book slowly became a genuine need as more people were asking more about it. Writing a book together encapsulated our mission to resolve the frustrations of working day in and day out with innovation, and make innovation a better engine for growth for retailers and for manufacturers.

FMCG innovation – in particular, food & drink innovation – has largely been in line with business school models of innovation over the last 40 years, namely the gate stage process (Waterfall), delivering a perception of steady innovation growth year after year, albeit single digit percentage growth. However, innovation has been promising double digit percentage year on year growth for decades, and consistently failed to deliver its own expectations because of the high innovation failure rate. Even the relatively limited innovation successes come at a high cost both in absolute terms (we estimate for every successful product it requires an innovation investment of £41m in a traditional waterfall approach). In the last 10 or so years, technology companies have demonstrated a new way to innovate products that allows companies to invest more into innovation and be more confident in the results. However, FMCG, and in particular food & drink, has been slow to pick up on the Agile Innovation trend. Given our experience in both food & drink and technology, we can demonstrate how Agile Innovation can transform the consumer products industry into a more dependable engine for growth, which is cheaper, faster and better than the old Waterfall approach.

The state of innovation, by any reasonable metric, is more of a failure than it is a success, albeit the limited successes pay handsomely for the failures. What causes innovation in FMCG to be in a high state of failure is systemic and not down to any one thing. Whether it's a failure of launching the wrong product to the wrong consumers at the wrong time with the wrong marketing activation support. Or a failure of management to understand what drives successful new products and to support structures that enhance autonomy and authority to develop winning innovation. Or a failure of innovators to not look for a different way of doing things other than what they've been taught for the last 40 years. Or a failure of consultants to not advocate for innovating innovation with a clear pathway that drives things forward. Or a failure of self-interested agencies to not challenge clients and their runaway flights of fallacy that support, perhaps even enable, the feebleness of innovation execution. The way we innovate is broken, and we can't tinker with the current way to make it any better. We need a new way to innovate.

There is little to cheer about from the sidelines when it comes to innovation, other than that this broken down, failing discipline still manages to deliver growth for business with a fairly respectable return on investment of 185%.[1]

To coin a phrase, failure is no longer an option for innovation: significant pressure is being applied to costs, and development time is being squeezed in order to generate faster profits. For more than 12 years we have been looking for a new way to innovate, a way to safely generate more growth and profit from innovation by being clearer on what works and what doesn't work. We tested, again and again, different approaches from different disciplines and industries, using our own money and skills, to prove what works. We now want to bring this to you as part of our mission to eradicate innovation failure.

We outline the case for innovation in and of itself; the costs of innovation; the reasons innovation fails; and then explore how to apply Agile Innovation in a way that offers clear management practices through benchmarking and applied scientific method to test all the decisions in the process.

We are heavily influenced by approaches and thinking in other sectors outside of CPG and FMCG, including Eric Ries's *The Lean Startup* as well as other works covering entrepreneurialism such as SSRN's *Value Lab: A Tool for Entrepreneurial Strategy*. We have a full list of books, papers and reports for further reading at the end of this book for those who wish to explore more.

The big innovation picture
The biggest challenge facing businesses, whether it is a startup or an established company, is working out how to add value – that is to say how to make money. Even well-established brands constantly have to re-evaluate their business model to better understand how they can add value. In our experience, that hypothesis of the business' value is set by the senior leadership team, perhaps solely the

---

1 Internal calculation, see Chapter 2

founder or owner of the business. When value hypotheses are expressed by senior leadership, they are rarely communicated as a 'hypothesis' or even a 'belief', but rather phrased as an absolute certainty with high degrees of confidence and authority. The confidence is summed up in a declaration such as 'Consumers want healthy milkshakes' or 'Consumers want healthy rice'.

But these absolutes often rely on the direct experience of the individual proposing the approach, otherwise known as 'a sample of one'. And as we can see from the failure rates of innovation, a sample of one isn't big enough. We recently – in the height of Covid-19 – had a senior leader in a client's business brilliantly demonstrate the 'sample of one' by expressing to his team that everyone was buying into a new category that was adjacent to the products this company sold. He confidently predicted that the growth in this aligned category during Covid-19 presented an opportunity for their business to pivot into this adjacent category, moving away from their traditional heartland upon which their entire business model rested. The senior leader spoke with confidence and gave examples of how they and their friends and family had bought into this particular aligned category during Covid-19, and that therefore it was a great opportunity. Everyone in the organisation took this at face value with energy and resources now focused on deploying activity towards this new category opportunity, all of it based entirely on the hearsay of the senior leader's friends' claimed behaviour. However, even a cursory glance at Google Trends[2] (which acts as a proxy for consumer penetration, as it measures the relative change in what people are searching for on Google) indicated that the number of searches for this new category hadn't changed in any significant manner in the last five years. It was a well-intentioned observation of a contrarian view of the current market in a time of turmoil to give direction to a business, but a colossal misstep from senior leadership in failing to understand the wider world – and more importantly a misunderstanding of the impact their observations and statements have in an organisation. It was cheap talk, underwritten by blind authority in the organisation, that cost the company large chunks of cash and wasted time.

Theory of value
So how should a company work out how to add value? Research from a study by the Universities of Oxford, Bocconi and Utah[3] shows that having a detailed theory which can be proven one way or another is the most efficient and effective way of discovering and exploiting value for an organisation or entrepreneur. Provocative or contrarian views of behaviour are not enough; having a way to prove those views is absolutely necessary, which requires a dose of humility. A leader should

---

2 https://trends.google.com/trends/?geo=GB
3 https://papers.ssrn.com/sol3/papers.cfm?abstract_id=3684428

be able to prove that there is a specific problem, and then to prove that a specific solution provides the best way of solving this issue, in order to ensure the business provides value. This is borne out in our experience of many businesses – both our own and our clients'.

Presenting an opinion as a theory that needs to be proven overcomes any bias in an organisation for blind obedience to the senior leadership team. It may dent the ego of the senior leadership, who want things done at their own behest, but it avoids lengthy and expensive forays into useless notions while at the same time building a more robust culture of diverse opinions and critical thinking.

Framing an opinion as a hypothesis that needs to be proven helps firstly to signal to your colleagues that this is not an order or an edict, but rather a thought. When it is a hypothesis, it shows that it needs to be proven, and the power comes not from posing the hypothesis but in proving the hypothesis. Once the hypothesis is proven, it then unlocks the potential of the opportunity. The opportunity does not exist until the hypothesis is proven, but posing the opportunity as a hypothesis offers an incentive to test it.

In 2019, we had a beverage client passionately tell us they had engaged an insight agency to inform them of the latest trends in non-alcoholic drinks, and were proud to share this agency's work to us to help develop new products. The trends seemed to highlight things that had been in style magazines or presented by influencers on Instagram, and did so in a compelling and stylish way – everything from activated charcoal and turmeric through to insect protein such as cockroaches(!). Upon closer inspection, however, we noticed that there didn't seem to be any hard data to back up the agency's insight or trends; we challenged the clients as to whether these 'trends' were relevant in their category, and suggested a hypothesis that these were less motivating to consumers than existing products in the category. We asked 500 consumers whether they would buy the product 'with added turmeric' over the original, and more than double said they would rather buy the existing product than the product with added turmeric. The insect superfood trend performed even worse, with less than a fifth of people who would normally buy the existing product saying they would buy the product with added insect protein. Activated charcoal was no more appealing than turmeric, although it did have a better result when we described the charcoal as a filter for the product; nonetheless it was still significantly less appealing than the current product.

The point of this example is to show that there was no guiding theory behind these trend insights. We instead came up with a theory that trend reports like these are fanciful at best and deliberately misguided at worst, and we could test our hypothesis by asking consumers whether or not they would buy a product that contained the specific 'trendy' ingredient or the product claim. We have yet to find an example from the deluge of annual insight reports in over a dozen categories that stands up to a benchmark that would make them sustainable. We even looked at trend reports from five and ten years ago in case the trends took time to enter the mainstream, but again despite asking in dozens of categories, no trends came back as being sustainable in the mainstream mass market, and therefore would in all likelihood fail if launched.

Not only has our theory of 'snake oil' trend reports been proven through research; it is also borne out in real life, as only one (seaweed) of the products from the Independent's[4] trend report of five years ago is still on shelves in your local supermarket. There were plenty of launches of products that sought to capitalise on trends, such as Birch Water, Baobab fruit, and Freekeh (all of which were touted as the big trend of 2015!), but none of these are available in Tesco today.

Understanding what is trending is necessary, however we would argue there is a need to be sceptical of these trends, and to test the trend transferring into into the mainstream on a regular and ongoing basis, rather than blindly assuming an view from a biased opinion maker. What our research highlights is that it is imperative for organisations to develop their own theories about their consumers, shoppers and customers, and to then set out a robust way to test the theory. It is not about blindly accepting the prevailing wisdom from 'trend experts' or even from buyers or NPD experts. The risk of following any and all trends are that finite innovation resources are focused on starting points that are significantly flawed. However, by quickly proving or disproving a "trend" theory, businesses can grow adeptly at reduced risk of failure and with reduced cost, and focus on what will work. That growth is called Agile Innovation, and we set out in this book how to bring Agile Innovation into your organisation.

Innovating innovation

This book represents not only our theory for the future of innovation in CPG, but also the implementation of Agile Innovation, including the resources you will need and how to go about it.

Our first sections explore a range of common beliefs in CPG innovation, in particular that innovation drives growth through consumer engagement and that the costs of innovation are high, as well as the reasons innovation fails.

---

4   https://www.independent.co.uk/life-style/food-and-drink/features/
    tastiest-food-trends-2015-9953124.html

We outline our contrarian beliefs that despite innovation delivering growth, innovation processes in FMCG are largely broken, failing shareholders, employees and consumers. We believe that marketing in general, and innovation in particular, is open to deliberate or well-intended maleficence, as it has, until now, been impossible to prove that any innovation beliefs, opinions or thoughts are actually wrong. Innovation, because of its high failure rate, is open to people looking for a solution, and people pushing a solution. And we, as authors, could be seen as no different in pushing our theory of innovating innovation.

However, we are different. We are willing to prove our thoughts, beliefs and assumptions are accurate and consistently applicable We stand behind our hypothesis with facts and consumer research to show that the hypothesis is correct, and that our theory of innovation explains the current situation and future opportunities in innovation.

The core problem for the current state of innovation in FMCG is that too much is assumed, and not enough is checked. We assume our insights to be true, but how often do we check whether our insights are more motivating than other insights or other proven beliefs? We have seen a rise in the biasing of data through advanced storytelling techniques, selective data interpretations, and impressive infographics, all designed to persuade and extinguish any critical thought.

One sub-problem with innovation is that organisations are too often programmed to respect high authoritarian figures, and default to accepting their opinions, irrespective of the facts. This lack of autonomy and accountability leads organisations down the rabbit hole with no clear sense of direction, and further entrenches the lack of assumption checking, as assumption checking is tantamount to challenging the powers that be in an organisation, people that may be intimidating to others in the business. Another sub-problem in CPG has been the time and cost of checking assumptions. Current mMarket research has been the standard approach for decades, and takes tens of thousands of pounds and months to get results.

All of this leads us to our theory of CPG innovation – that if we can prove every assumption is more motivating than incumbent products, then failure can be eliminated, and growth for the company, the people and the shareholders can endure.

To make this work we need a method of testing assumptions that is relatively quick, rigorous and cheap. We need senior management in organisations to be humble with their ideas, to ensure the company doesn't go down the wrong path. Senior management need to restructure their innovation teams to be more autonomous and have more authority.

Perversely what works for FMCG innovation are the governance structures that ensure products, and in particular food products, are still safe to use and consume. We say perversely as governance is one of those things that can often be seen as a driver for 'zero out of ten' innovation, and it is often governance that senior leaders in the organisation try to bypass to speed up projects. Governance is needed to ensure that limited investment in innovation is not squandered on the wrong projects or that investment is made at the wrong phase of product development, and that all inherent quality & safety standards have been met, especially in food and drink. The current methodologies for governance, especially food and drink safety, would in our view, not need to be changed or amended.

What also works is having great people working on innovation. We would go further in fact and say that the best people in your organisation should be working on innovation, as it is the most challenging and complex area of your business. Every product launch is, in many ways, relaunching your business again and again.

The final thing that works is understanding human behaviour, and applying that understanding of human behaviour into driving value for the company, whether that be in insight, product development or marketing communications.

Our *Agile Innovation Playbook* is a book written to be used in real life and adapted to your organisation. We have deliberately left space in the margins for your notes, thoughts and actions, and there are resources available to download and use on our website (www.agileinnovationplaybook.uk). Most importantly, this book will help you and your business to not only accelerate innovation, but also multiply growth from innovation.

Setting the scene: Common innovation terms
Throughout the book, we refer to some common terms and popular innovation models. Before we go into the detail of Agile Innovation, it makes sense to define these terms and models to avoid any confusion, and so that we don't distract from the case for Agile.

Consumer packaged goods (CPG) and fast-moving consumer goods (FMCG)
The scope of our book is innovation in the consumer packaged goods (CPG) world, which encompasses many sub-segments such as fast-moving consumer goods (FMCG) or food & drink. CPG covers anything that is manufactured and presented to consumers in a retail channel, whether that retail channel is a bricks and mortar shop, an e-commerce retailer such as Amazon, or a direct-to-consumer e-commerce site where the manufacturer sells their own products.

Consumer, customer or shopper

Throughout the book we refer to consumers, customers and shoppers. This may be confusing, as there is a difference between retailers' use of these terms and how manufacturers and brand owners use them. In this book, we have taken the view of brand owners and manufacturers. To clarify, this means that consumers are the end users of the product, shoppers are the people who buy the product from the retailer, and customers are the retailers. The shopper and the consumer may be the same person, but this is not always the case. For example, with baby food the shopper is never the consumer (excluding the jar of apple baby food used for a roast pork dinner in an emergency!). An example where the shopper is also the consumer would be buying a can of Diet Coke from the convenience store to drink at lunchtime. A distributor may be involved, and they act as an intermediary between the retailer and the brand owner or manufacturer. The distributor may be formal distributor or an agent acting on behalf of the brand owner for fee, or a wholesaler who resells products to retailers to make a profit from the reselling. In short, the consumer consumes the product that the shopper buys from the customer of the manufacturer / brand owner.

Range review

A process run by a retailer to define what products it stocks, which products it no longer stocks, and which products it will introduce into its stocks. Range reviews typically have different numbers of products dependent upon the types of stores in the retailers' estate. The range review is the main time where new products are introduced to the shopper, and are an important timing for manufacturers to plan their launch. Range reviews are also points in time where products previously introduced as new may no longer be considered new and may not continue to be stocked by the retailer, either in totality or in the number of stores previously stocked. Range reviews represent both an opportunity and a threat for manufacturers and need to be considered both in terms of timings and also for the metrics being used by the retailer to ensure the new products listed can survive for as long as possible.

Innovation

Innovation means different things to different people. There are arguments for innovation to only mean substantially new products which have never been seen before. There are other views which say that even if a product changes slightly, perhaps only a recipe change or a design change, then it constitutes a new product, and is therefore innovation. Our definition of innovation in this book is anything that is intentionally developed to generate profitable growth, and covers everything from breakthrough innovation to product extensions, flavour additions, pack size changes, and product engineering to reduce costs.

Innovation success

Innovation success is again another thorny subject, as different companies or retailers have different definitions of success. Some may think that it is successful if the innovation adds value to their existing portfolio. Some may view it as a success only if it pays back more than it cost to develop. Others might think it is successful if it gains a listing in the first place. Throughout our book, we define successful innovation as being innovation that at least lasts for one year in market, and we would want to push that out to three years. One year assumes that the innovation has survived at least one range review, thus proving that it has some form of sales base. However, given that more than 60%[5] of innovation that survives the first year will not survive beyond the second, it is more realistic to use a three-year timeframe to measure long-term innovation success.

Innovation failure

There is consensus amongst academics, market researchers, innovation commentators, and industry practitioners that innovation fails more than it succeeds. However, it is also fair to say that the level of failure differs depending upon the sources. The range we have found varies from 95%[6] to 76%. To illustrate the challenge in finding a hard data point of innovation failure, AC Nielsen state innovation failure rates of 85%[7] and 80%[8]. IRI state that up to "80% of innovation fails in some way"[9]. We asked AC Nielsen and IRI to provide a robust failure rate for this book, but none was forthcoming from either source. This makes it challenging to have an established, empirically-based absolute data point for innovation failure. Based on the data we can find, we would expect a failure rate of 90% to be approximate across the entire CPG landscape. We have used a figure of 90% in the book to allow for simplicity of communication and calculation of costs and opportunities. However, we would caution the reader to independently investigate their own category's failure rate as measured by EPOS or Panel data provider to have a more robust model for their own individual business opportunity for decreasing the innovation failure rate.

Insight

Insight is defined as a penetrating discovery about consumer behaviour that unlocks

---

5   https://www.nielsen.com/uk/en/press-releases/2014/nielsen-cracks-the-dna-of-breakthrough-innovation-success-following-study-of-12000-product-launches-across-europe

6   https://www.inc.com/marc-emmer/95-percent-of-new-products-fail-here-are-6-steps-to-make-sure-yours-dont.html

7   https://www.nielsen.com/us/en/insights/article/2014/how-to-flip-85-misses-to85-hits-lessons-from-the-nielsen-breakthrough-innovation-project/

8   https://www.nielsen.com/eu/en/insights/article/2018/three-common-causes-innovation-failure/

9   https://www.iriworldwide.com/en-gb/solutions/market-performance-and-strategy/innovation

profitable growth. Insight can come from multiple sources, but most often consumer understanding. Insight is often used to label up data, or to emphasise a point of view. Insight is often offered as term for an emotionally engaging statement, rather than a validated and proven discovery that demonstrably grows profit. Insight needs to be more than a pithy statement about consumers' needs, wants, and beliefs; it needs to be proven that the need, want, and belief not only exists, but is motivating enough to drive profitable growth

Existing product development (EPD)

Existing product development (EPD) is where new elements are added to an existing product. It is the classic 'new recipe' or 'new formula'. Some businesses call this 'renovation'. EPD makes up the majority of all innovation launched, accounting for 70% of all innovation.[10] EPD typically is a function of marketing to defend market share, looking to add product features that other competitors have and negate their advantage. EPD takes up the majority of manufacturers' resources, yet delivers the least incremental profit margin of all innovation. EPD is perceived as being low risk, as the capability to update the product already exists in the organisation, or is easy to bring into the organisation, to update the product.

New product development (NPD)

New product development (NPD) for us is the development of a new product in its entirety but within existing manufacturing capabilities (although those existing manufacturing capabilities may not be within the control of the company developing the NPD). A classic example of NPD would be Fairy Liquid moving into dishwasher tablets. Other examples would include Mars ice creams and Mars milkshakes, expansions from the traditional Mars confectionery bar. NPD is designed to gain market share by expanding into new categories and/ or attracting new shoppers. NPD is generally highly accretive, as it is driving incremental purchases, but requires high investment, especially in insight to discover opportunities for brands.

Breakthrough innovation

Breakthrough innovation relates to wholly novel products, starting a category that previously never existed. The printing press, semi-conductors, vaccination, automobiles, telephones, airplanes, trains, flushing toilets, mobile phones, compasses, fax machines, to name a few, were all were all breakthrough innovations when they were launched. Breakthrough innovations are distinctively highly incremental profit generators yet highly expensive as they require significant development.

---

10 Estimate based on our experience

Waterfall innovation

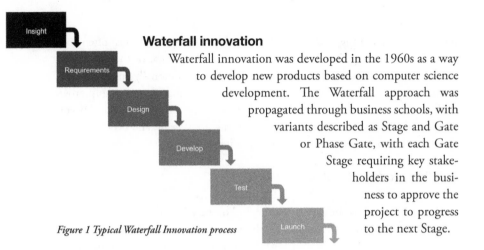

Waterfall innovation was developed in the 1960s as a way to develop new products based on computer science development. The Waterfall approach was propagated through business schools, with variants described as Stage and Gate or Phase Gate, with each Gate Stage requiring key stakeholders in the business to approve the project to progress to the next Stage.

Figure 1 Typical Waterfall Innovation process

Waterfall innovation is so named because the work is done in sequence, with the resulting project plan looking like a series of waterfalls. These programmes work well on developing defined technology, as the project can only progress once one element has been built, ensuring that dependencies are built on solid elements. It also reduces risk, so that problems are identified at earlier stages of development. The governance that the waterfall approach ensures is a strength of the process, offering clear investment decision points, and ensuring that development and therefore middle-class investment does not proceed until the completion of preceding functions. The governance also ensures there is sufficient documentation to support the progress of the development, as well as ensuring that all the steps taken are noted, thus reducing the risk of the overall project should any of the innovation team members change. Classically, the shopper or consumer is only engaged at the end of the process when the new product is shipped and launched. There might be some market research with shoppers or consumers at an early stage, but it is frequently limited in scope and scale.

Waterfall is exceptionally poor at building in consumers' expectations and desires into product innovation, as the consumer is left until the very end before they can have a say. Consumer research and co-development programmes have tried to overcome the challenges of consumers' not being involved in the process, but the amount of research or co-development that takes place has always been veneer-thin.

Minimum Viable Product (MVP)

Eric Ries coined the term Minimum Viable Product (MVP) in his book *The Lean Startup*. A MVP is an early product that is at its' most early form. It is most likely to be terrible in it's first instance, as it is bereft of features. But by launching an MVP, it allows for testing of the product's biggest assumption (i.e. will it sell) in a behavioural contex (i.e. do people use it and how do people use it). Further iterations of the MVP are developed and tested using the *Build Measure Learn Loop*, which allows for the features that are most valuable to be added through the *Pivot or Persevere* process. We've used real products as MVPs (e.g. relabelled existing wine bottles – see Chapter 7) or even things like Google AdWords as MVPs or visual product concepts as MVPs. What you use as an MVP is dependent upon what you want to achieve and the level of risk you want to take – the more you spend on developing the product before you test it, the more you risk losing.

Pivot or persevere

A common term in Eric Ries' *The Lean Startup*, pivot means to move away from a previously held assumption, and based on the learnings from the test of that previously held assumption, develop a different hypothesis to test. Persevere on the other hand is the positive test of an assumption that allows you to progress onto testing the next level of assumptions about the innovation.

Build Measure Learn loop

Again a concept presented by Eric Ries in his book *The Lean Startup*, the Build Measure Learn Loop is the quintessential process for Agile where a leap of faith product is built (aka *Minimum Viable Product*), that is then tested and measured with real consumers in a real world environment. Using the the metrics from the test, we learn whether or not that particular product's feature is viable and motivating for consumers. We then *Pivot or Persevere,* and build a product feature, which starts the feedback loop again.

Category Average Cash Unit Rate of Sale

Category Average Cash Unit Rate of Sale (CACUROS) is the amount of money the average product in a given category sells per week per store that it is distributed in. It is a readily available data point from EPOS data providers such as AC Nielsen or IRI, although they may name it slightly differently. It is the key component in benchmarking for Agile Innovation.

Figure 2 Build Measure Learn loop

Section one –

The Innovation Landscape

Chapter 1 – Why innovate?

Innovation for decades has helped businesses grow, whether they be small businesses launching their first product that propels them into greater significance and out of the incubation phase, or big companies growing through sequential new products that build upon their existing offering both in terms of features and also hopefully in terms of income.

Irrespective of their size, most companies appreciate that they have to continually develop their offering, adding more features or looking for new ways to reduce cost. Governments incentivise companies through research and development (R&D)[11] grants to invest in innovation both in terms of developing their innovation capability and incentivising the adoption of new technology to boost performance. Governments incentivise R&D as they know it grows businesses and therefore the economy.

But how can innovation help and support growth?
Innovation and growth are inextricably linked. If you want growth, you must innovate. Innovation seeks to improve the effectiveness and efficiency of an operation by using novel approaches. In time, even the most successful products and business models will atrophy as the market – and the competition – moves on. The ability to innovate, experiment and evolve is, therefore, an essential characteristic of the companies that are most likely to survive and thrive for years to come,

---

11 https://www.ons.gov.uk/economy/governmentpublicsectorandtaxes/
researchanddevelopmentexpenditure/bulletins/

ers and markets adapt to competitive pressure.

n is more than just product innovation or developing new products;
being innovative across several functions and at every level. Innovative
marketing campaigns to communicate better the product's features and benefits.
Innovative sales channels to better access shoppers and consumers. Innovative
manufacturing solutions to make existing products more straightforward and
quicker to deliver. Innovative finance tools to allocate resources more efficiently
and timely. All of this facilitates growth.

Innovation is not ethereal or an abstract concern; it delivers results for companies
around the world. For example, in the UK grocery market, innovation accounts
for 7% of the average category turnover according to AC Nielsen.[12] Without
innovation in FMCG, there would barely be any growth, as consumers would
be resigned to accept the current offerings. 97% of all growth in FMCG categories comes from innovation.[13] And arguably even 97% does not show the whole
picture of the value of innovation, as this only includes product innovation and
does not concern itself with marketing, manufacturing or finance innovation. A
97% growth figure from innovation is a staggering amount of value generated,
and highlights the need to have innovation as a key capability in any business, but
especially FMCG organisations. It also highlights how poor sales drivers other
than innovation are in generating growth.

The FMCG industry is renowned for developing major brands, with 23 of the
top 100 global brands coming from this sector.[14] FMCG companies constantly
innovate, building bigger and bigger brands, and generating greater shareholder
returns. So much so, in fact, the FMCG industry for the last 45 years has had the
second highest total shareholder returns of any industry.[15] Basically, innovation
has driven enough growth for CPG brands to ensure they are big global megabrands, and shareholders are happy with that level of growth, so there has been no
pressing need for the process of developing innovation to be changed.

---

12 AC Nielsen 2018 Market Report
13 https://www.nielsen.com/uk/en/insights/article/2019/announcing-the-top-25-breakthrough-
    innovations/
14 https://www.mckinsey.com/industries/consumer-packaged-goods/our-insights/the-new-
    model-for-consumer-goods
15 https://www.mckinsey.com/industries/consumer-packaged-goods/our-insights/the-new-
    model-for-consumer-goods

Lego case study

The ubiquitous children's toy company, Lego, is a great example of adapting innovation to change a business' fortunes. Despite strong early growth, The Lego Group's success started to plateau in the 1990s, as lower cost competition such as Megabloks entered the market, pushing down prices and volumes, thus reducing Lego's margin. Margins were further squeezed by manufacturing complexity and the high cost of a Danish operating base. Lego also expanded it's innovation beyond it's core range and diversified into theme parks, and had invested in hiring creative and diverse staff. It had followed all the rules on innovation, and double down on innovation as future growth driver. But the investment was not focussed behind a clear goal. The Lego Group slid into irrelevance with its core consumer base as their innovation failed, and it spent a fortune in doing so. Ultimately, Lego made a loss of $240m in 2003.

The company needed to change.

It changed CEO, away from the traditionally family-led business. It clarified it's goal to be the best company for family products. It changed the strategy of diversification by selling theme parks. Lego reinvented a better way to innovate by being more consumer centric with contributions from all parts of the business, and introduced a range of innovations such as Lego Factory, which was a form of co-creation with users. With the Future Lab, innovation culture was allowed to flourish with success and failure against the company's goal. Lego's broadening of innovation led them to expand its user base from solely young boys into young girls with Lego Friends, and also adults with their Architecture range. Lego started to work with third parties in open partnership, from videogames like Minecraft to movie franchises, including Star Wars, Jurassic Park, Marvel and National Geographic. But it did so in a more risk-averse way, keen to avoid the troubled waters of doing too much innovation. All innovation, no matter where the idea originated, had to prove it would work towards the company's goal.

Emboldened by their success, Lego began innovating into new sectors such as new media, with apps, games and movies such as their game Lego Brawls. Having an innovation focus as part of its business model means that Lego has made a profit of over €1billion every year for the last five years.

Lego is a great example of how a different mindset to innovation can dramatically change the fortunes of a business - by making it more consumer centric combined with a powerful innovation culture and focused on a long-term sustainable goal.

The above case study highlights the opportunities for innovative businesses, especially those that can build a sustainable culture of innovation against a clear goal, and have the ability to test all innovation against what consumers actually want to buy. But what about the opportunity cost of not doing innovation?

Let's look at organisations that have failed to have a sustainable culture of repeatable innovation, perhaps resting on their laurels, feeling they have climbed to the summit of their respective category. For whatever reason, they fail at large-scale innovation. They excel at tinkering around the edges of their products and brands, perhaps with brand extensions, flavour extensions or pack size changes – classic EPD. Growth is hard to come by organically, and subsequently activities that show a more promising return on investment than innovation, such as price promotions, are selected.

However, the drivers of category growth are the organisations that don't rest on their laurels and decide to rethink their culture of innovation. A study by Nielsen in the US found that the 25 largest food & drink brands only accounted for 3% of the growth of their combined categories.[16] 97% of the increase in their categories came from smaller, nimbler brands. In other words, out of the $35bn in sales from new growth in 2019, only $1bn came from those top 25 brands – the rest came from startups or smaller brands.

Big companies like those in the Nielsen US study are being outmanoeuvred across several different areas despite having deeper pockets, more people and a wealth of data. The opportunity cost of not applying a long-term sustainable culture of innovation is effectively no growth, and therefore a loss of market share.

Because innovation has begun to yield such low returns, many of those big brands adopt behaviours designed to mitigate the risk of innovation failure. They have adopted a practise of launching safe, 'iterative' products instead of pushing for bold game-changing innovations. The game-changers currently come from start-ups, the outsiders who have been prepared to think differently and embrace risk.

From a highly simplistic point of view, there are incentives for having a long-term sustainable innovation culture – as it creates growth – and there are also penalties for not implementing the long-term sustainable innovation culture, i.e. a loss of market share.

---

16 https://www.cbinsights.com/research/circleup-guest-post-product-launch-fallacy-big-cpgs/

But how does innovation help drive growth in the FMCG sector?

Product lifecycle

Retailers and distributors just like manufacturers want year-on-year growth, and most are ambivalent as to how they achieve that growth, whether it is through existing or new brands. Over the lifecycle of a product, distributors and retailers all seek to squeeze the manufacturers' share of the value pool further and further. Manufacturers that have sufficient brand strength are able to deflect the demands of distributors and retailers, thus maintaining their share of the value pool, either by price increases or by resolutely holding to terms of trade.

Innovation helps defend the margin pool of manufacturers, as new products can deflect the retailers' and distributors' demands for increased margin by being more motivating to shoppers as well as having fewer promotions, higher growth rates and generally higher prices. In a mature, "competitive retail" world, retailers and distributors who want growth are prepared to sacrifice margin for the growth that comes from new products. Instead, they seek profit generation from existing mature products whose growth is driven by price decreases, and increased promotional spend or calls for increased margin.

Innovation defends manufacturers' profit pool by attracting shoppers and consumers – but how is innovation motivating for consumers?

Rational and emotional benefits

Innovation can offer a rational benefit to consumers, such as an appropriate pack size or convenient packaging format. A rational benefit is a demonstrable and tangible feature that meets a specific consumer or shopper need. Let's take an example of a rational benefit – that of smaller sized toiletries. After the heightened terror threats in the early 2000s, governments around the world mandated a ban on large volumes of liquid in hand luggage. Brands were able to offer a convenient solution with product volumes that were comfortably well below the regulatory requirements, such as 20ml toothpaste tubes or 90ml shampoo bottles. This innovation gave consumers a rational benefit in terms of time and hassle in finding an appropriate container, decanting from the original container into the smaller container, and ensuring it was below the mandated levels. It also was a rational benefit against having to buy new toothpaste or shampoo at every destination they flew into.

But there are far stronger drivers than rational benefit; the emotional benefit can be more powerful. Emotions drive human beings, and emotions are evident in what we purchase as well as in our everyday lives. Emotional benefits are what people *feel* when they buy a product. To use a Star Trek analogy, rational benefits are like Mr Spock in that they are logical and reasoned, whereas emotional benefits are more like Captain Kirk, more instinctive and sentimental. Emotional benefits are the differentiator of a brand from a commodity. Emotional benefits tap into our human spirit, attaching feelings to inanimate objects. Emotional benefits are defined by how they make us feel, and are described as such. Examples of emotional benefits are when a product is 'cool' or 'distinctive', 'traditional' or 'luxurious'. These feelings mean different things in different categories; with milk, for example, being 'old fashioned' is seen as more motivating than 'modern', according to our research.

Emotional benefits are valuable for transforming simple homogenised commodities into value-adding brands. Some see that 'happiness' transforms a fizzy cola into Coca-Cola. Some view the emotions of 'fun' and 'comfort' as transforming cocoa beans, sugar and fat into Cadbury's. Emotions are huge drivers for brands in and of themselves, with the delight of discovering a new product being a key boost in the first place.

Durex case study

Durex, now owned by the consumer giant Reckitt Benckiser (RB), is a steadfast brand in condoms, in around 30 large markets globally prior to 2010. After RB bought the brand in 2010, they sought to re-position it to focus more on the emotional benefits, rather than the rational benefits of safe sex, comfort and family planning. The emotional engagement sought marked a strategic shift away from safe sex to more magical sex for the brand – literally from 'Feeling is everything' to 'Love Sex Durex'. The purposeful repositioning of Durex to make it more emotional shortly after it was taken over by RB led to NPD outside of the core area into personal lubricants and vibrators. The focus on the emotional benefits not only allows for a wider base to innovate from, it also allows Durex to be a lighthouse for sexual and physical health, as well as generate increased sales to become the number one condom brand worldwide.

Chemistry of new

A Trading Director at Asda said at a conference in the early 2000's that "New is the second most motivating word for shoppers after FREE". One in five consumers, according to AC Nielsen[17], buys a new product simply because it is new

17 https://www.nielsen.com/us/en/insights/report/2019/total-consumer-report-2019

in and of iself. In effect, they are buying a new product simply because of the obvious novelty.

Lab researchers[18] have indicated that experiencing new things, such as a new product, generates a dopamine hit, the pleasure hormone. Consumers feel happy with new products, and attribute that happiness to the product itself when it is actually a physiological reaction to the new stimulus. Consumers are willing to pay more for joy.

Innovation driving margin

In addition to the dopamine effect, an innovation drives more value the more emotionally in tune it is to what people expect. For example, pizza is perceived by consumers as being highly sociable[19], and that makes sense as we share portions with friends and family. Developing pizzas that focus more on the sociability of pizza can have a positive effect. We see that in our research into the number of pepperoni pieces on a pizza, where we found that the optimal number of pieces is nine.[20] The trend for the number of pepperoni pieces was inversely related to the purchase intent for the pepperoni pizza, that is to say the more pepperoni pieces the less likely the respondents were to buy the pizza. We saw that even numbers of pepperoni pieces had higher purchase intent than the odd number of pieces either above or below it (e.g. twelve was more motivating than eleven or thirteen). Our hypothesis is that pepperoni pizzas that appear more sociable and fair, are more motivating than pepperoni pizzas that appear more random. This emotional benefit of fairness and sociability drives a higher perceived value to the shopper.

This propensity for consumers to want to pay more for an innovation that connects emotionally helps companies see innovation as margin accretive.

Innovation is not only accretive from a price point of view, but innovation also grows profit margins by reducing the investment in price discounting. Generally in the UK new products are not promoted as highly or as aggressively as existing products in the category, as shoppers will forgo discounts for newness – that is to say they trade a rational decision-making process for an emotional 'dopamine' effect.

The ability to charge more for innovation enables companies to generate more profitability, which in turn leads to higher investment back into innovation, resources and growth.

---

18 www.sciencedirect.com/science/article/pii/S089662730600475
19 https://creatingpossibilities.co.uk/portfolio/innovation-insight-emotional-drivers-for-pizza/
20 https://creatingpossibilities.co.uk/portfolio/innovation-insight-optimising-pizza-pepperoni-slices/

Innovation drives innovation

Categories that are perceived by consumers as being more innovative than others tend to have more innovation. As part of a study we undertook in May 2017,[21] out of 39 FMCG categories we tested, we found that consumers expect categories like ready meals, crisps & snacks, and nappies & baby food to be more innovative than milk, bottled waters or oils. This consumer expectation of new products means that brands that are in categories perceived as more innovative need to innovate more to meet the expectations of the consumers. Our current hypothesis is that marketeers have programmed consumers to expect innovation in specific categories, in effect creating a cycle where new products are provided, and so expected, and so provided again.

Innovation also affects different consumers. Older consumers tend to purchase brands that they have trusted for years habitually. Young consumers, on the other hand, want to find products that help them 'find themselves' and differentiate them from their parents or older siblings, as well as better meeting their perceived needs versus the standard product. This helps explain why younger consumers tend to look for more innovative products. We've seen the innovation of 're-introduction' of many nostaligc products such as Wispa's, Monster Munch and Pimm's Number 3 to engage specific older consumers. M&S's core consumer is the middle-aged to elderly and middle class, but they need to appeal to younger, less affluent shoppers as their core group die out. Whilst the food part of M&S is to some degree achieving this with innovation in food & drink like vegan and food to go ranges, their fashion and homeware are still targeted at middle-aged, middle-class shoppers (I should know – I'm sitting on an M&S sofa whilst wearing M&S clothing, and I am definitely middle-aged!).

But it's not just younger consumers that are looking for new products; all consumers' needs change over time – just think about how we used to eat 20 years ago. Over the last 20 years, there has been staggering growth in food and drink from all over the globe as people seek to explore the culinary world from the comfort of their own home – Japanese gyozas, Indian bhajjis or Italian arancini. In the last 70 years, we have moved away from meat and two veg for every evening meal to 'Taco Tuesdays' and Vietnamese hot spring rolls. Our research has identified that North African, Filipino, German and Korean cuisines have been growing rapidly over the last five years in the UK, resulting in opportunities for innovation within these cuisines.[22] Consumers are happy to pay more for the emotional benefit of discovery rather than have the same reptitive traditional meals . These

---

21 https://creatingpossibilities.co.uk/portfolio/innovation-insight-consumers-expectations-of-new/

22 https://creatingpossibilities.co.uk/portfolio/innovation-insight-cuisine-trends-in-the-uk

changing consumer needs offer an opportunity for manufacturers, as well as a threat for any manufacturers that do not change.

For those manufacturers that have an innovation capability, it represents a conundrum for their competition – do they follow with innovation or drive their existing products harder? Innovation can be a definitive competitive advantage if executed well, so if one manufacturer is good at innovation they will accelerate market share gains and multiply their profits more than manufacturers who simply discount their brands as consumers flock to products that are more relevant and motivating for them. Therefore manufacturers are incentivised to innovate so as not to be out-competed by their rivals. We see this in highly competitive categories such as soap powder, and see the inverse in categories that are less competitive such as wine (there is limited wide-scale innovation in the wine market, mostly limited to varietals).

Drive for differentiation

It's not just rivals that are pushing manufacturers to develop more new products. Multiple grocers in the UK have been able to drive growth for decades through improved logistics and store development. As those long-term benefits are now providing diminishing returns, retailers are looking for reasons shoppers should come to their – rather than their competitors' – stores. Moving or developing stores is an expensive way to drive sales, and gaining a long-term marketing advantage in retail is also tricky, so retailers are now looking for differentiation in their range of products – effectively exclusive products that are not available in any other stores or channels.

This drive for differentiated products from retailers again presents a quandary for manufacturers as to whether they should back retailers with innovative products or drive their existing product portfolio as hard as possible. Given the relative power of retailers in some categories, retail range differentiation can very quickly become a dilemma for manufacturers around whether or not they should innovate for specific retailers. Manufacturers have to work out whether it is better to work with individual retailers on specific innovations or whether it is better to offer the innovation to all retailers.

Innovation and profit

The compound effect of all of the innovative forces outlined above means that innovative companies tend to enjoy higher profit margins, because customers are willing to pay higher prices for more innovative products perceived to offer more value than plain 'vanilla' products. A report by BCG in 2019[23] showed that

---

23 www.thinkergyus.com/how-innovation-affects-financial-performance

the 'Top 25' most innovative businesses had a higher median profit growth than industry benchmarks (3.4% vs 0.4%). Having higher profit growth in turn drives up the valuation from shareholders for future potential. Innovative companies achieved significantly higher total shareholder return premiums 4.3% higher over their category competitors over three years according to the same study in 2009.

We found through investigating UK companies' annual reports using Companies House data that businesses that invested in R&D five years ago had grown their gross profit by 14.9% over the last five years.[24] Furthermore, Innovative companies can charge even higher prices for their more innovative value offering (products, services, solutions and experiences) if they also invest in standout design, which further magnifies the perceived value in the eyes of their customers.

And it is not just the direct financial benefits that come from innovation; there are indirect economic benefits such as the City's perception that companies with long-term sustainable innovation cultures have a higher price–earnings ratio. In 2006, Boston Consulting Group[25] found that innovative companies tend to grow faster, have richer product mixes than their peers, expand into adjacent or new categories (especially if these promise higher margins), and produce more patents than less innovative companies.

With innovation as a driver of business success, it is not surprising to find that there is a financial metric that looks precisely at the investment opportunity of innovation, namely the 'price-to-innovation-adjusted-earnings' ratio.[26] Companies with a long-term sustainable innovation culture tend to have a higher price to innovation ratio, meaning they are better regarded by analysts, investors or potential partners.

Innovation develops people

It's not just financial benefits that innovation drives, but also softer benefits such as to your people. Innovation is good for your people's development, giving new challenges and opportunities for career growth . Working in a successful innovation business makes people feel confident about their employer and their employment prospects. It gives people a reason to stay for the longer term, reducing employee turnover and recruitment costs, and leading to higher productivity.

---

24 https://creatingpossibilities.co.uk/uk-companies-latest-investment-and-returns-on-innovation/
25 https://thinkergy.com/2017/08/17/how-innovation-affects-financial-performance/
26 www.investopedia.com/terms/p/pricetoinnovation.asp#:~:text=Key%20Takeaways-,Price%2Dto%2Dinnovation%2Dadjusted%20earnings%20is%20a%20variation%20of,of%20its%20products%20and%20procedures

3M case study

Most people who know about 3M know it for its Post-It notes. 3M is renowned for its innovation, receiving a National Medal from President Clinton in 1995. The story of the inventor of the Post-It Note, Art Fry, is often touted as an example of both serendipitous innovation and allowing employees freedom to follow their interests and passions for the benefit of the company. Most innovation specialists are familiar with Google engineers having time to do their own thing, with Gmail, Google Earth and Google Labs based on the work of those dedicating 20% of their time to exploring their own ideas. But it was 3M who, in 1948, launched their 15% programme, where all employees, not just engineers or technical people, spend 15% of their time supported by the company in chasing their passions and their ideas, to see if there is any value there.

That 15% investment of employees' time has led to innovations such as Cubitron II, a sandpaper that acts like a cutting tool and generates millions of dollars in revenue. But more importantly, this programme to indulge in pet projects does two things that symbiotically drive up profits – they reduce labour costs by increasing talent retention – through more satisfied and autonomous workers – and also reduce recruitment of talent costs, as highly talented individuals *want* to work for 3M versus their competitors. 3M balances off this 15% time by setting bonuses based on innovation – 30% of sales turnover has to come from products launched in the last four years for bonuses to be paid in specific divisions.[27] Therefore, a virtuous cycle is created in the culture of 3M, harnessing a spirit of innovation. 3M have also created organisational structures that feed and grow innovation to ultimately drive revenue, but at the same time to support and satisfy colleagues. For example, funding for pet projects comes from multiple potential sources, with avenues left open to the individual. Recruitment is done simply by colleagues putting together posters to recruit other specialists onto their project. 3M has innovation at its heart and soul, which is an incredibly compelling environment in which to work; 'What you're offering is essentially freedom, and that is very attractive for the right person', says Henry Chesbrough, a professor at the Haas School of Business at UC Berkeley, and the father of open innovation business practices.[28]

---

27 www.innovation-portal.info/wp-content/uploads/3M.pdf
28 www.fastcompany.com/1663137/how-3m-gave-everyone-days-off-and-created-an-innovation-dynamo

Innovation drives growth

In summary, Innovation drives growth, and substantial growth at that – for all sizes and types of companies, from start-ups to global megabrands. Innovation drives higher prices and higher margins as consumers want new products, either just for the sake of having new products or because the emotional and rational benefits of a new product better meet their needs. Innovation growth drives shareholder value, and metrics exist to help identify efficient, innovative businesses that drive higher earnings per share. Innovation growth drives people and talent growth, helping people develop, and organisations increase capability. In short, innovation and growth, however growth is defined and valued, are inextricably linked.

However, there can be costs associated with innovation when it's poorly implemented in a business, as we will explore in Chapter 2.

Key takeaways from this chapter

- Innovation links empirically to growth, for companies large and small.
- Successful, sustainable innovation can have a positive impact on profitability, which in turn leads to higher investment in innovation, leading to sustained growth.
- Consumers actively seek innovation and are willing to pay a premium when they find it.
- Innovation offers growth potential for employees.

Chapter 2 – What are the costs of innovation?

As we have seen in Chapter 1, innovation is a crucial driver of business growth in many forms, but that growth can have risk associated with it. The risk of innovation is that long-term innovation failure can wreck the profitability of any organisation. Not only can innovation failure increase financial risks and costs, but it can also increase cultural risk and people costs, which we'll explore later in the chapter.

As we saw in *Common Innovation Terms*, Innovation failure rates are significant, although varying failure rates abound, and Innovation failure has multiple different definitions. A number of these failed products may be seasonal or limited edition promotions or simple product extensions, all designed to be short term, but their cost of development is still incremental to the existing products, and therefore we should expect a return on those development costs.

For some perplexing reason, the CPG industry – and within that the FMCG industry – is very comfortable with a 90% failure rate for all its innovation. Over 20 years, the innovation rate failure rate hasn't changed, and talented individuals still fail more often than they succeed. We see no reason why a 0% failure rate is not achievable in the future, where every new product launched generates a return on investment.

Failure is our current default

When discussing with friends in other industries such as construction or medicine that there is a 90% failure rate in CPG, they are astonished. One friend, a civil engineer, could not comprehend having a tolerance in that kind of range. If he did, nobody would ever enter a building, drive over a bridge or travel on a road. Similarly, if doctors had a 90% failure rate, we would not consult them about whatever ailments we might have and probably view them in the same way as psychics or astrologists.

From our personal experience of being involved with large and small businesses, the failure rate remains relatively consistent irrespective of the size of the company. However, larger organisations can make a louder bang with their launches and have more extended patience levels (i.e. deeper pockets). All companies we have dealings with have an innovation failure rate over 50%, with most being in the high 70% to 90% range, which hardly inspires confidence that the capability to innovate is somehow linked to scale. It's rare to see a company be aware of the relevant success or failure rates of its products relative to the category. It's just not tracked as a measure, as it's assumed to be wrong, or it's embarrassing, or perhaps both.

Given that the majority of innovations in FMCG are small tweaks,[29] the costs of innovation are, one would think, probably relatively small. But that's not the case in our experience. We have found that a simple project to change the packaging on a product might require nearly 100 days of numerous people's time and tens of thousands of pounds in design and packaging costs.

Stripping down the cost of innovation

In 2015 we consulted for a FTSE 250 consumer goods company on their innovation pipeline, looking at the time recorded on innovation projects for the preceding ten years. Each of the innovation projects was grouped into high, medium and low complexity by the R&D department. Each project recorded the stage in the process reached, including whether it was launched. Some were simply ideas explored to an early stage, whereas some were complex products that required multi-year investment and had a successful launch. In total, we reviewed 163 projects. The average time spent on a launched project was 296 working days, with – unsurprisingly – more simplistic projects such as renovations and line extensions took less time than the average, and more complex projects took more time. This only included projects that eventually launched, but if we include all innovation projects even those that didn't launch, it would assume an average of 427 days, with an average of 749 days for complex projects.

---

29 https://creatingpossibilities.co.uk/balancing-the-innovation-pipeline/

With this data, we can calculate costs. We know that people do not work 100% of their time exclusively on one project, so we modelled that an individual would work on three projects at a time. We estimated £600 per day to include personnel costs and fixed costs such as R&D equipment and manufacturing equipment. Thus we reached an average innovation cost for a FTSE 250 company of £177,600 per project that was launched. If we look at the average of all projects irrespective of whether they were launched or not, that rises to £256,200, because of a high number of complex projects that were exhausted before being cancelled prior to launch. If projects are complex, then the costs jump up £449,400. This also does not include any direct sales or marketing costs associated with the launch of the project, such as advertising, promotional investment, or even listing fees with retailers or channel partners.

Hurdle rates

The above average costs are substantial investments in themselves at a base level. As part of the project, we assumed that for every incremental £1 in cost, the company would have to make an incremental £2 in revenue, meaning the revenue targets for innovation had to be double the costs. Targets for all innovation projects were to achieve at least an incremental £300,000 in revenue or they were deemed not worthy to invest in. For highly complex projects, we recommended at least a £500,000 revenue hurdle rate.

These hurdle rates generated a great deal of pushback internally, especially from the marketing and sales functions who felt that they would stifle the brand and growth of the company. However, the hurdle rates agreed above were very conservative base numbers using data from launched projects, and we would have recommended a number almost double those proposed to ensure that any innovation investment took account of weighted average costs of capital, with a positive net present value.

This project offers two opportunities for the client and other similar FMCG businesses. Firstly is the benchmark for innovation costs. Initiating our project was the first time that the Exec of this business had considered costs and hurdle rates for innovation, and the daylight that we were able to shine on their innovation cost base helped them change their innovation strategy, becoming more successful overall with innovation. They became more ruthless early on and wasted fewer resources on projects that were unlikely to return a positive impact. Quite understandably, previously innovation had been undertaken by both the marketing and sales community as a way to grow their respective elements in the business, as the costs weren't precisely tracked or allocated to their budget, but rather were hidden in personnel costs.

Secondly, it highlighted the opportunity costs of innovation to the Exec, that is to say, how else could the people and the costs associated with innovation be used in other parts of the business, and could that return a higher ROI than innovation. People were re-focused onto activities that could drive a higher return, and direct marketing costs for innovation, such as design costs, listing fees etc., were redeployed to more effective sales-driving activities.

The overall innovation budget for this client was in the region of £5m, as stated in its annual report, which corresponds to the average innovation spend for a large organisation, according to UK Government figures.

Calculating innovation investment

Based on November 2020 Companies House data,[30] companies in their latest year of reporting have invested on average 2.9% of their revenue into R&D, or £8.32m per company. Medium and large companies (those in excess of £25m turnover), spent an average of £15m in R&D each in their latest financial year, or 2.7% of their revenue.

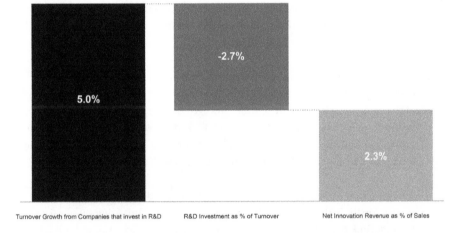

Figure 3 Innovation ROI

The level of R&D investment as a % of turnover differs significantly across industries. Manufacturers of food and broad consumer goods only invest 0.8% of turnover in R&D. Sports & recreation services (Standard Industrial Classification[31] or

---

30 https://creatingpossibilities.co.uk/uk-companies-latest-investment-and-returns-on-innovation/
31 https://www.gov.uk/government/publications/standard-industrial-classification-of-economic-activities-sic

SIC 9300) invest 44% of turnover. Financial services (SIC 6400) invest 23%, and education (SIC 8500) 21% of turnover.

R&D AS % OF TURNOVER
FOR THE LATEST YEAR AVAILABLE

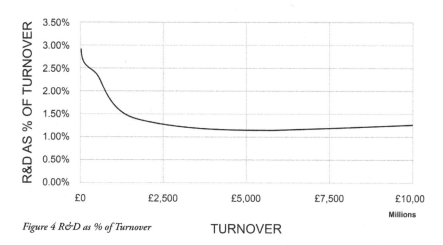

Figure 4 R&D as % of Turnover

Size of company also has a part to play, in that the percentage of turnover invested in innovation declines as turnover increases. Large companies with a turnover in excess of £1bn report investment in R&D of 1.7%, whereas companies under £25m turnover report R&D investment of 11.2%.

Innovation return on investment

Again using data from Companies House in November 2020,[32] companies that invested in R&D five years ago have grown their turnover by 5.0% and their gross margin by 14.9% over the last five years. Using that data, the ROI for innovation is 185%:

$$\text{Return on Investment} = \frac{\text{Innovation Contribution to Sales}}{\text{Innovation Investment as \% of Sales}} = \frac{5.0\%}{2.7\%} = 185\%$$

Figure 5 R&D Investment as % of Turnover
Source: Companies House Data November 2020

---

32 https://creatingpossibilities.co.uk/uk-companies-latest-investment-and-returns-on-innovation/

Although on the face of it, the ROI of 185% would appear to be healthy, when overlaid with the 90% failure rate, a different view comes into focus. Innovation is a powerful way to grow, but it is highly risky with a 90% failure rate. Only a small number of products actually generate high sales from innovation. For example, Kantar[33] reported the top ten innovations in FMCG contributed only £114.4m of retail sales in 2019 from a category worth over £110 bn.[34] Finish Powerball Quantum Ultimate was reported by Kantar as the biggest innovation in 2019 with £20.3m of retail sales, or 17% of the Top Ten products. In contrast the tenth biggest innovation in 2019 was only £6.5m in retail sales value or 6% of the total from the Top Ten. In other words, big successful innovations drive up the average contribution for innovation, so the 7% contribution of innovation is driven by a small number of highly successful products, and with an 90% failure rate, the majority of innovations is likely to not make an incremental profit.

Not only is there high failure with innovation, but those innovations that are successful may not be generating incremental sales or incremental margin, with Kantar[35] reporting that two thirds of innovations fail to be incremental to existing products.

Relative innovation performance

These numbers start to help organisations understand how they are performing in innovation relative to other companies. Are they generating better or worse ROI on innovation? How does their innovation budget stack up against others? How does their failure rate impact their delivery of innovation?

We drew up this simple matrix to aid the thought process of what to do when you review your innovation spend versus your innovation returns.

The matrix opposite uses the average R&D spend of 2.7% (rounded to 3%) of turnover that we found from Companies House on the x axis or horizontal axis. On the vertical axis or y axis, we have used the contribution that innovation makes according to AC Nielsen.

Other costs of innovation

The costs associated with innovation are not solely financial. There are also intangible costs for organisations that cannot successfully innovate, some more damaging than the financial costs.

---

33 https://www.kantarworldpanel.com/global/News/The-UKs-most-valuable-new-FMCG-brands-of-2019
34 https://www.thesterlingchoice.com/fmcg-around-world-compare-uk/
35 https://www.kantar.com/inspiration/fmcg/5-factors-for-successful-innovation-in-the-uk/

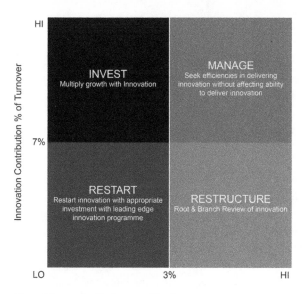

Figure 6 Innovation Performance Matrix

We've met leaders from hundreds of companies, from those that have a strong innovation capability through to those few that have zero innovation capability.

Where we have found companies that have limited long-term innovation success, their lack of success impacts them in unintended ways. These companies tend to be more conservative in their approach, not just to innovation but also to general management. They defer decision-making to the HiPPO (Highest Paid Person in the room's Opinion) in the room, and therefore innovation is slower as it requires the HiPPO to have time to make a decision, and riskier as there has been no diversity of input from a wider audience. It is slower as not everybody has bought into the project but has simply been told what to do. Running all innovation decision-making through or by the HiPPO we find develops a 'doom loop': a cycle of negativity in the business that comes from failure, and an attitude that anything attempted will lead to more failure, so therefore we should only do things that are less likely to fail, become more conservative, and invest less in riskier areas such as innovation. However, this results in lower growth, which continues the negative spiral.

These types of businesses become less motivating to work in, with knock-on effects of lower productivity and higher employee turnover, as nobody wants to work for a losing company. These factors then further increase costs directly, such as through recruitment fees, or indirectly through lower productivity.

Innovation doom loop

It is not just internally that the doom loop can occur, as external stakeholders such as retailers, distributors and suppliers see no advantage in low growth companies. Retailers and distributors demand higher listings fees and guarantees to clear stock should it fail and are less likely to push distribution to a higher number of outlets, thus reducing the chances of success or the impact of any marketing activity. Shareholders are affected by the doom loop too, as they see their investments and growth decline.

But companies don't just pin their growth hopes on innovation. Where innovation fails to deliver, they look to invest in shorter-term ways to grow, such as promotions and discounts. Fuelling growth through promotions and discounts over the long term, however, often leads to brand equity challenges and lower accumulated returns, as the uplifts from discounts are lower as consumers become used to them and rebase the perceived value of the product in line with the new lower price. Retailers become expectant of the discounts and fixed costs of promotions to fuel their growth. As a counter-example, consider successful tech innovators – rarely are their products discounted, even the core products.

The costs and risks for innovation are stark: costing between 1% and 15% of turnover, with a failure rate of 90%. And then there are the indirect costs of poor execution such as a gloomy organisational culture. But not doing innovation also has costs – often intangible costs, but costs nonetheless.

From our modelling of ROI, we contend that the ROI for innovation is very precarious. If the sales contribution for innovation drops below 5%, then the ROI turns negative. Also, if the failure rate increases beyond 90%, then the ROI drops too. If the contribution from innovation drops and the failure rate increases, then the ROI is significantly impacted. However, the inverse is also true, that is to say, if the contribution from innovation goes up and / or the failure rate comes down, the ROI goes up.

Innovation as an engine for growth

But innovation doesn't need to be so precarious. Imagine innovation as an engine for the growth of your company. This engine takes in three units of fuel and generates seven units of energy (i.e. 2.7% of turnover and 7% of innovation contribution). And it delivers that seven units of energy even though it only works one time in six. Innovation has consistently been in the 2%–10% growth range for the last 20 years.[36] And we have accepted this for decades as best practice. Frankly the current innovation process can hardly be a shining beacon when it could be described a "bit better" than doing no innovation at all.

---

36 https://home.kpmg/uk/en/home/campaigns/2019/07/kpmg-organic-growth-barometer-2019.html

Over the last 20 or more years, we have ended up in this precarious position for a multitude of reasons. Many companies don't know (and therefore don't track) their innovation failure rates. The road to innovation failure is paved with the good intentions of exploiting consumer truth and applying logical scientific rigour, but these are at the whim and favour of confident, charismatic leaders who effectively are working, more often than not, on a hunch or a guess. In our experience, the most common practice for FMCG innovation is – to borrow a phrase from Kevin Costner's *Field of Dreams* – 'build it and they will come', based on the HiPPO in the room's wishes, and then go hell for leather, raining incentives down on the teams to make the innovation materialise with little to no tracking of the ROI, as the majority of the costs are hidden costs such as personnel. 'Build it and they will come' is how we as an industry end up a vulnerable knife-edge for Innovation's ROI that could quickly crash into a doom loop.

We'll explore these and more reasons as to why innovation fails in Chapter 3.

Key takeaways from this chapter

- The financial cost of innovation can be both high and poorly measured or misunderstood – ensure you track your innovation costs properly when embarking on an innovation journey.
- The softer impact on people in an organisation underperforming in innovation can be significant.
- The opportunity for innovation success is significant given the size of the problem across the FMCG industry

Chapter 3 –
Why does innovation fail?

Innovation is a term used very liberally by executives across the consumer goods industry to describe the vast majority of their new product launches. In contrast, many industry commentators question whether there is actually any genuine innovation at all. When visiting high street stores or clicking through retailer websites, most consumers would be forgiven for thinking 'where is all the innovation?' The majority of what businesses refer to as innovation is, in fact, EPD – amended, extended or slightly improved versions of existing products and services. Iteration is a much safer game, far less risky in terms of investment but far less lucrative in terms of potential returns. Extending an already successful range of pizzas by one broadly accepted flavour variant is not really shifting the innovation needle. Relaunching last season's homewares range with the addition of a metallic stripe and a new name is not going to change the fortunes of the manufacturer, importer or retailer.

Iteration is a far easier course to follow as many of the uncertainties that accompany genuine innovation are not present; there is an existing pool of buyers; a known price point exists; the channel is well-defined; the packaging and promotional materials have previously performed. If you compare this to genuine innovation where none of these factors are known, you can begin to see why businesses shy away from product innovations looking to take a big step forward from the status quo. In genuine innovation there is uncertainty over the existence of or profile of potential buyers; how much consumers would pay for the new proposition is just guesswork in many instances; the best route to market is completely unknown; and you have no information about how to de-risk any elements of the packaging or promotional proposition.

So where has all the innovation gone? Why are very few consumer goods businesses coming up with genuinely new ideas anymore? Have we already had all the good ideas?

The answer to this last question is no; it is clearly still possible to launch strong, innovative new products and services that will have a transformative impact on the category in which they are released. It is however arguably harder than ever: competition is higher than it used to be, categories are predefined and hard-wired in the eye of the consumer, prices in consumer goods have become lower, new routes to market have opened up, meaning the choice available to consumers is massive and arguably overwhelming. To succeed in innovation and gain cut-through, businesses know that they need to invest properly in tools and resources that will as far as possible de-risk the decisions being made in the uncertain conditions previously outlined. The investment levels required are substantial, and the returns variable. It is our experience that many businesses will start out with good intentions but begin to water down the approach they take as soon as they witness the investment levels required to ensure success and a return on the investment made. As a result, processes are introduced that are comforting to the executives involved in the innovation, yet do not make the conditions for decision-making any less uncertain. The processes add layers of supposed safeguards and fallbacks, giving executives insurance policies to defend their decision-making should the products not work as anticipated. This comforting effect waters down and distils the innovation, eroding any incremental value to the end customer.

Researchers at the LEAD Innovation Management Institute[37] cited five reasons why innovation often fails. Despite talking about the broader industry and business model innovation, there are some points common to the decision-making issues we identify in this chapter. They said the reasons innovation often fails include;

- Meticulously detailed planning – drawing too much comfort from upfront planning and scoping, leading to overly detailed planning activities that leave no scope for pivoting or iterating based on the live testing data. Being fleet of foot at the start of a project may appear more risky but it leaves far more room for mid course adjustments as the products begin to be tested

---

37 https://www.lead-innovation.com/english-blog/topic/agile-innovation-management

- Adherence to assumptions – teams working with assumptions, not data-driven facts.
- Acceleration of the innovation process – a belief that first to market is best, and quicker at any cost is in fact 'Agile'.
- Control with financial figures – senior executives are asking innovation teams to make market share and growth projections for innovation projects to justify the investment in innovation in the first place. The level of uncertainty in innovation makes any exact forecast of any share gain or intended profits completely pointless.
- Project completion with product availability – the belief that the innovation process is complete at the point the product hits the market. This isn't true – the hard work really starts here in persuading internal and external stakeholders to back and invest in the product live in the market. The project is only finished when it's reached the desired level of customer adoption.

The key to success in genuine innovation comes down to confident, bold decision-making in highly uncertain conditions, decisions that are validated by robust testing data from the agile innovation process. To try to improve this decision-making environment, businesses throw structures, processes, data and resources at teams and individuals in order to de-risk it. However those attempts to de-risk it often result in poorer output than if no investment had been made. The drivers behind innovation failure can be put into three broad buckets:

- People and process.
- Data and testing.
- Budgets, resources and structures.

Let's take each in turn to explore in more detail what dynamics are at play.

People and process

Companies, much like society at large, have a tendency to accept the views of confident people, especially leaders. The phenomenon of the HiPPO can drive a lot of good things, such as the founding vision for a company, but equally can drive the wrong behaviours when innovation is being scaled beyond that first successful product. The HiPPO's view is perceived as fact, is rarely or never challenged, and before we know it these opinions become innovation projects that lack consumer truth, and failure beckons. Many executives at businesses we work with often refer to the HiPPO effect as a major drag on genuine innovation. This phenomenon is where the HiPPO overrides the data-driven empirical decision-making displayed by teams who have spent weeks or months developing products. When asked for sign-off, HiPPO's rarely just say 'yes, perfect' – their belief is that they have to have a suggestion, an amend, or a change – they feel they have to challenge or input on everything. Having a committee of HiPPO's being required to sign off new products or ranges is often the death knell of consumer goods innovation; the watering down of the innovation to a 'safer' proposition at this point is inevitable.

But how can executives and companies overcome the HiPPO effect? You need data to depersonalise decision-making – it can take the emotion and opinion out of the process; counteracting opinion with yet more opinion is just not going to work. Although the reality is that decision-making in organisations will still rely on gut instinct in some way, decisions should be informed by insights provided by data. When you depersonalise decision-making, it's not about you or what you think or what the HiPPO thinks. It's about what the facts state. Be focused on what your customers are saying, and get competitive data and other external benchmarks in your analysis. With this data available, far punchier, more empirical discussions and approval processes are likely to happen.

Linked to the HiPPO effect is the fact that we witness too much subjectivity in the innovation decision-making process, with a corresponding lack of objectivity. In some instances we have witnessed or been part of the approach that has been as follows: have an idea, sense check it with some colleagues and suppliers, and simply develop it six months out from your pre-existing range window. If we could replace this subjectivity with empirical evidence, we would see: 1) far fewer products reach the market; and 2) those products that do hit the market perform far higher on average than current rates of success. Removing the long tail of unsuccessful innovation is one of the principle goals of Agile.

We also witness a lack of commerciality within the teams responsible for new product development. Many new product developers that we work with are not targeted on margin (more on that in the next section), and therefore only pay vague attention to the price point they think this new product should sit at. Rarely do they challenge the pricing ceilings in a category by developing genuinely innovative products that consumers are willing to pay for in the context of existing products in the category.

All of this is partly linked to historic innovation processes, often referred to as Waterfall processes. As we defined in the Introduction to this book, a Waterfall process is where a product or range of products are scoped and heavily documented right at the start of the innovation cycle. Everything is prescribed upfront; formulation or recipe, price point, pack format, target customer, launch date and much much more. The innovation team then works with its suppliers to develop the product over the next 3–4 months, with the final 2–3 months left for technical testing, first production, logistics planning and merchandising. At no point during the process are any of the product concepts tested in any robust or consistent form, either with target consumers or internal 'customers' such as supply chain, finance and store colleagues. A Waterfall process leads to a total lack of flexibility and 'pivotability', and what can be manufactured is manufactured, rather than what consumers want being manufactured. The Waterfall process has numerous repeatability benefits, but it is not able to respond to changes mid-process. It is a methodology that prioritises the process over the outcome, and as a result is extremely rigid. Little thought is given to the question of 'should we be building/developing this product' and reviewing it from an end-consumer perspective. The only time everything is viewed as a whole is at the end when it's developed and produced, at which point it is often too late, and the business just shrugs its shoulders and launches the product anyway.

The software industry moved away from Waterfall development processes many years ago for the following reasons:

- It makes changes very difficult at any point after the initial scoping is complete.
- It excludes the end-user (in our case, the consumer) until far too late in the process.
- Nothing is tested until after development completion, by which point costs and time have all been used up.
- Problems can remain unnoticed until completion and launch.

Beyond process, we also witness a bias of action; namely many companies in consumer goods are biased towards developing and launching something, as they view inactivity as worse than poor activity. They believe that doing something would be better than doing nothing; after all, they are a product developer, they are paid to develop products... However the innovation statistics of the consumer goods market contradict this; it could be far more profitable for many businesses to launch nothing at all in the long-term, based on the innovation failure statistics of the industry. Whilst this wouldn't result in growth, it could result in less losses in the short-term, despite being a guaranteed route to long-term decline... Well planned, properly resourced innovation processes that result in far fewer launches by volume, but far greater launches in terms of impact would be more enhancing to shareholder value and thus the preferred route to take.

Within larger organisations, one of the issues we regularly encounter is senior individuals not willing to fully commit to backing genuinely innovative ideas or products. Whoever got fired for launching 'safe' new products that neither lose money nor make money? In larger organisations, careerists tend to shy away from the risk that accompanies genuine innovation as they climb the corporate pyramid. Contrast this to startups where entrepreneurs drive and own a big, bold vision for an innovative product or service that will shake up their market, and you can see how large organisations lose market share left, right, and centre to more nimble and ambitious startup companies.

Data, metrics and testing

One of the key issues with the Waterfall process is the paucity or lack of robust consumer intelligence or testing until far too late in the process. In numerous examples we have been involved in – either as a buyer or innovation controller – there was no insight or testing whatsoever all the way through individual private label development projects. Formulations weren't tested, price points weren't validated, consumer pain points weren't considered, the impact of neighbouring products was not tested. Sporadically retailers or manufacturers will research a new range refresh at a very high level, but very rarely will they do individual testing or validation. This is partly because the sheer volume of private-label launches in the grocery and apparel sectors render many testing approaches prohibitively expensive or slow, even if there was an appetite for them. If private label launches are to be justified at such scale, cost-effective and rapid – almost real-time – testing mechanisms need to be procured and rolled out across all teams.

Outside of private label in the branded world, it's not necessarily a lack of insight that is the problem, but the wrong insight. Traditional methodologies from expensive consulting agencies are used that are not in line with the latest thinking on behavioural science. And they continue to be used because they've always been used, and they give innovation and research teams the get out of jail free card of 'we tested it using the accepted means, don't blame us that it failed'. We still see questions being asked of consumers such as 'How likely are you to buy this product?' (it's binary – you either buy it or you don't) or 'Would you buy a protein-infused snack bar?' (a leading question to which most respondents would say 'yes'). Whilst we aren't writing a book on behavioural science (we have suggested some excellent books on Behavioural Science in the 'Further Reading' section and an introduction here - https://vyprclients.com/science/), this is a vital field to have a basic understanding of so that innovation teams can quickly flag if their testing methodologies are likely to produce robust results or not.

In many instances, we see the poor interpretation of data as the issue, where solid data sources are misread to back up the confirmation bias of individuals in the teams. Misreading statistical signficance is a common issue, and we delve into that in a little more detail in Chapter 11. We've also seen the narrative around the testing data being interpreted to retroactively fit the worldview of the innovation teams and justify the decisions they have already made, and even in some instances teams asking for products to be retested until they get the result that they want.

In a science laboratory, experiment after experiment would be conducted until a final outcome was reached empirically. That lab-based approach is just not seen across the consumer goods industry; the mindset of testing everything rigorously as early in the process as possible is not one that has ever caught on. In the absence of data and facts, subjectivity, gut feeling and opinion have stepped up to become the currency of iteration and innovation decision-making. R&D teams experiment their way to developing workable solutions that fit the manufacturing criteria; innovation teams tend to build products on flimsy untested assumptions.

Rarely are product ideas aimed at a significant consumer pain point; rather they fill some vague, unspecified need that in reality has little impact on consumers' lives. This anti-lab-based approach results in a lack of understanding of target consumers – their habits, behaviours and lifestyles. True empathy is exceptionally hard to attain, meaning that the idea is often poor and does not resonate or motivate consumers to change their behaviour. Product ideas are mostly forcefully generated six or nine months out from a launch window, rather than to address a shift in consumer need that has been witnessed by the individuals or teams.

To help move away from HiPPO based decision making to more empricial decision making, we need to introduce more accessible and robust data. Data sources for most businesses operating in the consumer goods industry should include, but not be limited to, some of the following:

- Consumer behaviour data sources such as video from in-home or in-office to truly understand how consumers are behaving around the pain point the business is innovating on.
- Comprehensive purchase intent simulation across all ideas being considered.
- More complex predictive analytics – pricing, cannibalisation and range impact can all be mapped ahead of launch.
- Statistically robust trending information to spot and track ingredient / colour / format trends in other parallel markets that are genuinely impacting consumer behaviour.

Data sources that we see readily available across the industry but which we don't feel offer a great deal of value to the product developer include:

- EPOS data (i.e. sales data) – all this does is tell you what is working now in-store or online. Tracking this too closely as a product developer just leads you to make more iterations of what is working now.

- Loyalty data – as above, this tells you what is happening now. It is arguably potentially a richer data source for the innovator as you can begin to map consumer behaviour, but it must be treated with caution, and it must be comprehensive and broad in nature.
- Market share data – most grocery chains are obsessed with market share, and it is the death knell of innovation. A bigger driver of short-term market share than innovation is selling more products on promotion or dropping prices to drive volumes. Any listed business (particularly any retailer) that is in a highly competitive, market-share obsessed sector can kiss goodbye to becoming an innovative business; the conditions just will not allow it. Making innovation decisions that will impact the long-term in an environment like this is difficult and rare.

The above can be considered lag indicators as they look backwards and lag beyond the consumer experience, rather than being lead indicators that look forwards and help indicate what will happen

The early triggers of an innovation process in many instances are also very misleading; a phenomenon referred to as signal vs noise. If businesses witness a high volume of specific product concept launches in the category in which they operate, they tend to read that as a trend that must be consumer-driven, and so feel that they must jump on the bandwagon too. A recent example of this is cold brew coffee; the sheer volume of product and brand launches in this space in 2019 suggests it was an unstoppable trend. In fact, the opposite was true; it was a trendy but peripheral product in foodservice that for some reason gained multiple listings in retail, but very few if any of the individual products or brands impacted the market in the way that innovation in the drinks category should. Coconut water was another product that trended and grew through listing proliferation, not through an unmet consumer need. Kombucha is a trendy non-alcoholic drink that has far too much exposure compared to the actual level of consumer demand.

But how can this happen? What we see across the industry are the wrong measures being used to judge the success of innovation, allowing instances like the proliferation of unsuccessful cold brew coffee to happen. Product developers are often given targets on the listing: getting the product on the shelf on time and on spec is the success metric, not how it performs commercially or what impact it has on the consumer. Launching new products that do not hit commercial or consumer penetration targets serves very little purpose whatsoever, either for the retailer, manufacturer or, importantly, consumers. KPIs on innovation need to be far more consumer-oriented and commercially focused, rather than the internal ones we see across the industry today. These erroneous innovation KPIs include:

- Percentage of overall sales from new products (which basically incentivises product developers to launch a wall of average iteration).
- Percentage of new products launched on time and on spec (how does this impact the consumer positively?).
- Total sales from new products (as opposed to incremental sales, or growth from innovation).
- Number of new products launched (no reference to the quality of the innovation, just the volume).
- The KPIs rarely have any link to consumer metrics such as consumer satisfaction or engagement. Equally, they are rarely targeted at things such as margin. It is very sector-dependent, but stronger innovation KPIs could include:
- Incremental sales from innovation.
- Incremental cash margin from innovation.
- Accretive % gross margin
- New customers brought into the business/category/range by innovation.
- Return on investment of the innovation launched by the individual/team.

We explore KPIs in much more detail in Chapter 10 because we feel it's such an important area to get right.

We rarely encounter any innovators or product developers who are commercially targeted; many would argue it would result in counterproductive behaviours. We disagree; anyone accountable for bringing new products to market should be commercially targeted – the key is on what timescale. Giving a new product developer six months to make a return would be foolish; giving them 18 months would result in confident, bold decisions being taken that would see a hockey stick style growth curve emerging if the right decisions were taken early on. The hockey stick growth curve is one often seen with disruptive technologies. When they are first launched they take some time to bed in, being targeted at a small niche of early-adopting consumers. Market share of the business that has launched the innovation would stay neutral or potentially even drop if they have abandoned a more successful mass market proposition. But once the product catches on to a broader audience, moving from just early adopters to a mass market audience, all of a sudden the growth accelerates rapidly, far outstripping competitors and setting a new benchmark for the category or market. It is sometimes termed the 'Nike swoosh' – a growth chart that dips down and to the right after launch before accelerating in a glorious straight line of growth up and to the right (and off the page, if you're lucky).

Budgets, resources and structure

There is a very common doom loop that we witness across the industry: a lack of profit generated from failed or average innovation launches, leading to lower investment in innovation processes, leading to even poorer innovation outputs, until businesses stop innovating in all but name. It's a cycle that is very hard to break.

But what happens is that at some point far more innovative startups or competitors come along and begin to eat away their market share. Smaller entrepreneurial companies tend to be much flatter in structure, following the vision of the founder or co-founders. Decisions get made much more quickly, and it's much easier to pivot; "sign-off by committee" is non-existent. Contrast this to the hierarchical pyramid structure of many large organisations, and it's easy to see why startups and SMEs consistently out-innovate them, even with far smaller budgets and resources.

Large companies lack of innovation success compared to startups need to think about their innovation capability and structure. Large companies are prone to turning to innovation agencies for help in filling in their innovation capability gap on a project by project basis. However, the vast majority of these innovation agencies lack the very innovation capability required to grow in the same way as startups and SME's have proven to do, and are too focused on their interests, such as making the client feel good to winning the next pitch. Clients rarely have long term contracts with the agencies, and the model is a project based one with high cost and little, if any, accountability. Substituating innovation capability from third party innovation agencies that follow the same process and mindset as the client company, with incentives limiting them to self-interest, will not drastically change the fortunes of large organisations' innovation success. Large organisations need to think hard about what innovation capability they need and how to structure themselves for long-term innovation success, and to blend external and internal resources into a coherent mindset that is focused on proving innovation success.

Jon Erlichman ✔
@JonErlichman

Amazon's **R&D** spending each year:

2019: $35.9 billion
2018: $28.8 billion
2017: $22.6 billion
2016: $16.1 billion
2015: $12.5 billion
2014: $9.3 billion
2013: $6.6 billion
2012: $4.6 billion
2011: $2.9 billion
2010: $1.7 billion
2009: $1.2 billion

19:09 · 06/10/2020 · Twitter for iPhone

134 Retweets **23** Quote Tweets **547** Likes

Figure 7 Amazon's R&D Spend
https://twitter.com/jonerlichman/status/1313541801614233600?s=21

The well-regarded business book *The Innovator's Dilemma* by Clayton Chris-tensen shows how as companies grow and begin to make substantial profits from a once-innovative product that they have now scaled ruthlessly across all their target markets, they tend to completely lose sight of fresh innovation. Eventually, these behemoths get swamped by an army of startups who outpace and out-innovate them to previously unseen levels of growth. One of the hardest and least frequently seen things in business is for massive companies to set out on a fresh course of in-novation and move away from farming the profits of their first big hit. That's why Amazon is such an impressive company; they continually reinvent themselves and reinvest all their profits into innovation projects. Some are a hit, many are a miss, but this ethos and structure keep them growing at the frenetic pace at which they do. In 2019 they spent a whopping a whopping $36bn on R&D![38]

---

38 https://statstic.com/research-and-development-expenses-of-amazon-and-microsoft-compared/

Short-term thinking, particularly for listed companies or private equity invested businesses, is really not conducive to an innovation environment. Any genuine innovation is likely to;

1) take 18–24 months before turning a profit;
2) require significant investment; and
3) have a substantial impact on the market only after the CEO / senior team / PE firm has moved on to their next role.

The obvious examples from tech where companies like Amazon and Google have taken an incredibly long-term view on reinvesting profits into innovation show what timescales businesses need to operate on in order to innovate at scale. The prize when they do is massive: Amazon Web Services was started as a side project by Amazon that was completely different from their core business of e-commerce. It is now one of the principal drivers of profitability (and therefore value) in the whole group. Most listed businesses just wouldn't have given a project like that the investment and time it needed to deliver. In a world where companies are being judged by shareholders and stakeholders on a daily basis, teams feel like they need to show action, and therefore a bias towards immediate action can develop, promoting a culture of 'doing something is better than doing nothing'.

In short, the process of Innovation in CPG is currently broken –subjective decision making, self-interested actors, and structures and incentives that promote the status quo for innovation. Our case for Agile Innovation in Chapter 4 attempts to make the decision-making conditions more certain in order to embolden the teams leading the innovation process. It is an approach that allows for imperfection in decision-making throughout the innovation process when contrasted with other approaches taken historically.

Now that we've identified the reasons behind innovation failure, we now move forwards to articulating the art of the possible, what the authors have termed Agile Innovation.

 Key takeaways from this chapter
- People, processes and structure can be huge drivers or inhibitors of innovation in an organisation.
- Lack of data, or the wrong data and testing tools, can make Agile Innovation almost impossible to implement and lead to failure.
- Budgets and resources need to be carefully planned, supported and implemented if innovation is to succeed on a long-term timeframe.

Chapter 4 –
Flipping to success

We know from Chapter 1 that innovation generates growth opportunities in the region of 7% of category sales in FMCG in the UK, as well as helping to create long-term value for shareholders and positive cultural change in the organisation.

However, the cost of innovation, in particular the risk of innovation, can be substantial as we saw in Chapter 2, with an innovation ROI on a knifeedge, for reasons we outlined in Chapter 3.

Because of hazardous situation for Innovation's ROI, we need to ask ourselves 'could innovation be improved?' and 'what would the ROI of innovation look like if we could improve our failure rate?'. Because improving the failure rate dramatically and positively changes the ROI. Let's take the example of the engine from the end of Chapter 2 that uses three units of fuel to generate seven units of energy, but only works one time out of six. If we can make the engine work two times out of ten, we would expect the engine to generate double the units of energy without any increase in the fuel expended. That is what we are proposing here: increase the success rate, and with no extra investment innovation returns dramatically increase. The current ROI of 185% jumps to 370% if the failure rate reduces from 90% to just 80%. And that assumes no cost saving in how we innovate.

And these are the questions we have been puzzling over for the past dozen or so years – how can we change the failure rate of FMCG innovation? How could we invest in innovation differently?

Changing innovation failure rates

We have looked at different industries and looked at their innovation failure rates and how they go about innovation. We found that several industries have lower innovation failure rates than FMCG, and even more interestingly, that some of these industries used to have as high an innovation failure rate as FMCG currently has.[39] For example, Construction has a failure rate of 53%, Education 44%, and Finance 42%.

For example, the software sector historically had a high failure rate. Software engineers used to go about innovation using the Waterfall approach, with a Stage-Gate approach building on the technological features of the product, and then marketing it, and finally selling it. Innovation was about proving we can build it, not about asking whether or not we should build in the first place.

But in the early 2000s and 2010s, the view started to change in technology, in ways proposed by innovators such as Eric Ries. They sought to challenge the 90% failure rate and questioned 'why are we waiting until the end of the process to find out if consumers want this?', and instead sought to find ways to determine 'can we sell this and, if so, then can we build it?'

This radical approach dramatically changed the technology sector, helping to lower the innovation failure rate down to below 50%.[40] Not only did it reduce the failure rate, but it also drove up the efficiency of innovation, with investment only going into NPD that could prove it was popular with consumers. As Eric Ries points out in *The Lean Startup*, this way of thinking was not novel: the mail order industry had been working this way for generations; advertise a product, ensure enough people bought it, then make it.

Eric Ries's ideas were the stimulus for ours, thinking about how we can adapt the successful principles of *The Lean Startup* in technology into consumer packaged goods.

Examples of turning around failure rates in tech abound.

Amazon launched its Amazon Prime 'club' based on the 'Sam's Club' model, where

---

39 https://www.failory.com/blog/startup-failure-rate
40 www.telegraph.co.uk/finance/businessclub/11174584/Half-of-UK-start-ups-fail-within-five-years.html

for an annual fee shoppers receive benefits such as free next-day delivery. Amazon launched Prime in a matter of weeks after testing it online with consumers, and it is now a major driver for Amazon. The average Amazon Prime member spends $1,400 per year with Amazon, whereas non-Prime customers only spend $600.[41]

Spotify, the music streaming business, develops and launches new products every week, adapting and improving on features and functions that are proven to be of interest to consumers. They organise and structure their R&D team around the flow of these frequent launches, so they can learn quickly and in-depth. The results allow Spotify to thrive in a highly competitive world.

Tesla appears to be the most successful startup car brand ever, with a market capitalisation in January 2021 exceeding $700bn compared to Ford's market capitalisation of $23bn, despite shipping only a fraction of the total cars Ford has shipped. But Tesla invested in one model and invested heavily in features that were tested with consumers to see what they wanted, with those features launching frequently. Learnings from these frequent innovations showed what consumers valued and where to invest. But will Tesla continue to command such an advantage when it comes to price–earnings (PE) ratio over other automobile manufacturers? That question misses the point that innovation also drives shareholder value. The fact that the PE ratio is so high for Tesla versus Ford is because the equities market believes in Tesla's ability to execute innovation – and that innovation is what consumers want – which is therefore the biggest driver for the market capitalisation. Simply put, it is the expectation of future innovation rather than the current reality that is driving shareholder value. It may be purely coincidence that the founder of Tesla, Elon Musk, is a proven expert in Agile Innovation with Zip2 and X.com / PayPal, and is helping push less risky innovation further than incumbents anchored in their technology-led, hierarchical Waterfall Innovation approach that builds on thinking from the 1950s.

But it is not just the glitzy tech world of Tesla and Elon Musk where significant innovation change is being driven.

Within the automotive sector, John Deere – the manufacturer of agricultural and forest vehicles/machinery – has, for the last ten years, used an Agile Innovation approach to develop better innovation faster. Their software development team can develop and launch constant innovation to their vehicles, helping improve performance as well as tracking what people want from their agricultural products, further fuelling the innovation cycle in other areas outside of software such as hardware and remotely operated machinery.

---

41 https://marketrealist.com/2019/08/amazon-prime-integral-part-of-amazons-success-story/

Unbound is an example of Agile book development, where books can be funded in advance of the publication, helping authors and publishers understand the market for novel IPs or new ideas from big-name authors. In effect, Unbound sells the book before it is written, never mind published.

Kickstarter and Indigogo are an agile way for entrepreneurs to prove their product idea has consumer potential before they invest heavily in production. Successful companies such as Bragi, Oculus, and Pebble all started on kickstarter.[42]

Changing innovation in FMCG

The FMCG industry is not exempt from the challenge of launching products quicker, as P&G has shown with their three-year launch cycle for feminine care products being reduced to one year.[43] But successful innovation is not about speeding up an existing process for the sake of speeding up a process. Frequently we hear claims that 'Innovation Sprints' reduce the time for innovation, but all they are doing is stripping out rigour in the process, making the project riskier overall. Speeding up innovation is not in line with tech industry thinking or our thinking, as the innovation failure rate can only increase as a result: all that is happening is that more bad ideas go into the process, go through the process quicker, and have more risk of failure. This mindset assumes that it is the pace of the approach that is the problem, not the approach itself.

Using tech companies' and others' experience with Agile product development, combined with leading-edge thinking on consumer behaviour, we looked at FMCG innovation and how the frankly shocking failure rate can be improved and flipped into a success, helping garner not only financial returns but also cultural benefits that drive long-term innovation success.

Our approach is to make innovation better for consumers, which has as a by-product quicker, cheaper and less risky innovation – we don't start by simply making it faster or cheaper, as that increases the risk. We seek to sell the product first, ensuring consumers want it by parting with their hard-earned cash; and only then, if we can sell it, will we work out how to make it, as that proves that the innovation will work.

The FMCG industry has for the last ten years or so started taking on board the Moments of Truth following Procter & Gamble's lead. Moments of Truth are pivotal moments of a shopper's experience with a new product, first coined by

---

42 https://www.forbes.com/sites/amyfeldman/2016/04/14/ten-of-the-most-successful-companies-built-on-kickstarter/

43 https://hbr.org/2011/06/how-pg-tripled-its-innovation-success-rate

P&G. The first truth is the moment a consumer first sees the product and then chooses that product over the competitors' offerings. The second Moment of Truth is when a customer purchases a product and experiences its quality as per the promise of the brand, along with any further consumption of the brand. The final Moment of Truth is the consumer offering feedback on the product by re-purchasing it, becoming a positive advocate for the product, not buying it again, or becoming a negative advocate for the product. We underpin what we do in the Agile Innovation process by proving we are continually meeting, at the very least, the first Moment of Truth for consumers, if not the second and third Moments. Any ideas that don't meet the first Moment of Truth are binned.

Our searching and experiments applying Agile Innovation into the FMCG world have shown us the financial and personal benefits of this new way of doing innovation, and we want to share those with you in more detail in the remaining chapters.

Key takeaways from this chapter

- The innovation process is not static, and can itself be innovated. Other sectors have shown the possibilities for this.
- The future of innovation is about making better innovation products for consumers, proving that they are wanted earlier on, and binning those that don't motivate consumers.

Section two –

Agile Innovation: A Different Way

Chapter 5 –
The Agile Innovation vision

As we've highlighted, innovation drives growth opportunities, both financial and non-financial growth opportunities, from 7% of category sales, through to higher job satisfaction, higher employee retention, increased engagement scores, better suppliers, and a general air of the company going places.

Currently, FMCG is not incentivised to take advantage of these growth opportunities fully, as innovation requires 2.7% of revenues, and is extremely risky with a 90% failure rate and ultimately shareholders are happy with the returns of CPG companies. And the more a company innovates, and therefore fails, the more likely it is to stagnate and potentially fail. Like sharks, companies cannot stay still; otherwise, they atrophy and eventually perish.

Based on our work in 2015 focused on the costs of innovation, we modelled that for every successful innovation project, an organisation would require up to £41m of investment (which translates to roughly £100m–400m in sales). This level of investment is staggering and shows the compounding nature of failure when combined with the cost of product development – that is to say, the more you fail doing expensive work, the more expensive it becomes.

Multiply and accelerate innovation
So any change in the failure rate would both multiply and accelerate the performance

of any organisation. If we can reduce failure throughout the innovation cycle, there are significant savings to be made (we estimate 54% savings in product development alone, which accounts for 60% of all innovation costs).

Not only are there savings to be had from the innovation process, but reducing failure also speeds up the entire development process, as there are fewer projects in the pipeline, helping to focus resources and energies and making systems more straightforward.

Bearing this in mind, we debated long and hard about the appropriate vision we should have for innovation. We discussed the merits of various metrics, but wanted a simple metric applicable to all companies in all stages of growth. The debated centred around two sides of the same coin, namely 'innovation success' or 'innovation failure'.

Innovation success is a gloriously positive metric to have, but we also know 'innovation success' is difficult to measure, as success depends upon the objectives set, and it can become subjective very quickly. Some may see a product that only survives a few months as a success if it is to test the water for a significant introduction into a new market, or it may be a success if it blocks off a competitor from entering into the market.

Failure, although it initially seems to have negative connotations, is more accessible to evaluate. It is easier to show that a product is *not* a failure by it merely surviving beyond one or two range review cycles.

By having a metric of zero failure, it means we are producing better products that consumers love, that are incremental to the retailer and the manufacturer, demonstrating better returns for shareholders, and less impact on the environment.

We decided that our metric for Agile Innovation is zero failure.

Zero innovation failure target

This is achieved by simply making better products, products that consumers want to buy over existing products in the market. This means 100% of innovation launches surviving longer than one year, and ideally over three years. Take a moment to consider just how distant that prospect is compared to the current reality in your company. Most companies don't even evaluate their failure rate for innovation.

A company with a vision to have a zero innovation failure rate means they are focussed on only launching innovation they know will succeed, rather than hoped would succeed. They would only launch when the burden of proof was irrevocably on the chance of zero failure rather than on "taking a punt" or "building it and they will come".

And what would a company with 0% innovation failure look like? Suspend your disbelief for a moment and imagine it – a business that always succeeds. What would it look like? How would it feel to be part of that business? How would it feel to sell the products of that business? How would it feel to be a competitor to that business?

It would be utterly different from any organisation currently operating in the FMCG industry. It would be powerful yet humble. It would have the power to invest with confidence behind a key brand activation knowing it would drive value for shareholders, and be a place of humility where checking and double-checking assumptions with consumers and shoppers that this was the right thing to do would be the norm, and leaders' opinions would not just be taken as given.

It would be transformational. Suggestions and challenges from HiPPO's would evaporate, as objective data from robust contemporary methodoliges prove the first Moment of Truth for consumers would be met .

It would be effective. It would move the dial. Performance would be off the charts. Growth would appear to be effortless. It would be efficient in the use of resources of the company, leading to better financial results and less environmental impact.

But how much better would Agile Innovation be versus the current way of innovating? Let's look at the two different models in full to illustrate the principal.

Idea to innovation success funnel

Currently, innovation has a 10% chance of success: when launching ten products, one will succeed, based on the failure rate of 90% we identify in the *Common Innovation Terms*. And for every product launched, the innovation pipeline needs ten projects to be developed, as we see a failure rate during development of between 73% and 90%.[44] And for every project in the pipeline, there needs to be 30-100 ideas developed[45] from those rejected during ideation workshops to those formally rejected by Gatekeepers (Burley & Steven cite between 3,000 to 8,00

---

44 Internal study with FTSE 250 Food & Drink Company 2015
45 Internal Study with FTSE250 Food & Drink Company 2015 and 17 years experience of
    ideation workshops

or more).[46] Thus 10,000 ideas are needed for the 100 innovation projects in the pipeline needed to launch ten products, of which one will be successful.

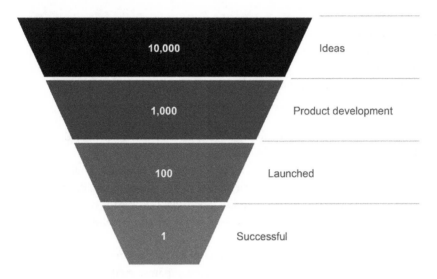

Figure 8 Current Idea to Innovation Funnel

Figure 9 Current Idea to Innovation Funnel

The cost of ideas

The cost of generating an idea is close to zero in the grand scale of innovation. The actual intellectual process in coming up with an idea is virtually free – the cost associated with the time taken to come up with an idea would be in pence, as ideas are momentary intellectual processes, perhaps taking less than a second to spark.

In 2016, an art exhibition at Popaganda in New York City by artist Saltinebomb summed up the thought of how disposable and cheap ideas are.

---

46 Greg Stevens and James Burley, "3,000 Raw Ideas = 1 Commercial Success!", Research Technology Management (May-June 1997)

But even if we took a worst case on the cost of ideas, it would still only represent a few hundred pounds for an idea.

Let's assume a traditional innovation agency has helped a company develop a host of ideas, say 100 concepts in total – a typical amount for an innovation workshop. The innovation agency would charge between £30,000 and £60,000 to facilitate the appropriate elements to develop those 100 ideas, including a typical two-day offsite meeting with stimulus sessions, breakout rooms, an illustrator – the list goes on. Each idea, in the most extreme example is between £300 - £600. But the cost of ideas is heavy because of the scale of ideas that are needed to find the ideas that have the potential to become successful products. For our model, we have assumed the cost of an idea is £600, and therefore that 10,000 ideas would cost £6m.

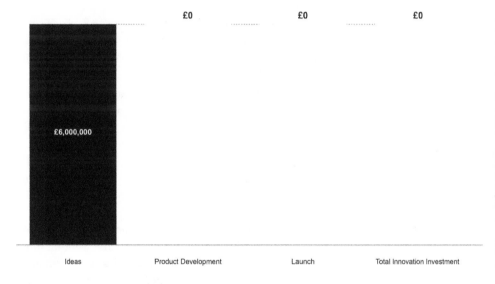

Figure 10 Current Idea to Innovation Funnel

Other innovation costs to launch

The highest cost in innovation is project management of the development of the ideas. In Chapter 2 we saw the average cost of product development as £256,200 per project launched, so therefore the cost to have 100 projects would be £25.6m of investment. To keep our model simple, we rounded down to the nearest million.

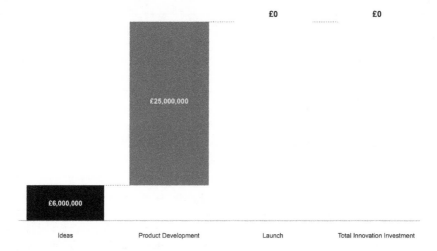

Figure 11 Product Development Costs

We assumed a launch cost of £1m per launch. This figure is a conservative estimate and does not include ATL advertising spend, which would multiply that £1m several times over. We assumed that not every innovation would have ATL support as the bulk of innovation would be EPD. Our assumptions for every launch are it would require at least one full-time equivalent (FTE) innovation team member to support the launch; at least six FTE sales team members, probably two FTE category team members; and one FTE supply chain team member, along with support teams behind the scenes of HR and finance. If we suppose it would take 13 weeks to sell-in a product from start to finish, and we assume a day rate of £500 per day per FTE to include all staff costs plus absorption of other fixed costs, then we come to £325,000 for every launch in people cost.

But it's not only the time of the people working directly on innovation that we have to consider; there's also the opportunity cost of their time spent on innovation, i.e. what would these people be doing otherwise and is that worth more than launching a new product? We have not accounted for this in our model as it would be done on a case by case basis.

In-store activity supports innovation, including simple promotions and merchandising to attract shoppers' attention to the motivating 'new' product. Typically we find support for new products in store with display features such as point of sale cards or gondola ends across all major multiple accounts in the £20k–£40k range, so across the top five significant multiples that would be £100k–£200k. The display feature may be repeated multiple times through the course of the year, usually three times per year. In addition to the display features bought, we typically find £20–£50k is spent per significant multiple on shopper marketing activation to encourage shoppers to try the new product, totalling £100k–£250k. Again, shopper activation might be a couple of bursts per annum, sometimes even three times per year. Display and shopper marketing investment would come to £600k to £1.2m alone.

We haven't included the promotional investment of discounts or retail price offerings (RPO) that are associated with displays in our analysis as it is too complex to estimate accurately. Still, we know that investment is an order of magnitude greater than the shopper marketing and merchandising costs.

Overall, we have conservatively assumed a cost of £1m per launch, but it could be considerably higher for some bigger scale innovations.

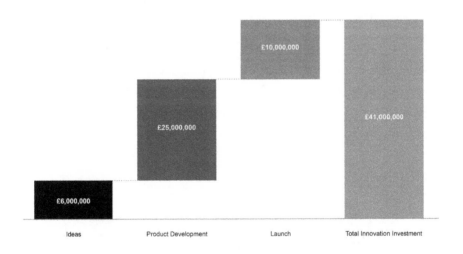

Figure 12 Current Idea to Innovation Funnel

Cost of innovation success

To launch one successful product in our modelling requires £41m of investment, with a view that companies waste 90% of that £41m, i.e. £36.9m wasted because of failure.

However, under our vision, we would spend considerably less, as we would cut the number of projects from 100 to 10 based on relevant and recent benchmarks (discussed further in the chapter on KPIs).

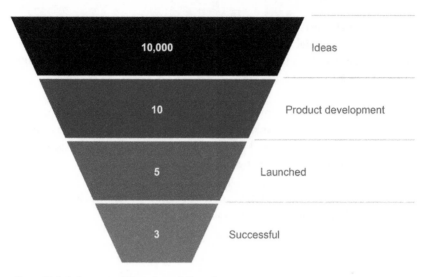

Figure 13 Agile Innovation Idea to Launch Funnel

Reducing the number of projects in development and focusing on a transparent commercial benchmark for innovation would save close to £20m alone. Our modelling would indicate that Agile Innovation can cut the average cost of successful innovation in half.

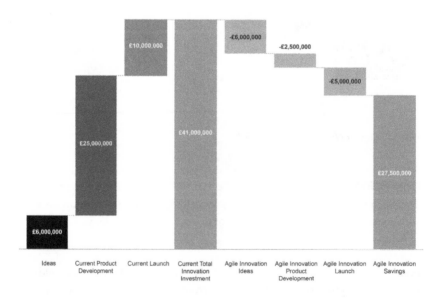

Figure 14 Agile Innovation Idea to Launch Funnel

And our modelling of £20m efficiency assumes there are not further efficiencies through this process. We know that this is conservative. We have found that by implementing this approach, reductions in the number of meetings and the length of meetings can be drastic. The provision of clear objective data against a pre-agreed action standard limits time wasted arguing on whther or not it could work – the data speaks for itself. Time is saved as there's no need to persuade others in the room to accept their point of view. Prioritisation of resources against innovation projects becomes clearer as consumer data points are met or fail to be met, and resources are moved accordingly. Time spent aligning stakeholders is easier as having a clear and aligned action standard has already been set, so stakeholder meetings are focused on updating stakeholders or improving the product. Let us be clear: we're not ruling out ALL meetings; there are still meetings; meetings where people look for creative solutions to improve the features & benefits of products or to explore different product directions. Using our Agile Innovation approach we have experienced significant reduction in time spent in meetings with people more focused on driving the product to the action standard, and thus allows for more significant efficiency savings, never mind enhanced effectiveness of having a better product.

As innovation risk is reduced, and innovation performance increased, investment in discounts and promotions could also reduce, boosting the overall margin. This is because the company's need for growth is being met by innovation, which adds more incremental value than price promotions (see Chapter 1). Retail customers would actively want innovative products, moving away from apathy for listings to the active solicitation of new products. Listing fees would disappear completely. Retail margins could conceivably shrink as retailers compete amongst themselves to offer their shoppers products in which they have absolute confidence.

Suppliers will be queuing up to work with this company to take advantage of the halo effect of being seen to work with growing companies.

Efficiency in reducing work (launching fewer products) would positively impact the supply chain, potentially allowing for more scale in supply agreements. With more efficiency in the supply chain, waste would be reduced, helping to improve any environmental impact – we'll look at this in more detail now.

Environmental impact of innovation

Discussing the impact of innovation failure on the environment is rare, as it is potentially embarrassing. Innovation failure in our experience has meant destroying and recycling complex electronic products, disposing of chemical waste from failed innovation projects, sending food products for animal feed, and destroying the associated sales and marketing materials employed for the doomed launch. By reducing 70%–90% of innovation launches we can eliminate a significant source of environmental waste.

The amount of waste generated by failed innovation is difficult to calculate exactly. The packaging from the produced products, and those packaging materials bought but not used, could be recycled, especially if they are glass, metal, paper or some plastics. Then there's the launch product itself. That would have to be dealt with, ideally with a remnant stock seller, who in turn sells it on to retailers, and eventually consumers. Excess failed products might be reused; for example in food & non-alcoholic drinks, it is frequently re-purposed into animal feed. Sometimes (in the instance of alcohol products) in order for the disposal of failed product to comply with environmental regulations, the product needs to be treated prior to being, which adds extra cost for failed products.

We are seeing innovative companies sprouting up to take the excess, damaged, or redundant products of failed innovation and re-use them, such as coffee beans into logs for wood-burning stoves, or excess or damaged fruit being used to make gin[47]. Perhaps innovation will solve all of innovation's own environmental problems, with a solution for failed new products. Then there are the launch materials, including the point of sale displays. We know from personal experience that a vast amount of promotional clothing for failed launches is given away to charities, and then in turn go to developing countries. And point of sale materials are mulched up and recycled in a similar way to the recycling of existing products.

Innovation needs to do more to reduce the impact on the environment. In our experience, we have yet to see any accounting for the costs to comply with environmental regulation for failed projects in advance of a launched product. By highlighting the costs in advance, and being clearer about what will work and won't work through Agile Innovation, then the environmental impact from innovation will reduce.

Employee benefits of zero failure

A company with successful innovation is a company that always meets its budgets and pays out on its incentives. In turn, team members will be happy in a job well done, and to be seen doing a good job, as well as a job that incentivises their efforts. Rewards and recognition symbiotically work together to generate high levels of productivity and job satisfaction.

---

47 https://www.foxholespirits.com/pages/our-story

The effect upon individuals in the organisation is not just at a financial level. There would be more job satisfaction and increased self-esteem as people see the impact of their behaviour in results. They would be less stressed overall and they would be expending less energy on fewer projects. This 'frictionless' working would mean less burnout of individuals and a more harmonious, productive culture.

We have also seen a further non-financial benefit of 0% failure, which is less management and more self-starting autonomous work. When there are precise data to make decisions that are independently verifiable, cheap and quick, people start to engage more through curiosity rather than being told to. It becomes like a game. 'How can I score higher?', 'What can I do differently?' It can, in some circumstances we have seen, become a challenge laced with fun. These self-starters require and desire significantly less management and want significantly less management. More self-starters frees up resources for managers to work on their own projects or potentially redeploy into other areas. This self-starting curiosity results in a compounded productivity – more people are working more effectively, needing fewer people to manage them.

The financial growth of the company means more recruitment over time, and that growth in employees drives more career opportunities in the organisation. The calibre of the candidates applying for roles would, we expect, to increase, as a company becomes renowned for job satisfaction, career growth, reward and recognition programmes, and increased investment. As the calibre of recruits increases, so too does the overall capabilities of the organisation.

Shareholder benefits of zero failure
A 0% failure rate would also mean that shareholders would be more confident about the long-term outlook of the company, therefore boosting the value perception of the company – i.e. the share price. The company would also be active in allocating more of their investment into innovation, driving a higher valuation for the company in the process.

Capability to manage complexity more easily
A further benefit of this innovative approach is that it would develop a capability in a company to manage complex projects and associated risks easily. Innovation is complicated, and currently prone to failure; it's perhaps the riskiest part of doing business in most organisations. If a business can control the riskiest part effectively through better management and culture, then it bodes well for other similarly complex challenges an organisation will face.

These 'network effects', although intangible and technically all non-financial, compound together to drive a higher return than just a 50%–90% saving in product development. When combined, the multiplied effect from better innovation is substantial.

Innovation growth, faster

And it is not only the multiplier effect but also the accelerator effect. Currently, there is massive waste in the innovation cycle, as multiple projects develop at different stages, each requiring attention and investment, with some of these projects requiring up to 700 FTE days. Our vision for 0% failure speeds up this process, partly because the decision-making criteria are readily available and less prone to being swayed by a single opinion (ideally they are not opinion-based at all). We can see from our work that we are saving hundreds of days from the idea and development stages, as the criteria are more prescriptive initially than the current method. People no longer have to invest time in thinking and persuading others as to whether an idea is likely to be a success when a simple metric can do the job better.

From this comes organisational agility. Fewer people are needed. Fewer decisions are needed to be made by senior team members. Decisions are local, where the data is. The organisation as a whole becomes more accountable as the centre of decision-making has moved lower down, creating a more motivating, satisfying, productive and profitable enterprise.

This pace of bringing ideas to market will also mean organisations can react more quickly to events and keep their products relevant to shoppers and consumers. The organisation can grab more of the overall opportunity from being both early and successful.

Overall, having a 0% failure rate creates a virtuous circle, where success breeds further success. The investment would flow from current sales drivers (e.g. promotions), that have relatively lower returns on investment, into innovation, where the return on investment is higher, creating an engine for growth: more success creates more demand for innovation, which allows for more investment in innovation.

An organisation with a 0% innovation failure rate as its vision will be a place people want to work and invest in, and an organisation where growth becomes more efficient over time. It would be a hugely ambitious and positive step forward for improved growth for the company.

In the next chapter we're going to illustrate how your business, which in essence is all of the people working in it, could look and feel if it were to embrace Agile Innovation.

Key takeaways from this chapter

- Currently, to have one successful product a company needs to have 10,000 ideas, 100 products in development, and ten launched products, costing over £41m, of which £36.9m is wasted.
- Agile innovation can cut £25m of development costs by 90% and increase the pace of innovation, as well as success overall.
- Agile innovation not only drives the financials but also improves the culture of the company and how the company carries itself in the marketplace.

Chapter 6 –
How does your business
look and feel?

A company that can eliminate Innovation failure can jump-start its performance not only through better innovation, but also by being more productive in its innovation. We've seen the virtuous circle opportunity that Agile Innovation presents for the organisation. But we haven't explored how an Agile-envisioned business would behave. What would it do differently? How would it actually work? Who would make the innovation decisions? Who would govern the process?

In this chapter, we explore the impact of Agile Innovation and of having a successful innovation track record, and how the Agile Innovation process and the ensuing pipeline can trigger a flywheel of momentum for a business. How does it feel internally, and what impact and opportunities does it begin to create?

There is a self-fulfilling prophecy that occurs within businesses that begin to innovate successfully, having invested upfront in structures, resources and processes to do so. Customers and clients begin to eagerly anticipate the next product release; innovation consistently generates a return on the investment made to create and launch it; investment levels back into innovation increase as a result; the press and markets begin to recognise the consistently high levels of innovation displayed; and talented people want to come and work for the business as it grows and expands.

From push to pull

The shift from a 'push' effect to a 'pull' effect is an important one to dwell on here. What we mean when we talk about push / pull is the following.

A push effect for innovation means that the business that is innovating has to work hard to 'push' the new product or service onto the market. If it's a manufacturer, they have to work hard to convince retailers to stock the new product. If it's a retailer, they have to promote the new product incredibly hard to get customers to pick it up in sufficient volume. Any attempts at PR fall on mostly deaf ears, and there is a collective shrugging of the shoulders from consumers and trade customers alike. Whilst the product may sell an average amount, it hardly blazes a trail for future launches of a similar ilk.

A pull effect for innovation is the complete opposite; the market effect is so strong that it 'pulls' the innovation out of the business. Anticipation is high, demand is strong, and it's a case of deciding whom to supply rather than desperately trying to force stock through the supply chain. For manufacturers, this means being in control of commercial terms with channel partners and retailers. It means guaranteed shelf space for new launches, which gives huge confidence in planning and forecasting. For retailers, it means footfall driving launches that bring in new customers and delight existing ones.

Some prominent examples of businesses that experience this pull effect are:

Apple – an obvious example, but one worth mentioning, nonetheless. The anticipation of their device launches, particularly back in the early to mid-noughties, was hyped to unprecedented levels. The subsequent financial impact (being the biggest company in the world by market capitalisation at certain subsequent points; massive profitability) set new standards on multiple levels.

Supreme – this youth fashion retailer has got staggered, limited edition, hyped product launches down to a fine art. If you walk through a city centre shopping area and see queues of fashionable looking young people waiting to get into a store, it's probably Supreme. They call it their 'drop' strategy; new product releases sell out almost immediately on limited stock runs, and then restocks to the inventory are done sporadically and without much fanfare. The hype around the drops builds on the psychology of FOMO – fear of missing out. This approach to stock scarcity is a strategy

---

scarcely employed in other parts of the consumer goods market yet is one that has led to Supreme becoming a billion-dollar business in the highly competitive street fashion market.

Nike and Adidas – building on the approach of Supreme, footwear giants Nike and Adidas ensure there is pent up demand for their products through limited edition lines, collaborations with artists, and re-releases of old models to drive 'collectability' across certain parts of their range. They maintain a very high pace of innovation so that avid fans are constantly engaged, and there is always something new to look out for. They have also begun to experiment with personalisation – the ability to take a core model and adapt the colourways or add wording to the product, which could be a very big driver of innovation in the future.

Nespresso (Nestlé) – this has to be one of the more sustainably successful products launches within the food and drink industry in the last 20 years[48]. They followed the approaches used in other verticals (Gillette's razor blade strategy, Xerox's printer ink strategy) to create an ecosystem of products that create lock-in and repeat purchases. Once consumers have bought a coffee pod machine and tasted the quality, the only way they can continue is through purchasing the Nespresso coffee pods. The quality of the coffee, ease of use, and impact of the branding has led to a highly successful, profitable business unit being created and sustained within Nestlé. The initial push effect through Advertising with George Clooney has now developed into a pull effect for future launches.

Diageo – in the early 2000s Diageo had a string of innovation successes, one of the biggest of which was Smirnoff Ice. The success from Smirnoff Ice fuelled other successful launches such as Smirnoff Black Ice (a flavour variant of Smirnoff Ice and nominated by AC Nielsen as the best launch of 2004) as well as Archer's Aqua in 2001. All of these contributed to massive incremental innovation into the alcoholic beverage category. Unfortunately, Diageo was not able to maintain the golden touch for pre-mixed spirits, with a series of new product failures including Gordon's Edge, Baileys Glide, Slate 20, Archer's Vea and Quinn's. Diageo subsequently regained it's edge in launching innovation of pre-mixed spirits with canned spirits and mixers such as Gordon's and Tonic.

---

48 https://digital.hbs.edu/platform-digit/submission/brewing-a-successful-future-at-nespresso

Impact on talent

Working within a successful innovation led business has a very significant impact on talent. The social and professional kudos of working for a business that has a strong track record in innovation, and a strong pipeline of innovation projects coming up, is significant. Think for a moment how different it would have been to work for Apple with Steve Jobs at his peak circa 2007, compared to being an NPD manager at an underfunded, margin-deprived private-label goods manufacturer in 2020. It's arguably not a fair comparison, but from the perspective of talent management, let's dwell on it for a moment.

In Apple in 2007, every job vacancy gets hundreds of applicants, so the calibre of recruitment is extremely high whilst the cost of recruitment in relative terms is comparably low (few headhunters or job ads are required). Staff engagement would be incredibly high and churn very low. Expectation levels would be very high, with underperforming staff quickly managed out, either by peer performance or by management intervention. The excitement of getting involved across the business to manage the next big product release would result in staff enthusiastically learning about other parts of the organisation to become more rounded managers. They could learn from some of the top people in the business world just by observing their managers and leaders. Contrast that to the private-label manufacturer; job vacancies get very few applicants, so the business is forced to engage expensive headhunters to find good quality talent. When candidates are identified, they often have to be lured with attractive packages, so the costs of recruitment are proportionally far higher. Staff engagement is below average; excitement levels in the business are non-existent, and although churn may be low it's often the wrong people not leaving.

People want to work in successful companies – they desert sinking ships

Confidence is king. It sells, and people invest in it. This leads us onto the positive financial opportunities that can stem from Agile Innovation.

Profitability and growth that stems from innovation breeds confidence. Confidence leads to investment and a long-term view. The profits from innovation drive differentiation in the business, moving it away from competitors and into what business schools term 'red ocean' space. Those profits lead to investment in people; not only new people but upskilling the capabilities of the existing team. That confidence leads to a clear understanding and communication of the metrics that drive the business: what are the minimum profitable production runs, what is the lowest percentage margin they will sell at to a customer, and other decisions across the business that lead to a maximisation of profits and investment. This again drives the talent agenda, which in turn drives the innovation success, which generates profitability and kudos – you see where we're heading.

Successful innovation companies are perceived by stock market analysts as having higher potential future revenues, which will be reflected in their price–earnings (PE) ratio, and ultimately their market capitalisation. So a small amount of incremental profit, when magnified through a higher PE ratio, makes a very big impact for shareholders, with a higher price-to-innovation-adjusted-earnings ratio.

There are various ways of measuring innovation, from subjective judgement to the future premium investors put on a stock. These metrics, in turn, alongside the benefits from customers, would increase the return on investment of the company overall, in particular from innovation. More investment would be put into innovation, and more returns would be generated. Funding would flow into innovation from inefficient non-value-adding investments such as promotions and discounts.

And then there's the fame. Successful innovation companies will be more written about and more talked about. They would be invited to conferences and appear in business magazines to share how they innovate. Journalists would regularly ask them for sneak previews of upcoming products. Product launches are guaranteed coverage because the journalists and editors understand the demand. Product launches trend on social media and increase the pool of early adopters every time.

Even when you get it wrong, those mistakes trigger other companies to bring out better versions, and trends start, so the investment isn't lost on the market. The business becomes respected for understanding the consumer and the category more than before.

The personal impact of working in an Agile organisation

Working autonomously feels radically different from working in a directed, bureaucratic and hierarchical organisation. It isn't necessarily something that would suit all personality types: it would be liberating for many; however, some would find it unsettling and would crave more specific direction.

The professional impact

The freedom to make decisions, with strong boundaries and a clear sense of mission, would have a huge impact on individuals. Seldom is that witnessed in most traditional corporations. The feeling would be liberating, empowering and energising. A greater sense of ownership and responsibility would follow, leading to more entrepreneurial traits being displayed across the business.

The personal satisfaction coming from an environment like that is much more in tune with that of an entrepreneur than that of a corporate manager. That is part of what Agile Innovation tries to accomplish – decision-making and ownership more in tune with a tech entrepreneur than a faceless corporation.

On a more pragmatic level, you'll spend less time in meetings; that alone is a reason to do Agile. Sign-off by the organisation's innovation committee will be less and less common, which means not only fewer meetings, but also less time in meetings or preparing for meetings with senior stakeholders. The day-to-day role will actually be just that – doing the day-to-day role, as opposed to sitting in meetings justifying your existence and pipeline. In short, more time doing the actual work that you signed up for in the first place.

An Agile business is a lean business, so it'll simplify organisational structures and reporting lines, reducing meaningless office politics, and gives you more time to do the elements of the job that you enjoy. It'll probably mean less office space needed too, with fewer meeting rooms, which reduces administrative overheads, making innovation cheaper.

Working closely with key cross-functional colleagues in a common way means enhanced learning opportunities for everyone. Challenges being overcome results in fulfilment and collaboration; everybody has a voice in an Agile environment. Debates only centre on the interpretation of the data used for decision-making. It makes managing teams and projects easier as there are clearly defined metrics and schedules to be used.

And when it comes to innovation, in an Agile organisation, it becomes safe to be bold. It becomes normal; leaders empower autonomy and trust teams to make decisions. Bold decisions supported and evidenced by the data become the norm across most teams and individuals. Bold innovation that is backed up by the data all the way through its development journey becomes more and more common. And the return on investment kicks on from there – this is the self-fulfilling prophecy we have previously spoken about.

The personal impact

Work–life balance becomes far more attainable as you can achieve your KPIs in a more realistic timeframe. Working from home is accepted as a key approach to the successful delivery of KPIs as it's an Agile organisation based on trust. That means less commuting, more exercise, more time with family and friends. It means better rested executives who are more focused and energised when they do work. Employees are more likely to work from distinct and diverse locations than all be in the same geographic area, which results in more diversity of stimulus and therefore better ideas. Ideas are not limited to London.

The widespread use of transparent data for decision-making results in far less anxiety and stress. If the data is effectively driving team decisions, not one isolated individual, there is far less pressure on any individual's shoulders. And that means a feeling of winning (and learning) together, without the sense of isolation experienced by many executives in traditional corporations. The feeling of going out on a limb to take a risk would be massively reduced.

It helps progress their career as they have more successes and they develop new cutting-edge skills. They learn how to manage projects and they manage diverse teams with high autonomy and alignment.

Happy and proud team members are more engaged, which ultimately benefits both the individual and the business itself, as more contented staff are more likely to stay. These super-engaged employees can be given the opportunity to be mentors and coaches in the organisation to help develop less experienced or newer colleagues, further helping to instil the culture, as well as rewarding the high performers with social recognition.

Retention and recruitment

What happens to retention and churn in an Agile organisation?

As staff satisfaction increases, so too does employee engagement, as employees are more satisfied with their jobs, and satisfied employees are more engaged. Equally an engaged workforce is a more productive and happy workforce – this isn't rocket science we're revealing here.

From a business perspective, an engaged workforce equates to far lower staff turnover levels. This reduces costs quite significantly as you're not recruiting for new people in the same role every couple of years. This means far lower recruitment costs, and a smaller HR team to manage the workforce.

Instead of looking for jobs elsewhere, Agile organisations are able to offer individuals roles in new teams and departments due to the high level of cross-functionality and sharing seen in these businesses. That means those team members who are looking for a new challenge can find it internally rather than externally. It becomes much easier to build a substantial career in Agile businesses as you can build experience in areas that you wouldn't get exposed to in traditional siloed corporations.

And what is the recruitment impact?

It doesn't take a PhD to figure out how easy it will be to attract superstars to a business that is constantly in the trade press because of the quality and hype surrounding its new product releases. You're also more likely to be able to attract high calibre candidates who thrive on autonomy and really driving forward towards a clear objective and mission.

This influx of talent further heightens the high-performance nature of the organisation, driving even stronger behaviours and output from existing teams. Underperforming individuals stick out like a sore thumb, and it becomes much easier for organisations to identify them, performance manage them and then, if required, move them on.

Existing team members talk glowingly about life in the organisation to their friends and family, and this, in turn, has a positive effect on the calibre of candidates applying for roles. Net promoter scores improve; stellar ratings for senior management on sites like Glassdoor drive candidate calibre. This is why investment in innovation should be prioritised by senior managers across all functions of the business – it improves their KPIs too…!

Now that we've explored what your business could look and feel like, we'll get into the nuts and bolts of implementing Agile Innovation in your business. This is the focus of the final chapter of this section, Chapter 7.

 Key takeaways from this chapter
- Embracing an Agile Innovation approach in an organisation will result in a different look and feel within the current organisation.
- Innovation moves from 'push', where the organisation has to reach out to customers, persuading them to take the product, always looking for extra distribution space; to 'pull', where customers are actively looking for your innovation to help them grow, knocking down barriers for your organisation to have more distribution and promotional space.
- There are professional and personal benefits to an Agile approach, which when all combined within the organisation means more happy and productive teams and easier recruitment of better candidates.

Chapter 7 –
Bringing Agile Innovation
into an organisation

Innovation for growing a business and its people is a necessity, although the costs and risks of innovation make it challenging to achieve growth, let alone long-term sustainable growth. We've shown how the lack of innovation in innovation has meant that the risks and costs associated with it haven't changed in the last 20 years at least, and we've outlined the need to move away from the current and inefficient way of innovating.

We've shared our vision for the benefits of moving to an Agile way of developing new products, creating an organisation that drives long-term sustainable innovation and is a better company for employees, shareholders, customers and consumers.

Now, in Chapter 7, we explore Agile Innovation in detail, outlining what it takes to bringing agile innovation into your organisation, in particular the differences in mindset and process, and also being clear on what doesn't change, such as governance. In later chapters, we'll explore how best to structure your teams for Agile Innovation.

What is Agile Innovation?
Agile Innovation is the development of new products based on responding to

continuous consumer testing, eliminating failure with a pace and efficiency not found in traditional models of innovation. It is the application of Lean Startup methodologies, in our case into a consumer goods world.

Why is Agile Innovation different?

Traditional innovation is one where an idea is the first phase of development, and then the product is developed in a sequential manner, usually through a Stage Gate process. As previously discussed, this is sometimes referred to as a Waterfall approach, as when the entire project is reviewed on a Gannt chart it resembles a series of waterfalls.

Agile is fundamentally different from Waterfall in its approach, although all of the developmental parts are the same, in that there still needs to be packaging development and production trials etc. The 'what' of innovation doesn't change, it's the 'how' and the mindset that changes.

The mindset of Waterfall is about building a product based on an idea and ultimately selling that to consumers. This means products are generally developed with little or no interaction with the shoppers or consumers. It is only once the expensive development has taken place that consumers are invited to buy it in the store, amongst a plethora of other products competing for the shoppers' and consumers' attention. Only after investing hours and hours of product development time can a company following a Waterfall approach know whether or not an innovation product will actually work. The risks in following the Waterfall approach are huge and result in a 90% failure rate of all *launched* products[49] – let alone all those which never make it that far.

Agile works the other way around, seeking to establish whether a product can be sold to consumers, and then only when it's clear it can be sold should it be made. All decisions and assumptions throughout the development process are tested with consumers to ensure that they would continue to buy the product. This eliminates waste in the product development cycle as it gives a clearer and more confident brief, as well as eliminating elongated discussions of what should or should not be developed. It also ensures there are no material compromises made in the development versus what consumers are willing to buy.

When we first read *The Lean Startup*, we thought that this all made sense. Test and learn – how can anyone disagree with that principle? We reflected back upon our innovation projects and thought we had tested products with consumers before we started development. However, as we challenged ourselves, we realised we

---

49 Defined as any product that is withdrawn from sale within 12 months of launch.

hadn't been following a Lean Innovation approach. A number of projects had zero research at all. Most did have research, but the research was at best superficial in that the methodologies were old and unreliable, and the benchmarks were out of date or unrelated (at the time these were best practice quant studies). We only ever tested the concept, not the execution of the development, such as claims or designs. We would never test price, or test promotional execution, just rely on the previous understanding, and therefore assumptions. We were clearly not following a Lean Startup methodology in our innovation efforts but had deluded ourselves that because our strike rate was better than 90% failure (it was in the high 70s) that we were good at innovation.

So how does Agile reduce risk rather than increase it? Risks are tackled upfront in the process with the input of the people who will ultimately buy the product, rather than at the end, and *before* deciding to develop anything and incur costs. Risks include value risk (i.e. will customers buy it), feasibility risk (can our suppliers or our site make it) and stakeholder risk (will our business go for it).

Products are designed and defined collaboratively, rather than sequentially. The old way was a product manager defining requirements, a designer designing a solution for those requirements, and then production and technical teams implementing those requirements. Each person lived with the constraints of the decisions of the preceding team member. The new way is for product, design and technical teams to work side-by-side, in a give-and-take way, to come up with technology-powered solutions that are then tested: with consumers and shoppers to find out if they love them, and to see whether they work for the business.

Agile is about efficiency. About only developing product features of designs that motivate shoppers or consumers. If it doesn't motivate shoppers or consumers, it is redundant. Time and time again, we see over-elaborate solutions developed to problems that don't exist, or solutions shoppers and consumers don't value. This might be a graphic design where an overly elaborate design adds less value than a simple design. Or it might be in the expression of a product claim or a name that doesn't resonate.

Finally, Agile Innovation is about solving problems together by testing with consumers, not implementing features individually, inconsiderate of consumers' behaviour. Product pipelines are traditionally about output. However strong Agile teams know it's not just about implementing a solution; it's also about ensuring the solution solves the underlying problem well.

In short, it could be said that traditional innovation is 'make it then sell it', whereas Agile Innovation is 'sell it then make it': it seeks to ensure, as much as possible, that what is produced is what consumers want and at a price they would be willing to pay.

This is not straightforward; the change in mindset requires the discipline to test every assumption, and to engage teams of people who are humble enough to want to test their own ideas and expressions with consumers, risking failure via research.

How does Agile Innovation work?

Agile innovation seeks to verify the consumers' Moments of Truth earlier on in the product development cycle in a much more thorough manner and at a significantly reduced investment than the traditional Waterfall approach. By focusing on these Moments of Truth sequentially and testing them thoroughly with consumers, the risk is – as per our vision – reduced completely. Agile development aims to stress test a hypothesis or theory which has been worked up at the start of the project before ideating products that fit with the theory.

Agile Innovation is a scientific and test-driven approach throughout product development, where every assumption in the product development process is validated with consumers, starting with the biggest assumptions first, which are usually the first Moment of Truth assumptions.

Traditional innovation practices may only check some assumptions at the start of the process through consumer research, and that consumer research may be limited in both its scale as well as its efficacy. Traditional concept testing perhaps would only test a limited number of concepts, not every expression conceivable. The methodology of traditional research is a 'likely' question, such as 'How likely are you to buy this product?', with a scale of 1 to 10, frequently giving a measure referred to as 'Top Two Box', as the researchers aggregate results from 7 to 10 into the Top Two boxes. This means a person who says they are 7 out of 10 likely to buy a product is assumed to want to purchase it. All seems logical at this point. However, let me ask you this question – when was the last time you bought a product thinking you were 7 out of 10 likely to buy it? Shoppers who buy a product are 10 out of 10. Shoppers who don't buy a product are 0 out of 10. These types of questions are relics from antiquated research methodologies: they are using a Likert scale for a binary choice. It is yes or no question, not a maybe. Respondents to these research questions are at best being polite when they offer a 7 out of 10, or (more likely) they don't know if they would buy it, which is an 'I wouldn't buy it' by another name.

Even if the researchers adopted different questions, they have fallen guilty in the past of using out of date or irrelevant benchmarks. They quote category benchmarks, but these are likely to have been made in previous research in the category, which might have been a considerable time ago. So the ideas being measured seem to have a higher rate of success than they actually would.

Setting aside the efficacy points above, when using the Waterfall approach to test ideas it's only possible to screen a limited number of concepts as budgets don't allow for multiple testing rounds. This limits the opportunities massively. Agile Innovation looks to test dozens if not hundreds of concepts and ideas. Recently with a client, we tested over 10,000 concepts over two years, mostly because we had a higher KPI than traditional Waterfall businesses for progressing ideas, but also because we wanted to identify the best concept to progress.

Traditional innovation engagement with the shopper/consumer would stop here (assuming it had even started at all). In contrast, Agile Innovation sequentially builds on known facts about consumers and about what they are motivated to buy, rather than on technological know-how, assumed knowledge or opinion-based decisions. Agile Innovation constantly checks with the consumer that they would buy the product, as the product being developed might change, or the consumers themselves might change.

Agile seeks to ensure that *every* element of the product development stage is validated with a robust number of consumers at every turn. The testing is scientific, in that all the elements are controlled, and one element is changed systematically at a time to gauge the effect of the change. With the appropriate measure in place in advance, the decision-making process for product development is taken out of the hands of opinion and subjectivity and put into a rigorous, objective process that allows for either persevere, progress or pivot. Agile Innovation seeks to confirm the assumptions in order, with the biggest assumption first (e.g. is this idea motivating enough for consumers to buy it), and then through a range of other assumptions eventually building confidence behind a product concept that consumers have fully validated all the way along. Or, if the assumptions are proved wrong, to allow businesses to walk away from product ideas that would not have worked in the first place, allowing resources to flow to the products with the highest chance of success.

In an ideal world, this product testing would be in a store, with real products and real shoppers. However, for many reasons, this isn't practical – cost, time, secrecy, ease of measurement, product safety. We know; we've done it. In 2015 a client wanted to launch a new wine into the UK from Australia with a significantly different approach to wine labelling, using bold graphics. We sought to test this in the real world. Using sample labels from the client in Australia, we partnered with a local wine shop here in the UK to stock these dummy wine bottles. The dummy bottles contained real wine, just with a new label on them. We wanted to test the biggest assumption, that of the first Moment of Truth – would a consumer buy it! The wine was displayed in-store along with the competing products, and we worked in the store to covertly research how shoppers engaged with the product. We deliberately didn't advocate any wines during the test and left the wine to effectively fend for itself. We were able to watch as shoppers engaged in the category and how they would engage with the new product. After several weeks it was clear that this product would not pass the first Moment of Truth. This was an expensive way of testing the product, as it took a considerable amount of time and human input but it is the most realistic method.

In the 21st century, Agile Innovation tests products on a regular basis using tech. We have overcome the challenges of testing in the real world by developing a 'simulated world' where we can gauge consumers' behaviour, providing tools and techniques that mimic the real world in terms of results, but at a significantly lower cost, quicker turnaround, and with far more secrecy than in the real world.

Through this 'simulated world', we can test not only ideas, but the execution of the development of these ideas, and do so sequentially. In our Agile Innovation process, we can go from idea to concept, to pack design, to product claims, to price, and even brand positioning and brand development, all in the simulated world. We design, then develop: designing product specifications digitally, cheaply and quickly before developing anything physically. From recipe description and product formulation all the way through to pack design and price point, before anything is built or created in a kitchen or lab, we test. We create a hypothesis, take a set of assumptions, test them, iterate, reject ones that don't pass the success criteria, build on the ones that do. This massively reduces the risk in the innovation process. It needs a robust benchmarking or acceptability testing approach to work well (which we will explore in later chapters), but when it does work it means that propositions that are either going to fail or not sell more than the products they are replacing will be weeded out early in the process, at very low cost. Poor products don't even make it to the development lab, let alone the shelf. We will explore how we test in later chapters.

'Build–measure–learn' is the key learning and feedback loop. One of the main principles in Agile is the ability to test everything at a very granular level, repeatedly and almost daily throughout the process. Small micro-changes can rapidly be prototyped digitally and tested without incurring a high cost. Only propositions or elements of the proposition that pass the action standard can progress through to form the final product specification.

The two key phases of Agile Innovation are validation and optimisation. In validation, you can take hundreds of product concepts, ideas, trends, etc. and rapidly rank them to understand which ones are likely to generate a positive impact on the category. This continues into more granular levels with validation of myriad product concepts that can, during each stage of development called a Sprint, be ranked and whittled down. Once you have a set of top-level product concepts that have passed the acceptability testing criteria, you move on to the second phase: optimisation. This is the process of squeezing every ounce of commercial potential from a product proposition before you begin to physically develop it. The type of levers that would be optimised in this phase would be price, pack design, product title, pack claims and supporting comms.

Where appropriate this can be delivered using a Sprint approach to ideating and testing. Agile Innovation isn't a process with a set number of steps – a fixed process is completely contrary to Agile. Rather it is a set of steps for a team to go through as they refine and develop product specifications. Each Sprint is an individual phase in this fluid process. A Sprint would typically be one element of a set of assumptions, ideas or concepts that are all tested at the same time in high volume, often but not necessarily at high speed. Only the ones that hit the success criteria go on to the next Sprint. For example, on a set of products being developed for a retailer, one Sprint could be focused on price. The team would test tens or hundreds of product concepts using the same price criteria, and only the ones that match or exceed the required price point would pass to the next phase.

Sprints need to be run with cross-functional teams from individual categories, divisions or businesses. They can be run remotely or face-to-face. A typical Sprint with a category team in a retailer would involve the buyer, product developer, a graphic designer, copywriter, consumer insight analyst and a product technologist. Each product concept being tested during a Sprint must be represented in the testing in exactly the same format. For example, if you were using an illustrator to bring to life product concepts in a Sprint, you couldn't test the benchmarks in the same Sprint using photography, as it would introduce bias and imbalance to the testing. Sprints work well with a facilitator who can impartially lead the team through the phases at pace. An Agile Innovation journey for an individual business could be two Sprints, or it could be 200. There is no fixed set of steps; however most businesses will have an existing 'Gate' led approach to developing products, and this can be used as a guide at the start of an Agile Innovation experiment for most businesses. The testing is effectively recreating consumer purchase intent at every stage, as that is the core purpose of any new product – to appeal to the target consumer in enough volume to justify the investment in the design and development of the product.

We've made important distinctions between Agile Innovation and Waterfall / the Stage-Gate process. However, we are not suggesting throwing the baby out with the bath water when it comes to Stage-Gate. Stage-Gate is still an important tool in overall project management, and is especially good at governing the investment into innovation. Stage-Gate ensures investment is placed in projects at the right time, and if managed appropriately ensures the right resources are being funnelled into the best opportunities. We think Stage-Gate should still be used for governance, but the mindset should be that of Agile Innovation.

The result of Agile should be innovation done quicker, better and cheaper. Quicker – either quicker time to market in terms of shortening the development cycle, or moving faster through an existing process. Better – more revenue success, higher category impact, and stronger profit and growth for the products that launch through an Agile process. Cheaper – less cost incurred as investment decisions are only made on the back of successful, validated propositions.

These are all principles taken from the software development/technology industry, which now boasts seven of the eight most valuable companies on the planet.

How Agile reduces risk

The biggest difference between a Waterfall approach and an Agile approach is the handling of risk, via assumptions. In the Waterfall approach a number of assumptions are made through the process (people want your product, people want it in a specific colour, people are prepared to pay a certain amount etc.) and risk accumulates as the project goes on, with the real test of the risk only coming at the end when the consumers are asked to put the product in their grocery trolley or their online basket. At that point, if the consumer doesn't put it in their basket, all the hard work is undone, and worse yet, *nobody can identify exactly what the problem is*. Even if consumers do buy it, there is still an issue, in that there is little to no understanding as to why: the drivers of them purchasing it are completely unknown. So the Waterfall approach wastes time and money, and actually makes matters worse by not identifying the issues and drivers of the product development process. Agile, on the other hand, reduces the overall risk as it de-risks each element in the product development process as it goes, seeking to answer the underlying assumption of each element. Not only does Agile de-risk the overall project, but it also increases the opportunity of the product.

Agile does not seek to negate the Stage-Gate process, but rather break it up into a series of phases, with the assumptions in each stage being validated with consumers behind the biggest assumption of all – will people buy this product. It also seeks to use the good governance of Stage-Gate. You can then continually loop back and retest until you have a proposition that is resonating with consumers.

1) What can we learn from the world of product management, a discipline within software development that works within Agile? For a good product team,
2) Products are designed and defined collaboratively, rather than sequentially. The old world was a Product Manager defining requirements, a designer designing a solution for those requirements, and then production & technical implementing those requirements. Each person lived with the constraints of the decisions of the person preceding. The new way is for product, design and engineering to work side by side, in a give and take way, to come up with technology-powered solutions that customers love and that work for the business."
3) It's about solving problems, not implementing features. Product pipelines are traditionally about output. Strong teams know it's not only about implementing a solution, but they must also ensure the solution solves the underlying problem. Identifying and agreeing on customer problems and pain points upfront is a crucial step to building relevant solutions. If you don't know what pain point you're solving, your solution is unlikely to be successful.

Strong product teams talk about continuous discovery and delivery. What this means is that product teams firstly need to discover the product to be built, and then they need to deliver the product to market. Discovery and delivery become the two main activities of a cross-functional product team, and they should ideally be run in parallel to keep a strong pipeline of ideas and concepts flowing through. In a cross-functional team in a technology company, the product manager and designer focus on discovery, whilst the engineering team work on delivering production-quality products. This is a little simplified, and there is a fair degree of crossover, but at a high level, this is a good outline.

The purpose of discovery is to separate the good ideas from the bad; the output of discovery is a validated product pipeline ready for engineering delivery. Prototypes would be used heavily in the discovery phase of a software product development process, and the prototypes would be used to run experiments quickly and inexpensively. A prototype would be the minimum standard required for a user (customer) to identify and engage with. It wouldn't be functional, automated or intelligent at this point – the team are merely trying to identify whether users would choose to buy it or use it. Once the team have provided evidence that something is worth building, the delivery team takes over to build a production-quality version of the prototype that can be sold to users through the relevant channels at a price identified in the discovery phase.

And now onto the final section of this book, focusing on the tools and approaches needed for you to successfully implement Agile Innovation into your organisation.

Key takeaways from this chapter

- To bring Agile Innovation into your organisation, be prepared to change the entire organisation's mindset to innovation. Be prepared to have continuous product testing with consumers. Be prepared to focus teams on eliminating failure through granular understanding of what works and what doesn't work. Be prepared to do it with rigour that transforms your business from HiPPO based subjective criteria to an evidence based approach. And be prepared to have a pace of development that differs significantly from where you are now.
- Agile seeks to verify the consumers' 'Moments of Truth' earlier on in the product development cycle in a much more thorough manner and at a significantly reduced investment.
- Build–measure–learn is the key principle taken from the Lean Startup methodology that we have applied to Agile Innovation. A continuous quest for learning should be the backbone of Agile Innovation.

Section three –

Applying Agile Innovation

Chapter 8 –
Building your Agile lab

We've learned in previous chapters about the concept of Discover then Deliver, sometimes also referred to by us as Design then Develop. The Agile lab is the space (virtual or physical) that you and your team will use to run the discovery (design) phase of the process.

What is an Agile Innovation laboratory?

A laboratory is defined as a room or building equipped for scientific experiments, research, or teaching, or for the manufacture of drugs or chemicals. An Agile Innovation lab is a safe space with the right equipment and suitably trained team to conduct research and experiments based on that research. It is not necessarily a real-life laboratory (particularly in our post-Covid world). It doesn't even have to be a room. It just has to be somewhere where you can access specific tools. There are a multitude of different tools out there that would fit the purpose of the Agile lab: some are in a real-world environment such as a shop or a community hall, whilst others might be in a simulated world, where people can be asked questions in real-life scenarios. No matter where it is, it will need to be equipped with talented people who are happy to conduct experiments.

Equipping your Agile Innovation lab will need to be structured around some guiding principles, as follows.

Assumption is not knowledge

When reviewing proposed innovation documentation such as business plans or GatePapers, we're always struck by how much assumption there is in the documentation. Each untested assumption is an opportunity for overall failure because they can take product concepts off in directions that really aren't important to customers. Assumed pain points are a key example, where the product developer will project his or her own pain points across all consumers, and start building products to solve that one problem. We see things like 'a high number of launches in the category are vegan', making the assumption that because products lots of being launched are vegan, that is a trend that needs to be continued – without any digging into whether or not consumers actually want lots of vegan products. In our experiences, this would be an assumption that needs to be checked in EVERY category.

In effect, an assumption is a risk factor – the more assumptions, and/or the bigger the assumptions, the bigger the risk carried by innovation. Agile Innovation seeks to minimise, and ideally eradicate, all assumptions. Checking assumptions, in our experience, has been the biggest mindset challenge for innovation leaders when building an Agile Innovation lab. Especially because it is not just the assumptions made about unknown behaviours – in effect the 'guesses' – but also the long-established 'organisational truths' that have built up over time, left unchallenged. The risk is that too many innovations are built on foundations of failure, rather than on structures of success. Agile Innovation needs to have a myth-busting attitude to succeed. To challenge both the guesses and the long-term myths, and test them with relevant consumers in an appropriate context at the most up-to-date time. In summary, we move from guess to test, and reduce risk in the process.

When looking at an innovation project from end-to-end, a staggeringly large number of assumptions come to life, and it may seem daunting to test all of those, so we have developed an approach to consider when prioritising the assumptions. The first set of assumptions to be checked are those that are most vital to the long-term success of the project and are about how 'valid' the product is – will people buy it, do they like it, is it relevant in their lives, how much they would pay for it etc. The second set of assumptions to prioritise is on how to improve the product.

The overall objective for the Agile lab is to have an assumption-free, consumer-centric environment where product developers have all the tools they need to be in perfect harmony with their target customers. The core belief of Agile is that in this environment, the product developer can truly thrive. Outside this environment, the odds of success are just too low, which is sadly proven by the industry metrics in the consumer goods sector.

Theory creation

The second principle for an Agile lab is around the concept of theory creation. For an Agile Innovation project to have a really disruptive impact on a category, the product developer needs to start with a contrarian view of a particular category or channel, different to what most people believe. Only in this way can you create new value compared to what has come before. Coming up with a theory allows you to be more specific about value creation and to perform the right type of experiments through the development process. A theory can be the bedrock of upfront ideation: it can drive and direct the ideation process, giving it a purpose that can be absent otherwise. And whilst theories are not likely to be correct every time, they give a basis for rapid prototyping, experimentation and testing that can be quickly dispatched and begun afresh in a lab environment.

What are the main approaches and processes we are running in the lab?

There are five main phases to an Agile Innovation development cycle:

- theory development (where appropriate)
- ideation,
- validation,
- optimisation
- evolution

Theory development – as mentioned above, there are times when starting an Agile Innovation process that theory development can play a powerful role in setting the project off in a positive, potentially disruptive direction. It's not easy to take a contrarian position against a widely accepted view, but evidence suggests that it is a compelling way to begin an innovation cycle. Radical breakthroughs in science and technology come from theories, as they help people see the world differently and challenge the accepted norms. Through their theories, Galileo was able to see the earth going around the sun, Newton viewed light transform from colourless to colour-filled, and Einstein forged the first path that enabled later scientists to discover black holes. To come up with a genuinely contrarian theory, try answering this question: 'What do you believe that (almost) no-one else believes?' These don't need to be huge industry-changing theories. It could be something as simple as, 'I believe we can sell ready meals in a scaled mass market retail environment at 4x the price they are currently sold at', or 'I believe we can deliver at-home meal kits for households that will nullify their need to do a weekly shop'. Using these theories for the basis of ideation and testing can be really powerful.

Ideation – the subsequent phase of generating as many ideas as possible and crafting them into product concepts that a customer could recognise. There are myriad approaches to ideation so we won't list and dwell on them all here. However, four well-known ideation techniques we've seen over the years seem to be consistently more successful than others:

- Brainstorming – participants in a workshop or process generate ideas in a public forum and let the others build on them, challenge them or refine them.
- Brain dumping – an individual version of brainstorming where participants come up with ideas independently and present them back to the group. Time pressure (i.e. 'You have three minutes to complete this task!') often helps to generate volume and quality of ideas.
- Cheatstorm (terrible name, we know) – where you take ideas from other categories within your sector and figure out how to apply them to your space. For example, if you were an ice-cream manufacturer, you might look at the confectionary category and take successful ideas from there and then convert them to ice-cream variants or flavours.
- Mindmapping – participants write down the pain point in the middle of a sheet of paper and begin to write solutions or ideas that come to mind in a network around it. This illustrative and graphical approach seems to help the quality of ideation.

When looking at ideas, we start at the highest level possible, a few levels above what a consumer would yet recognise as a 'product', and come up with ideas in 'buckets' of topics that come out of previous strategy sessions. For example, if you work in the fresh food industry, 'healthy family eating' might be one of a number of strategies that the category has identified, and you would ideate within those boundaries. We will often use a Sprint-style process at this stage, working with small cross-functional teams in a workshop-style environment for two to five days.

Validation – this is the first testing phase of an Agile Innovation process whereby tens or hundreds of insights, ideas or concepts can be created and tested in a short space of time and checked to see if they resonate with consumers to the predetermined degree necessary. Insights about consumer behaviour can be checked here, to ensure that any ideas following on from these insights are relevant. These insights might be in the form of a question such as 'Are snack bars fulfilling?' or 'Is milk traditional?' By validating the insight, we can cut through swathes of ideas that are irrelevant, allowing us to focus on specific areas that are relevant.

The goal of the validation phase is to refine and test a far broader range of ideas than would have previously been considered, and using a robust testing process, whittle them down to a more and more manageable number at each phase. Remember the 'Design then Develop' mantra – we are trying to arrive at product specifications as rapidly as we can. In a typical consumer goods category we would aim to generate 300–500 ideas in the ideation phase, and exit the validation phase with roughly one-tenth of that – so 30–50 possible product concepts to put through to the next phases (this is an expectation based on our experience rather than a fixed KPI). Validate the right price to ensure that the assumptions in your business model around pricing and product costs are correct.

Optimisation – once a valid and motivating idea has been discovered, we move to the optimisation phase. This is where you take the bare bones of a product concept and stress test every key lever through which a consumer could consciously or subconsciously assess the product. Through this process, still working in Sprints, we will optimise (in no particular order) naming, messaging, pack design, formulation or recipe and pricing. In each of these phases, we will start with an assumption – let's say three possible names for a new product – test it using the benchmarking approach, and iterate based on the response data. The end goal for the optimisation phase is a product specification that you could hand to production and say – 'Build this, and I'm confident it will sell in enough volume to justify the investment we make', based on using volumetric assumptions from the benchmarks. Agile Innovation has a built in feature which helps idenitify the Size of Prize, as having an existing product or products as a benchmark, it is then possible to estimate the size of an innovation relative to the score versus the benchmark. So, for example, if an existing product has a Rate of Sale of £5 per week per store, and the innovation product scores a statistically similar amount in the digital MVP, it would indicate that the innovation product would have a ROS of £5 per week per store, assuming weight of purchase, frequency, and price per unit are the same (a safe assumption given the Byron Sharp in How Brands Grow indicates that frequency is a category dynamic rather than a user dynamic).

- Naming – here we would test three to four alternative names for each product concept using an AB testing methodology (this is explained later in the chapter). The names tested would range from the edgy to the more conservative, in order to see what was resonating with the target consumers. As always with Agile, take the winner, and keep refining and retesting until the results are close to the initial idea score. . What is key is to optimise to ensure a score as close to the original idea as possible. A score lower than the original idea indicates that consumers don't think the current expression of the idea meets the expectations they had in their head. Basically, the name isn't working unless the scores are similar.
- Messaging – similar to naming, we want to understand what on-pack messages and keywords are most likely to grab the consumer's attention.

- Pack design – design is such a subjective thing that consumer testing is often the only way to settle the argument. A rapid design resource needs to be available here, or you'll burn a lot of money on agencies very rapidly. This is about getting validation on design direction before committing to a final creative direction.
- Formulation/recipe – does organic beef have any perceived benefit over British beef? The former would cause a significant dent in the margin, so the consumer benefit would have to be substantial to justify it – test, test, test.
- Pricing – for this phase, our goal is to understand whether the product concept we have created will fit into the pricing hierarchy that exists in the category. If we want to break that pricing hierarchy, i.e. we have developed a product that we believe can sell for twice the category average price, now is the time to test that assumption. If it fails the pricing test, don't be disheartened – retest with different iterations of some of the key levers (a new name, an enhanced formulation) and see what impact it has. It's much better to know now than it is to find out on the shelf.

Evolution – once a product has been made and has had some time on the shelf, you continue to refine and develop it. The design and formulation can be enhanced. Very much like an application – Spotify would never just get launched once and left alone. It is improved and refined every few weeks with product releases.

There are challenges around this in terms of packaging design, ingredient changes, technical testing etc., but we would be able to evolve all products to make them more efficient and successful over a long enough time frame. We evolve the products in line with how they were developed using Agile Innovation – we design, test, then develop.

As a guide, we have been able to increase purchase intent on existing products by up to 20% by using a combination of cognitive biases across names, descriptions, claims, product design, colours and price[50]. The beauty of Agile Innovation in a simulated world of an Agile Lab is the ability to test these combinations at pace, without risking them failing in the real world. We can even make marketing communications better using the Agile Innovation approach of design, test, and develop.

What people do we need in an Agile lab?
The key approach here is cross-functionality; what we don't want is a single-skilled team. Agile in software development is at its most impactful when the team is

---

50 Internal data 2017-2021

made up of individuals from different functions and backgrounds. The same goes for Agile Innovation. Whilst there is not a fixed or finite list, an Agile lab team should be made up of four or five of the following individuals or functions:

- Product developer / innovation manager who is the specialist in understanding the product or the consumer. Typically a marketing type role. They understand the products in the current portfolio, as well as products in the marketplace. They have an understanding of how the product is made and the current capabilities of the organisation.
- Designer who work up designs and mock-ups that can be used in the testing, and to bring to life the final proposed product specifications. This might even be one of the other members of the team if they have sufficient Photoshop and Illustrator experience. It could also be a third party agency.
- Copywriter, depending on what the nature of the product is being developed. In many projects we work on we find that pack copy (i.e. the language used on packaging or online to describe and promote the product) is often overlooked until the very last minute of the product development cycle. This could also be an external third party agency or freelancer.
- Buyer / marketing manager who will be responsible for pricing and therefore price testing. They would also be knowledgeable about the market, customers (sales), and consumers. They will have contacts with agencies about developing visuals or copy, or even marketing communications.
- Manufacturing partner who is accountable for production feasibility.
- Consumer insight manager who can own the intelligence, and potentially be accountable for the testing.
- When running a Sprint, think about the flow of the decisions and appoint someone to be a facilitator – this can be internal or external to the project, but needs to be someone familiar with Agile Innovation.

What tools are required to operate it?

Digital product testing – it's vital that teams have access to a digital product concept testing tool that they can use consistently and confidently all the way through the innovation process. Most of these tools are self-serve applications that the teams can operate themselves. They are a crucial way to get consumer input into the process from step one. Without access to a product testing platform, it's impossible for the teams to validate any of their assumptions at the pace (and low cost) required by Agile. To make MVPs cheaper and quicker, we developed a "digital" version of a MVP for the CPG world, using best practice from the Tech sector and expertise from behavioural economics. In 2016, a series of product concept tests would have taken several months from starting the brief until receiving the results, and cost tens of thousands of pounds; now those same questions can be done in some instances in 15 minutes and for hundreds of pounds, with the same degree of rigour. What is important is that the predictive nature of the data generated on the platform is solid and has been validated, and the community of consumers they access is representative and relevant to the products being developed and tested.

In traditional research, a brief would contain assumptions about what would be discovered in research for follow-on questions as part of the research methodology. Agile insight is different – it only asks one question at a time, as the answer isn't assumed. Then, based on the answer given, the next question can be asked, building and reacting to the answers from consumers. This reduces time and cost, as unnecessary questions are never asked in the first place, and answers to those unnecessary questions don't then need to be interpreted.

Insight tools – to ensure the team are addressing relevant pain points, good quality Agile insight tools are needed to gain those unique insights into your customers. These tools will be digital versions of traditional qualitative research; frequently video-based insights to get a rapid understanding of the attitudes, behaviours and lives of your target customers.

Design tools for mockups and MVPs – a designer with rapid prototyping skills on something like Adobe is exactly what is needed in an Agile setting. We're looking for rapid, consistent designs being churned out to bring the ideas to life for the consumers receiving the tests. This is not expensive, slow, agency-style digital creativity. These are minimum viable designs being created for the hundreds of concepts being put into the early stages of the innovation funnel – 10 to 15 minutes per design.

Price testing tools – in an Agile setting, we should be looking to test consumers' appetite to pay for product concepts as early in the development cycle as possible. There is little point in building a strong product concept that scores highly all the way through the innovation process, only to fall flat on its face when consumers (and teams) realise it is 50% more expensive than the average price in the category. So having access to a robust, efficient price testing tool is important for an Agile lab.

And finally, some physical space will possibly be needed, particularly if you're likely to be running workshops. Whilst they can be run virtually, a physical get-together is hard to replace from time to time. And if you're running an Agile Innovation workshop then yes, you'll need a lot of Post-It notes and Sharpies...

MVPs should be quick and easy – an example

In early February 2020, we had a very interesting conversation with the head of R&D for one of the world's largest pharma companies. In an in-depth conversation over the course of a day, including lunch, we discussed many topics. Their expectations for an MVP had grown legs to such extent that it was less 'minimum', more 'maximum'. An MVP to them was a full-scale prototype that would take 18 months to go to market, and effectively be a mini launch, with full marketing support including field sales support. Sharing our experience of MVPs, from Google AdWords to Twitter advertising-based MVPs through to the Wine Shop example, the expectation in the pharma business was transformed into thinking differently, and viewing innovation – and therefore MVPs – as proving assumptions such as it would sell, rather than proving they could make it. The tough challenge for them now is to work out the assumptions that prove a product can be sold, as the Moments of Truth in Pharma are different from those in FMCG.

Key techniques for the Agile lab

Some of the key techniques and approaches that we have at our disposal during these phases include the following.

Benchmarking – this is the lynchpin of the testing ethos. Without it, it's a little like an archer without a target; you can shoot arrows, but if you've nothing to aim at, how do you know if you've been successful? Benchmarks can come in many forms, and they should change as you go through a full innovation cycle. Within the consumer goods sector, the obvious place to start when finding benchmarks is products that are already on the shelf. If you have a product, or set of products, that perform around the level you would need a new product to perform to justify its place in the range, then take those products as the benchmarks. The main thing to watch out for is this – the benchmarks need to be presented in the same format as the ideas that you are testing. So if you are testing early-stage product concepts which don't have any visuals yet, and you're using images from public sources like Google to represent them, make sure you 'deconstruct' the benchmark products and present them in the same way. Clearly, if you test a set of product ideas using stock images but use a benchmark that appear beautifully packaged and presented as if it were in a catalogue, it is likely to skew your data and conclusions.

AB testing – another extremely useful tool, specifically related to testing methodology, is 'split testing', or AB testing. This is a test taken from the software world that tests one variable at a time, in a statistically and behaviourally robust way. Let's say you have two possible product names for a product concept you're working on. The traditional way to test those would be to ask consumers, 'Which name do you prefer?' This is artificial – a consumer would never see two versions of the same product on the shelf and choose which he or she preferred. The split test approach is to split the test respondents into two equal halves, asking them both the same question with the same image, but changing the product name for group A vs group B. What this means is that any differences in appeal, assuming the question was something like 'Would you buy this?', can be empirically linked to the difference in name.

Price testing – it's crucial that the team in the lab can test and simulate price as early in the development process as possible. To do this, various tools are available from rapid, digital self-serve products through to more consultative approaches. Neither is right or wrong; budgets and time constraints are particular to each individual business. Different pricing methodologies are available such as Van Westendorp[51] or Conjoint Analysis[52]; again, neither is right or wrong, it depends on the context of the project. What is crucial is that price testing is conducted consistently across all product concepts, whilst testing product benchmarks for the price as well. We are not necessarily looking to establish the recommended selling price here; we are more interested in the difference between products, namely how much more or less consumers are prepared to pay for a product versus its potential competitors. We are also interested in price ceilings for products or product ranges – the price points at which large volumes of potential buyers drop off. This type of modelling tells us more than simply establishing a possible optimum selling price.

Brand development – when developing or refreshing a brand, we can use our Agile laboratory to check our assumptions about consumer insight, or even optimise the key brand benefit or brand essence. As an example, one of our clients wanted to refresh their brand: we developed over 60 brand statements, and through rigorous testing, we found a statement that was 11.5% more motivational than the current. Furthermore, as the design process developed, we were able to ensure not only that the brand redesigns were hitting the targeted consumer scores, but also that the designs delivered against the new brand statements through brand association work.

Launch plans – taking the decision about whether it's a big bang launch or a more traditional seeding launch through product lifecycle (see Chapter 6); we

---

51 https://en.wikipedia.org/wiki/Van_Westendorp%27s_Price_Sensitivity_Meter
52 https://en.wikipedia.org/wiki/Conjoint_analysis

can look at the most effective communication activation for the brand at launch in a similar way we develop product names, descriptions or pack design. We have tested different Marketing communications routes to find out what is more effective. We can test positioning, media choices, ad creative. For example, should the brand communicate the award winning taste or how it helps save the bees? We found in the Summer of 202 that our client should communicate how it helps save the bees!

An Agile laboratory, no matter whether physical or virtual lab accessed via cloud and remote working, it is a crucial piece of the puzzle for a business attempting to embrace Agile Innovation. Without a formal/tangible 'thing', it is likely that old habits will re-emerge, and comfortable processes will be re-embraced. An Agile lab is a step forward that can break old habits and build new ones.

Adoption Curve Portfolio

We now turn our attention to what we have coined 'the Adoption Curve Portfolio'. Generating a return from short-term innovation gives the ability to invest in a dynamic long-term innovation portfolio that will sustain the business for many years to come. We call this pipeline the Adoption Curve Portfolio. What this means is a pipeline of innovation that is mapped across a typical consumer adoption curve like the one seen in Figure 10.

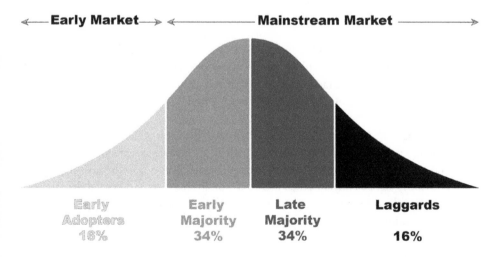

Figure 15 Product Adoption Curve

Profitability from innovation will come from having products that sit in the two highest parts of the chart above; early majority and late majority. All new products must pass through the stages of the adoption curve in order to be successful. Those early phases can be very rapid in the case of a small handful of products, but on the whole, they take weeks and months to pass through the early market stages and into the mainstream market. The key to successful long-term innovation is investing not just in innovation for the mass market, but seeding and tracking projects and products that the business knows will take time to catch on, but with the right level of patience and support will become the next big drivers of profitability in a business.

To invest in an Adoption Curve Portfolio takes confidence, belief and a long-term view of the market. It also requires patient shareholders who don't just want to take the first heady wave of profitability generated by the initial innovation. Amazon is an excellent example of a business that has continually invested its profits into early market projects and services and reaped the rewards later. Their founder and CEO Jeff Bezos spends very little time working on anything under a timeframe of 18 months out. He is constantly planning, seeding and investing in future projects that will drive the profitability of the business five to ten years from now.

Too many businesses that we see in the consumer goods industry try to rush or completely ignore this adoption concept, and push products straight into the mass market. Building a solid base of early adopters through niche partnerships before hitting mass-market channels is a much more solid way of building a consumer brand. Haagen-Dazs is a good example of a brand that built patiently and really seemed to understand this adoption curve. In the UK, they got listed in all of the convenience store channels and built a core following of consumers that created hype and kudos. As a result, when the big supermarket chains came knocking, they were able to dictate the terms of their expansion into the mass market, ensuring the brand would be priced and supported for the long term. The brand is still benefiting from that solid base in the UK today.

A strong innovation portfolio should sit across all five areas of the Adoption Curve and be constantly tracked and measured. There are many, many examples of businesses that have had a successful piece of innovation, scaled it to the mass market extremely competently, but then milked the profits for years and not fed the early stages of the curve with new ideas. Those businesses, without exception, all end up disappearing from view. In time, even the most successful products and business models will atrophy as the market – and the competition – moves on. The ability to innovate, experiment and evolve is, therefore, an essential characteristic of the companies that are most likely to survive and thrive for years to come.

IRI, the retail and FMCG market intelligence company, ran a study based on around 3,000 product launches from 2013–2015 across food, soft drinks, confectionery, personal care, health and household categories. In the IRI study[53], they determined that two factors contribute to long-term innovation success: relative rate of sale to the category norm, and weighted distribution. The higher both of these are, the greater the chance of success. That is the primary driver of big bang launches for big brands. They want to gain distribution quickly in order to be able to build high volumes and justify the high ad spend needed to drive the higher rate of sale.

Data suggests that the innovation launch model is predicated on the purchase cycle of the category overall. Milk has a very short purchase cycle with virtually all households buying their milk more than once per week (basically every five days). New milk brands or new milk propositions grow very quickly, albeit to a small share of overall milk. Spirits have a very long purchase cycle, with most households only buying a handful of bottles per annum. This then means there is little opportunity to try new products, so the time to move through the early adopters and into the mature phase is measured in decades. It is often said in the spirits industry that it takes 20 years to be an overnight success. Examples abound from Baileys to Captain Morgan to Hendricks.

Interestingly, some products require considerable time to grow through the stages when they are first launched, but subsequent launches can be done at a higher pace. When King Gillette started his razor business back in 1901, he sold a measly 51 razors and 168 blades. Gillette Fusion, one of the company's most recent innovations in shaving, sold millions of blades, with the support of a multi-million dollar launch programme that saw it gain massive distribution and motivate millions of men to go out and replace their incumbent razors.

Ultimately the launch model is a reflection of the risk and reward of innovation. Big brands can afford a big bang launch, not just in a financial sense, but also from what Byron Sharp in *How Brands Grow* calls a 'mental availability and physical availability' sense. Smaller brands with less awareness and distribution may not be comfortable taking on that risk. Brands with longer purchase cycle categories such as spirits may adopt the more traditional approach. Even in those categories, the innovation of using celebrities to launch their own brands has accelerated and multiplied the growth trajectory of spirit innovation. Effectively celebrities have innovated innovation in long purchase cycle categories.

---

53 https://www.iriworldwide.com/IRI/media/IRI-Clients/International/uk/new_product_ study_wp_july16-Final.pdf

Now that we've outlined how to build your Agile lab, we move onto the structures and management approaches needed to facilitate and support Agile Innovation.

Key takeaways from this chapter

- Theories can play a crucial role in giving direction and momentum to ideation and ultimately innovation.
- Consistent testing methodologies play an important role in the Agile lab.
- Key approaches for an Agile Innovation lab are ideation, validation, Optimisation, and Evolution.
- Key techniques to master for an Agile Innovation lab are benchmarking, AB Testing, Price Testing, Brand Development, and Launch plans.
- The Adoption Curve Portfolio is a compelling way for businesses to begin to build long-term innovation success.

Chapter 9 –
How to structure teams to facilitate an Agile culture in your organisation

In this chapter, we look at the Agile Innovation structures and management practises required to unlock the benefits of Agile for all people in the organisation. We assess the impact on the individual and link it back to the impact on the business from a personnel perspective.

Unfortunately, despite looking very, very hard, we have yet to find a one-size-fits-all golden structure that will cure the innovation ills of most businesses. We can tell you about some that work, and many structures that are destined to kill any sniff of disruptive innovation. One thing is for sure; pyramid-shaped structures do not lend themselves to successful innovation in any form. A pyramid structure means multiple levels of sign off, which in turn means multiple opportunities for products to be watered down. Pyramid structures typically have a 'designed by committee' approach, where all senior leaders input their ideas, and the innovation either becomes a hodgepodge of features and ideas or is diluted so as not to offend any one party, which perversely is unlikely to motivate anyone to buy the product in the first place. A hierarchical pyramid structure is the very opposite of what is needed; for a successful Agile Innovation environment to flourish, a flat and empowered structure must be put in place.

The ideal Agile Innovation structure

But what could a non-pyramid structure for innovation look like? We often use the example of Spotify[54] as a truly Agile business: their main focus is on community and knowledge-sharing to drive the structure, in place of hierarchy. They have found that a strong enough community can get away without rigid structure in the traditional corporate sense. If you need to know exactly who is making decisions, you are in the wrong place at Spotify. They believe that most organisation charts are an illusion. As a young business, they were created from day one with Agile disciplines, and as a result, do not necessarily have a structure that large existing corporations can easily copy. However, some of the main principles are easily leveraged:

- Autonomy.
- Alignment.
- Trust.
- Knowledge sharing.
- Community.
- Cross-functional teams.

We will touch on some of these in a little more detail as we go through the rest of this chapter.

Management approach required for leading Agile Innovation

We would outline two key management traits that are required to enable the successful implementation of Agile Innovation:

- Clearly articulated and communicated vision or mission for at least innovation, if not the whole company.
- Transparent, data-led, rapid decision-making.
- The impact of a clearly articulated vision was brilliantly illustrated through President Kennedy's declaration in 1962 that America would 'go to the moon this decade', which was made *before* the USA had even sent a man into orbit. This assertion led to nearly ten years of unprecedented levels of innovation, not only impacting the moon landings but filtering through to many technology products we know and love today. A clear, bold vision can really empower teams to make the unthinkable happen, provided the vision is tangible enough to stimulate action immediately. Clear direction on goals

---

54 https://medium.com/pm101/spotify-squad-framework-part-i-8f74bcfcd761

from management is crucial for a successful innovation culture to be created. A woolly, unsubstantiated goal is of little use in Agile Innovation; the target values need to be apportioned across the various business unit leaders and cascaded across all their teams in the form of targets and timelines: anything less pragmatic risks inactivity and navel-gazing.

In the absence of a singular all-encompassing business mission, a divisional leader's job in an Agile organisation is to focus on what problem needs solving, and why. The job of the team is to collaborate to find the best possible solution, considering product innovation but also business model innovation at the same time.

The leader must provide guidance so people know where to go, and then leave them alone to get on with it.

Decisiveness is a crucial behaviour for managers in an Agile organisation. In a successful innovation business, more projects or products must be constantly set in motion in the early stages than the business could feasibly launch. Leaders then have a strong, broad portfolio from which to pick and tell their teams to focus on. Most established companies err on the side of overloading their innovation pipelines with relatively safe, short-term and incremental projects that have little chance of achieving their growth targets. We see time and again clients' companies having innovation projects to shore up sales targets for the current financial year or having an innovation project to overcome poor performance in advance of range reviews – all doomed to failure before they are launched. Many retailers that we work with spread themselves thinly across too many projects instead of focusing on those with the highest potential for success and resourcing them to win.

The strong leader in an Agile Innovation team should have a compelling roster of products to choose from in every early stage cycle, and then make strong, transparent decisions about which ones the teams should back. Leaders can easily harness rapid testing formats to improve and refine product concepts. As American chemist Linus Pauling said, 'the way to get to good ideas is to get lots of ideas and throw the bad ones away'.

Alignment and Autonomy

There are two useful criteria to think about when reflecting on the management approaches needed here; alignment and autonomy. Alignment is the responsibility of the leadership – making sure that teams are clear on the overall mission, and what the major problems are that need solving. Autonomy means empowering teams to be left to get on with the task in hand.

Alignment and autonomy are the two key pieces of the puzzle when setting up Agile in an organisation. High alignment and high autonomy enable high-performing teams to face problems head-on and collaborate to find the very best solution possible. Low autonomy and low alignment, which we find in an alarming number of businesses, is a dangerous combination. Low alignment effectively means it is unclear why a business exists (what its mission is) and what people should be working on and why. Low autonomy means managers who like to micro-manage or individuals in teams who are incapable of making decisions and acting on them.

However, to build autonomy in an aligned organisation takes high levels of trust. And trust stems from culture – the people in the business, how they behave, what examples their leadership set, and how clear their mission and purpose is. Agile at scale requires trust at scale; trust is absolutely paramount as it binds the teams together, and tight teams knit the organisation together, which helps build alignment. If we reflect on innovation, an increase in trust allows for people to take risks without fear of blame; only in a trusting environment can failure be seen as an opportunity to learn, not a black mark on the book.

Let's think for a moment how alignment and autonomy could impact the day-to-day process of developing products. If as a senior innovation manager you were given a cross-functional team, a whole uninterrupted year, and crucially a very clear objective then the potential for true innovation is very high. Let's imagine the CEO says to you and the team 'Increase our market share in this category by 10%' – that's a hugely motivating remit for the manager and team to tackle. Instead of launching iterative products in fixed launch windows, you'd be far more likely to think differently, and really reframe your channel or route to market. For example, you might launch a subscription box, or a direct-to-consumer website, instead of just a new set of packaged products. Conversely, imagine how difficult that sort of thinking and action would be in a traditional top-down Waterfall environment, you just wouldn't have the time, trust or headspace to propose those sorts of innovative leaps forward. We believe that type of innovation environment, if fostered correctly, results in far higher growth than could be achieved through the typical Waterfall approach of fixed product launch windows.

What does this mean for senior leaders or execs for innovation? Ensure alignment to a long-term agenda, with a crystal clear vision for the company, or at least for innovation. Don't interfere once the teams have been set up. Govern within the aligned and agreed frameworks, and check-in as per the agreed timeframes to course correct or break down barriers.

Spotify's innovation structure

Spotify uses structure in an interesting way in their organisation; most of their product teams are constructed as follows:

- A Squad is a small cross-functional team of fewer than eight people. The members of a Squad have end-to-end responsibility, and they work together to solve their long-term mission.
- Each Squad is grouped into a Tribe, which has a Chapter.
- A Tribe is a lightweight matrix containing a number of Squads, who are all aligned in one particular product area.
- A Chapter is the group structure for competency-based areas such as quality assurance or mobile development. Here you will find functional line managers.
- They also have a Guild, which is a community interest group that uses informal communication methods to share best practise on particular topics of interest.
- Chapters and Guilds allow for cross-pollination of learning to other project teams. They also mean that individual members can change Squads without changing line manager every time.
- In a Squad the team members have end-to-end responsibilities, and they work together towards a long-term mission. For successful Squads, the key driver is autonomy; they need to decide what to build, how to build it and how to work together in building it. Each Squad needs to remain aligned with the mission, product strategy and short-term goals. The leader's job in a Squad is to communicate what problem needs to be solved and to be clear on the mission; for example 'We're going to increase market share by 10% and here's why I believe we can do it'. The Squad's job is to collaborate with team members to find the best solution. To bring some sort of structure, each Squad is grouped into a Tribe which forms a Chapter. In this environment, you can change your Squad without changing your manager, allowing for a significant level of flexibility and agility.

Let's try to bring this back into life in the world of consumer goods. What if you gave a cross-functional team a simple market share growth target, telling them to operate within broad business guidelines and leaving them to it, giving them 12 months with all available Agile business tools at their disposal. A cross-functional team would be established to look at the traditional category they operate in. The team, headed by the product developer, supported by a technologist, supply chain expert, designer and copywriter would begin work on the task of increasing market share in this category by 5%. Without the impending date of a large window, the team would be likely to take a more considered and hopefully long-term, bold approach to product innovation. A far broader range of ideas could be generated, tested and refined than was previously possible. At the end of an Agile Innovation process, the performant ideas could be tested on a very limited (single store) scale quickly and cheaply. That live data could then be used to evidence further investments that the team want to make during the course of the 12 months.

The team would be more likely to make confident and considered decisions and be genuinely excited about the project experiments they want to test. Collaboration should be high, along with engagement and trust, and knowledge flow would improve exposure to the different functions on a team. Our supposition is that there would be a higher chance of the market share objectives being achieved compared to a traditional Waterfall approach, and is achieved in a generally impact-differentiated and sustainable way.

The reality will probably be that your company either doesn't have an innovation team currently or the structure for the current innovation team is hierarchical, and so moving to a flatter Agile team could have serious implications for the team and the wider business.

So what other techniques are used within an Agile Innovation structure to facilitate Agile behaviours? There are three ideas from the technology world we'd like to cover briefly:

- Sprints – phased bursts of ideation, testing and refinement activity centred around one particular topic each time and typically done over a period of two to five days.
- Release train – flipping the concept of fixed launch windows, this idea gives teams one day per fortnight (for example) on an ongoing basis in which they can launch products in-store or online, either as a test, expansion or rollout.
- Blast radius – all products first launch in a handful of trial stores so as to give teams early data through which they can make product iterations before broader exposure to the full estate.

Agile Innovation sprints

In terms of how we would apply it to innovation, a Sprint is a two to five day process for answering critical questions by prototyping and testing product ideas with customers. When structured and facilitated properly, Sprints can give teams the confidence, momentum and focus to really make a dent in an innovation project. They can enable teams to focus on what is important in a given project, generating lots of ideas and giving rapid clarity about which to concentrate on. If they have robust data and pre-agreed KPIs, they can significantly sharpen the decision-making process, not only making it quicker but also more consistent and empirical. Sprints allow a culture of continuous improvement as they can form the perfect environment to build–measure–learn, making concept development a truly iterative process.

Ultimately Sprints allow cohesive teams to develop the most valuable products possible in the least time to market if they are facilitated and focused on in the correct way.

A word of caution on Sprints, however; they are not the Agile Innovation silver bullet. They can be poorly applied when speed is given as the central tenet. And when robustness or consistency of decision-making is sacrificed in favour of speed, they lose all benefit. Sprints, and in fact Agile, are not about speed. Speed can be a by-product if Agile is delivered well, but it should never be the sole focus.

Whilst Sprint workshops can benefit from being structured in, say, five continuous days, consider structuring an innovation Sprint as one day per week over five weeks to allow time for reflection and robust testing. Even done in this way, you are far likelier to get a more robust and pacier outcome than by following a traditional Waterfall process.

Release train
Now we turn to the idea of the release train[55]. The central idea of the release train is to give far more fluidity and flexibility to teams as to when they can release products to market. The industry currently is very fixed and rigid in terms of how it releases products. Fixed launch windows are fine for Waterfall, but give rise to so many anti-Agile behaviours that it becomes nearly impossible to break out of the cycle. What if innovation teams could release products with much greater regularity and fluidity, and only once they had passed all the testing criteria? It would relieve a huge amount of subconscious pressure, and enable much longer-term and bolder products to be developed.

Let's say each category team has a release train (launch window) that departs on a particular day of the week or month in each cycle. The release train works on a regular schedule that gives cadence and predictable planning. Stores and store clusters have to be set up to receive much smaller numbers of launches on a more regular basis; this is in contrast to the infrequent large-scale approach normally taken by the retail sector.

---

55 https://medium.com/pm101/spotify-squad-framework-part-i-8f74bcfcd761

If a product isn't fully ready for launch, it can either launch in a limited test environment, knowing that it is incomplete so that learning can take place, or further development can take place without any launch.

Releases or launches should be common and routine, not rare and dramatic like many are now, with the associated costs. The release train concept can also be brought into the digital testing environment where simulated stores and ranges can be stress-tested. Virtual product concepts can be 'released' into the digital environment with other existing products to see how they perform in context; they can then be withdrawn and iterated on based on the testing learnings and resubmitted before release to the live environment.

The release train concept works seamlessly with the blast radius idea presented in the next section.

Blast radius

A blast radius[56] is about limiting the impact of new products to only a handful of trial stores or web portals before they are fully tested, iterated on and optimised. It gives teams the ability to gather further customer data in a controlled manner before they release products for full store estate or web launch.

If something goes badly, it doesn't impact the brand and provides a massive live learning opportunity to optimise products before the full launch. Release phases could go something like this:

- Phase 1 – MVP release in a single dedicated web test or lab or stores near to the company headquarters.
- Phase 2 – a small cluster of stores or web portals with a similar profile to the test stores from Phase 1. It gives products the potential to be refined based on the data from Phase 1 before being exposed to a broader audience.
- Phase 3 – a full store or digital release for products that have successfully passed through the first two stages. This will result in a full estate launch with strong sales, low wastage, no markdowns and delighted customers.

As an example, we recently developed a new direct to consumer brand of speciality coffee, and as part of the development we built a fully functioning website, but with a previously rejected brand name. This website allowed the client to test various different elements of the website, the product offering, the pricing, and promotions, without impacting the new brand. This dummy website simultaneously

56 https://medium.com/pm101/spotify-squad-framework-part-i-8f74bcfcd761

gave permission to the team to play with the brand without having any blast back onto the brand. The learnings from this "sandbox" have gone on to help launch the brand successfully

Agile Innovation culture

Finally in this chapter, we are going to examine the culture required for successful Agile Innovation to thrive.

As Peter Drucker sagely advised, 'Culture eats strategy for breakfast'. You might want to bring Agile Innovation into your business, but how do you do it to ensure success? How a company behaves will help entrench the Agile process, as will adopting the KPIs, workflows and governance of Agile Innovation. What will help more in the establishment of Agile Innovation is the behaviour and values of the business towards innovation, especially those behaviours and values of the senior leadership team. The senior leaders in the business must ensure a culture of humility, autonomy, and delegated authority for Agile Innovation to succeed in their business.

It is crucial to ensure there is a culture within the innovation function that is focused on the company's purpose, and that the roles within innovation are clearly aligned to the company purpose. Where companies only have the purpose of generating profit, it will be harder to have a clear guiding light for Agile Innovation, as ideas will have to be evaluated against wider criteria and more obscure benchmarks. In comparison, a company with a clear purpose has a simpler set of measures to gauge innovation success, allowing for more autonomy and faster decision-making.

It also means developing a culture where failure is not only allowed but widely expected, perhaps even incentivised, as validation and optimisation stages will have significant numbers of failures before they have any successes. Remember the vision for Agile Innovation is zero launch failure, not that there is no failure in the process. In it's simplest form, Agile Innovation seeks to push the failure as far up the process as possible – fail more at the early stages of development where the costs are smaller, and only be left with products that are more likely to succeed. The benchmarks will be a challenge to meet in the first instance, and there will be a temptation to lower the benchmarks to reduce the failure rate. But if the benchmarks have been derived appropriately and reflect the real world, then they will tell you the story of what will happen when you launch the product in the real world – if they fail the benchmarks, they will fail when they are launched. Failure may initially be painful for both the individuals in the team and the function itself, and it will feel easier to revert back to the old system of innovation. But the culture needs to allow for time to fail and to be comfortable with failure.

The values and behaviours of senior leaders are absolutely critical at this stage, and encouragement to fail, fail safely and fail often needs to be given. Senior stakeholders need to ensure that there is compliance with the benchmarks and govern against the weakening or bypassing of benchmarks. A benchmark needs to be integral and not abused. For example, if the benchmark is 80%, and a product achieves 76%, it has not passed the benchmark, so should be rejected with a recommendation to review to improve the score. It should not progress, as doing so – even when it is so close to the benchmark – will undermine the entire process in the long run.

Senior stakeholders need to accept that their ideas must be submitted to the same rigours as anybody else's, and only proceed if they pass the objective benchmarks. It will be challenging for teams to say that a senior leader's idea has failed, but the senior team should look for this as a test of the system – if testers aren't telling you that your idea has failed, then what else are they letting through the system? Stop being a HiPPO. Be humble. Behave in an Agile way.

Agile behaviours:
- Humility – be open to consumer data proving entrenched hypotheses incorrect.
- Creativity – use the data to go in different directions that are opened up and made permissible.
- Open-mindedness – accept ideas from all areas; don't become tunnel-visioned.
- Live with imperfection – the MVP itself will not be perfect, as if it is perfect it's not 'minimum'! You will have to make decisions with about how to persevere or pivot on imperfect information – it is not a paint by numbers exercise, more creativity, but with testing if the creativity works.
- Understand the drivers of your consumer and target those drivers; don't tinker around with the baubles of the latest trends that don't drive consumer behaviour.
- Rigour – be clear on what really drives consumers.
- Integrity – ensure that tests are run fairly, and results interpreted without bias.
- Accept mistakes.

But when to go about this change? With Covid-19 as a driver to reduce costs, simplify working, structure teams towards more authority and autonomous groups, take hold of the opportunity right now to convert to Agile.

Having identified the structures and approaches required to facilitate Agile Innovation, we will next look at a crucial and often overlooked piece of the puzzle: KPIs.

Key takeaways from this chapter

- There is no ideal structure for implementing Agile Innovation. When considering an appropriate structure, it needs to consider autonomy, alignment, trust, knowledge-sharing, community and cross functional teams.
- Resourcing Agile Innovation effectively requires trust. Trust from the organisation that the right people are in the role, and trust from the team that the organisation will give them the autonomy to work.
- Spotify gives a great indication of how structure can work, with its Squads, Tribes, Chapters, Guilds, Sprints, release trains and blast radius approach.

Chapter 10 –
Innovation Benchmarks and KPIs

In this chapter we build the case as to why KPIs can be a key enabler for Agile Innovation when created using the structures we propose. Our starting place to bring KPIs to life means heading back to the laboratory from Chapter 8.

In a laboratory, any experiment has a clear objective accompanied by a theory to prove or disprove. An Agile Innovation lab is no different. A theory is a short statement that represents a major shift in mindset away from how the rest of the industry perceives a particular category or sector. A series of hypotheses, which in our Agile lab are more granular and lower level, then sit underneath the theory. Traditionally, consumer goods innovation would be drowning in assumptions that are not made clear and certainly never tested. In an Agile lab, the opposite should be true. Theories are clearly stated, with specific tests developed to prove or disprove the hypotheses that sit underneath them. Working towards proving a theory builds knowledge iteratively, which the Agile innovator can convert into recipes and formulations. The same approach is taken all the way through the innovation process, on all of the key levers of an individual proposition.

To implement robust and relevant innovation KPIs, we need to have a clear innovation objective and underlying innovation strategy. For example, is the innovation objective to grow profit by a certain amount? Is it to be a global leader in the market in which you operate? Or is it more about following the market to maintain market share levels? Understanding the objective and strategy is crucial to setting appropriate KPIs.

For complete clarity, let's define the word theory in the context of Agile Innovation. It is a supposition or proposed explanation made on the basis of limited evidence as a starting point for further investigation and subsequent testing. It is often contrarian in nature, taking a position that is different from the assumed thinking for that category or sector. A hypothesis would be at a lower level than the theory, and probably more practical in it's nature.

An example of a theory, contrarian in nature, is: 'We can sell ready meals for 5x the price they are currently sold at through mainstream retailers'. The underlying hypotheses for testing this could be:

1) 'Consumers will pay more for a takeaway-style ready-meal box'.
2) 'A hyper local range containing meat from no further than 10 miles away will encourage consumers to pay a higher price'.
3) 'Using the latest meat replacement technology to build a vegetarian equivalent range will drive up the price point'.
4) 'Partnering with renowned neighbourhood restaurants to build a retail range will encourage consumers to trade up'.

So how do you take a hypothesis, create a test for it, and link the output to the pre-agreed KPIs? Any hypothesis is likely to be aimed at either understanding the consumer pain point or maximising the potential performance (revenue or profit) of the innovation being worked on. Ensure any tests developed will help shift the needle in one of these areas. For the hypotheses above, the following tests could be created, with a potential KPI listed after each one:

1) 'Consumers will pay more for a takeaway-style ready-meal box'. Test – create a visual of a takeaway box format, and compare it for purchase intent versus the original using an AB testing methodology. Use price testing to understand the price ceilings that exist for the product. KPI – margin growth, profit growth.
2) 'A hyper local range containing meat from no further than 10 miles away will encourage consumers to pay a higher price'. Test – create a manipulated visual of a product from this category and artificially show the hyper locality of the meat. Test it against the target consumer profile, using other benchmark products to build a broader picture of purchase intent. KPI – product concepts created that score above the CACUROS target for the 'growth' consumer segments.
3) 'Using the latest meat replacement technology to build a vegetarian equivalent range will drive up the price point'. Test – create different pack mock ups with

the latest meat replacement technology listed heavily on pack and test them all for purchase intent. Put the products through pricing tests to see how they compare versus benchmarks. KPI – revenue growth, profit maximisation.

4) 'Partnering with renowned neighbourhood restaurants to build a retail range will encourage consumers to trade up'. Test – pricing analysis to see how many consumers drop off at the various price ceilings when asked how much they would pay for a restaurant-branded version of the product. KPI – profit growth.

Now that we've outlined how to build and test hypotheses, we need to understand how we decide whether the tests have been successful or not, and what impact they will have on the customer. This is where KPIs come in. Your Agile Innovation KPIs need to reflect and be aligned with the organisation's KPIs so that it is clear what innovation is being measured against and why it's being done. If your organisational KPIs are 'revenue growth of 5%' then it's easy to reverse engineer this and ensure your departmental or individual KPIs contribute to this broader goal.

We now know that the whole point of Agile Innovation is to make the investment for innovation work harder over time, so before an investment is committed, either in terms of cash or people, any innovation product should have a better than average chance of meeting the organisation objective. To that end, we need to understand the likelihood of success.

To do this we break Agile Innovation KPIs down into four areas. The first two are KPIs that help manage and focus activity before products are launched; the last two are KPIs that monitor how products are performing in the real world. These areas are:

1) Customer (pre-launch).
2) Pipeline (pre-launch).
3) Commercial (post-launch).
4) Financial (post-launch).

Let's summarise and then explore in further detail each area in turn in the natural order that they would occur.

For clarity, when we refer to pre-launch and post-launch, we mean the period of development before new products are launched, compared to the period of analysis that happens after a product has launched and is in the hands of customers.

Customer KPIs (pre-launch)
Suggested KPIs in this pre-launch area are listed below. They are designed to help

drive behaviours that positively impact the top end of the innovation funnel. The innovation funnel is the pipeline of product concepts that are being developed through different phases moving towards eventual launch. Managing an innovation funnel well at the start with lots of well thought out product concepts gives the rest of the innovation process a far higher chance of success.

- Category average cash unit rate of sale (CACUROS). In short, this is a metric around the rate of sale that can be very useful in early-stage testing when used to create a set of relevant benchmark products. We talk about benchmarks in more detail in the section below
- Purchase intent (PI) score to 'nurture' customer segments – as in how motivating are the new products you're creating to the existing group(s) of customers that your business relies on for profitability. We will compare these PI scores to the benchmarks identified
- Appeal score to 'grow' customer segments – as in how appealing are the new products you're creating to the group(s) of customers that your business is trying to attract for long-term growth. This could well be a more important metric than the one above.
- Relevance to people's lifestyle – relevancy correlates well to frequency, as the more relevant a product or category is to someone's life, the more often they buy the product or category.

But why are benchmarks important, not just in the whole Agile Innovation process, but in the use of smart KPIs?

Without benchmarks in the early stages of product development and testing, it's a little like being a competitive archer who doesn't have a target to aim at. What does good look like? Have those changes brought me closer or further away from success?

But what benchmarks should be chosen, and how should they be measured? We recommend a five-step process to choose and use benchmarks consistently throughout the early stages of development and to build some of the relevant KPIs:

- Choose relevant benchmark products from the target or neighbouring categories.
- Record the CACUROS for the group of benchmarks.
- Select benchmark products that are on or around the CACUROS.
- Put those benchmarks through the same testing and scoring methodology being used on the new products.
- Use those testing equivalent scores as your target for testing the new products, and for building the relevant KPIs.

Based on great work by IRI, there are clear benchmarks that can apply across most consumer goods companies. The benchmarks apply broadly on two levels, rate of sale and distribution. Distribution is a measure that is applied rather than researched, but the rule of thumb is the more confidence a buyer has in the product, the more likely higher distribution will be given. Therefore predicted rate of sale has a large bearing on both distribution and overall success. Using IRI's work, we advise looking at the CACUROS.

CACUROS can at first seem a daunting measure, but it is relatively simple to handle once the concept is understood. Imagine a category of products, perhaps including 40 or so products. Virtually all categories behave in a way where there are a small number of products that deliver a high volume or value share of the overall category. For example, Coca-Cola would be expected to have a high volume and value share of the carbonated drinks category. The other products have small volumes and sales values, and the further down the list of products in the category you go, the smaller the ROS would be expected to be. We don't want the benchmarks to be so high that innovation is never done as it's almost impossible to develop concepts that hit the Purchase Intent score. Nor do we want them to be so low that any product concept would be stronger than the Purchase Intent required. The IRI benchmarks look at the category average, which means looking at adding up the ROS for all 40 products and then dividing it effectively by 40 (it is slightly more complicated than this as levels of distribution have to be taken into account), effectively giving the average for that category. We use a measure of cash unit rate of sale, as not all categories are measured in volume in the same way, from beer to butter or from paella to dishwasher powder. But cash is a universal metric from one category to another.

The work from IRI highlights that new products generally behave in a similar way in the rate of sale: a high burst at the start then settling down into a long term behaviour. Their analysis shows that products that achieve less than 80% of the CACUROS will not survive more than one or two range reviews. And this makes sense for the retailer, as shelf space is limited, so they have to prioritise shelf space to products that have a high rate of sale or are bringing new purchasers to the category. Thus products that don't have a high rate of sale will probably be dropped over time. And it seems from IRI that 80% is the bottom rung of the ladder; any lower than 80% risks the product falling off entirely. IRI recommends 120% to the CACUROS to ensure long-term success, which again makes sense given that they should survive a number of range reviews.

Let's work through an example of how to use CACUROS. Let's say you've taken the sales data from the last six months (to flatten any peaks or seasonality) for a sub-category of 50 products in a typical convenience food category. The CACU-ROS comes out as £10 (we're going easy on the maths!). This £10 figure is £10 worth of one product sold in one single store in one single week. So the products to take as a benchmark are any that have a CACUROS in the range of £8 (80% of the average) to £12 (120% of the average). Let's say you've now got 12 benchmark products that sit in that range. We take those 12 benchmarked products, and in the same visual format as you are testing your new products under development, you put them through the same testing methodology being used to assess everything. That testing methodology, most likely digital at this early stage in the process, should spit out some sort of PI score. So you should have 12 sets of PI scores for those benchmarks, and they should broadly be in rank order of the rate of sale (giving the testing methodology some leeway for statistical significance for tightly grouped products).

This is now your target. Any PI scores for your new products that fall significantly below the target? Ditch them. Any PI scores that fall just below the target? Keep them, and think of what hypotheses and changes you could make to improve them. Then retest them. Any PI scores for your new products that are within the range? Great job, keep them but again see if there is anything you could easily iterate and test again to try to improve them. Any PI scores for your new products that are above the range? Amazing job! But you're not finished. Arguably these are the product concepts that now need the most attention. Come up with a hypothesis to improve them, retest them, and keep on iterating until you think they're as strong as they can be.

Clear KPIs that are linked to matching or exceeding the benchmarks identified around this early stage of the product development process will pay dividends in the long run. Be prepared, and be confident enough, to put to one side ideas that just aren't hitting the PI levels required to make a dent on the category. Double down on the ones that are on target or even above target. Less is very much more when it comes to maximising your energy and resources in these crucial phases.

Pipeline KPIs (pre-launch)

In this area we're creating KPIs that drive behaviours to improve pipeline efficiency – i.e. the number of product concepts being managed through an innovation process by individuals or single teams. These include:

- The ratio of product concepts scoring above the CACUROS target compared to total product concepts in the pipeline. This shows the number of successful ideas.

- Pipeline efficiency. The number of successful product concepts per team member (less is better). Could be done overall or by pipeline stage, if the pipeline has been broken down into stages.
- Percentage concept elimination per Sprint cycle to ensure only high-quality ideas are moving through the process.
- Speed of decision-making (how long a product has languished in a particular stage of the innovation pipeline) – what we pretentiously term 'pipeline cadence'. Given product development is the most expensive part of innovation, if we can speed this up it results in lower costs and also allows for more time to generate sales.
- Percentage of products that exceed the benchmark.
- Speed through the Agile Innovation process.
- The number of concepts developed that score above average for target growth in the consumer segment / category strategy.
- Cost per product specification created.
- Overall pipeline value by developing models for volume and price using benchmarked products' volumes and the index to the benchmark of the new ideas.

Managing the pipeline – by constant reviewing of products entering the marketplace – an Agile Innovation lab would have more predictive powers about what the next 'big thing' was going to be. One of the advantages of Agile Innovation is the pace and certainty that can be applied. Applying a product lifecycle view on the pipeline would traditionally mean looking for breakthrough for early adopters and more incremental innovation on more mature categories. Traditionally breakthrough innovation would be seen as big risk, big reward, as these are currently not known products and would tap an unmet consumer need with a new product. Conversely, incremental innovation on mature products would be seen as less risky with a lower return. Innovation pipeline management seeks to balance both breakthrough and incremental innovation to manage the level of risk and return.

Using Agile Innovation approaches, the risk of failing on breakthrough can be reduced whilst at the same time maximising the opportunity of incremental innovation on mature products. Breakthrough can be managed by long-term reviewing of product concepts in the breakthrough area and comparing their purchase intent with known products, and when they hit a 'trigger point', i.e. a predetermined level of purchase intent, then they can be launched. This can be tracked over a long timeframe allowing for a regressive analysis and future predictions. With incremental innovation such as flavour or format extensions, using Agile Innovation approaches the number and breadth of extensions can be prioritised to those that will make the biggest bang for the buck rather than executing anything over a threshold limit. For example, imagine you are an ice cream manufacturer, and rather than just launching a product that hits a predetermined benchmark, you create in your lab literally thousands of product ideas and take the best ideas forward.

Innovation pipelines can, and arguably should, be broken into stages using the same principles as sales team pipelines of customer prospects . By having differently labelled stages moving from the left (speculative concept ideas) to the right (fully specified validated products ready for physical production) it becomes much easier to manage innovation and development teams. KPIs can then accurately be applied, just as they would be to a sales team, that help product developers manage correctly shaped pipelines. Having too many product concepts in the early, unvalidated stages means the developer is clearly guilty of starting too much and finishing too little. An overall lean pipeline in the early creative stages will mean the developer will be unlikely to launch enough products of the required volume or quality.

To bring an example to life, let's say there are six pipeline stages from left to right in a typical innovation pipeline:

- Ideas – this is the first, speculative stage where all potential ideas are captured.
- Product concepts – any ideas that the product developer likes can be refined into a product concept, a level that a consumer would understand.
- Propositions – at this stage, the product concept has been tested with consumers, it has a product title that has had multiple variants optimised, and packaging format and design have been tested and refined.
- Commercialised – as we move into the second half of the pipeline, the number of products should shrink dramatically as the barriers to success become higher. Here, all products should have been tested for price suitability in relation to the categories they are likely to sit in.
- Performant – all product concepts at this stage have been tested and performed better than the benchmarking target (or CACUROS).
- Ready for launch – fully validated and optimised product specifications ready for manufacture.

We see some clients using Excel or generic project management software to apply some of these principles already. The shape of the pipeline should be broad to the left, becoming narrower through the stages to the right.

Sales pipeline software such as Pipedrive will apply a percentage likelihood to the deal value in the different stages of the pipeline to spit out an overall value of the pipeline using a Monte Carlo simulator (a sophisticated algorithim that uses random number generation to solve complex problems, such as the likelihood of a range of variables becoming a given number) . We can apply the same principles to the innovation pipeline: anything in the first speculative stage should have a projected sales value, but a 0% factor applied to it. As you go through the phases from left to right, the percentage factor increases through to 100% in the final column. This gives the product developer and their manager an overall pipeline value KPI that can be used. Effectively it's similar to working out the payout to a very long accumulator bet, with each individual bet having different odds, and where the overall completion of the accumulator is a compounding of the individual odds.

Commercial KPIs (post-launch)

We now move onto KPIs that measure individual products' performance once they have been launched into market. This is a simpler area to outline but it's surprising how many product developers we encounter that don't have commercial targets. Suggested KPIs include:

- Sales per new product versus the category target (i.e. the expected rate of sale for a strong new product in that particular category).
- Return on investment per product (sales minus associated costs).
- Return on investment per product developer, judged by relevant time period (quarter, half-year etc.).
- Number of launches per month/quarter/year versus target/competitors.
- Market share penetration achieved through innovation over one year and three years.
- Sales per square foot (for physical retailers).
- Sales compared to existing products.
- The average rate of sale per new product launched (versus category target or average) over one year and three years.
- Incremental profit per new product.

In this KPIs list, we're mapping the performance of the individual products along with the impact they have had on some of the key corporate customer metrics such as footfall, the weight of purchase etc. What we are looking for here is an understanding of the impact of individual new products as part of an overall category and business strategy. Not every product is going to be a record-breaker; some products can be launched to attract new customer segments to the category or store. Some products are very expensive to develop, but that heavy upfront investment leads to further similar products being launched at a much lower cost. Some products are very cheap and quick to develop but are launched just to capitalise on a growth opportunity. Overall, we need KPIs to help the product developer understand the balance of their portfolio, and how each product will therefore feed into a strong overall set of numbers on the contribution that innovation is making to the category.

Financial KPIs (post-launch)

And finally we move onto KPIs that measure performance at category or grouping level post-launch. Whilst somewhat more obvious, there are very easy traps to fall into here that reward volume of innovation, not quality of innovation. We suggest:

- Total revenue generated at the category level by new products, broken down as an average over one year and three years.
- Incremental revenue generated at the category level by new products over one year and three years, arguably a far more important metric than straightforward sales. This can be represented in percentage terms to show the amount of growth achieved through innovation.
- The profitability of new product innovation both in cash and percentage margin terms across the whole category over one year and three years to ensure an accretive profit.
- Incremental profit generated at the category level over one year and three years – again, arguably more important than a straightforward profit figure. We need to know how much profitable growth the product innovation has created.
- Cost of the innovation in totality across the category over one year and three years – not just the cost of goods, but the salaries of the product developers, any testing resources etc., represented as a percentage of overall category sales. There should be a target that the business sets for each category. Most companies will have this as part of their R&D tax credit submission.
- ROI on innovation for the category represented as a percentage of sales over one year and three years.

In this high-level list of KPIs, we're looking to track the performance and impact of innovation on the total category, rather than by individual product. Here we need to be able to map the incremental impact of the innovation, i.e. what would the category look like without the innovation that had launched in the last 12 months (hopefully much worse). This shows the business how much sales and profit their innovation investment (people, resources, tools) is generating. To gather all this information accurately, however, everything must be tracked and monitored at the individual product level, which is where the commercial KPIs come in.

Conclusion

KPIs are an easy win for businesses looking to embrace Agile. They can really help shift the mindset of innovation teams, allowing them to flourish under clear guidance from the senior leadership. Without them, it will be a struggle to get Agile going in an organisation.

The key to KPIs is to review them regularly and intervene when they start to deviate from the objective or the expectation. In essence, course correct, which is the focus of Chapter 11.

Key takeaways from this chapter

- Innovation KPIs can act as a substantial enabler of Agile Innovation when structured, implemented and monitored properly. Our suggested areas for KPIs are the following.
- Customer metrics that help the Agile innovator develop a high-class set of product concepts in the first part of the funnel.
- Pipeline metrics that ensure robust, consistent and rapid decision-making is used to develop an efficient, impactful pipeline of product concepts.
- Commercial metrics that monitor the individual impact of products once on the shelf.
- Financial metrics that help the innovator and business understand the incremental impact of innovation on a category, division and company.

Chapter 11 –
Charting your course
with course correction

When sailing a yacht, unfortunately navigating from one point to another is rarely as simple as drawing a straight line between two points on a chart. Consideration for wind, tides, equipment and crew capabilities must be thought through when plotting the course. However, we cannot successfully take into account all the components involved at the start of the journey: navigation must constantly make corrections in real-time with real data. Success in reaching the destination is dependent upon interpreting the data available at the time and blending that with the experience of the crew and the capabilities of the yacht.

Planning a sailing voyage is similar to the Agile product development process; we may have a broad understanding of the product we want to achieve and a clear understanding of the consumer's 'problem to solve'. However it would be considered poor practice to have a final product in mind before the Agile process started, as that would leave its development open to confirmation bias (the tendency of human beings to look only for information that supports their existing beliefs).

Instead, what happens in the development process is similar to what happens when we are sailing. We review the data from our tests, and if it works, we persevere, and if it doesn't, we change tack to see if that works better, which we call a 'pivot'.

The Agile process of Build–Measure–Learn has been widely distributed and commented on since Eric Ries outlined it in *The Lean Startup*. At an abstract level, we build products, then test the products and measure results against the previously set benchmarks/KPIs. We use the data to learn and iterate on the product, changing elements to see if it improves results with consumers. We repeat this process for multiple iterations, perhaps dozens, in some cases thousands of times.

When we first read *The Lean Startup* in 2012, we fully understood the abstract idea of the process, but it probably took four or five years to understand how to bring Agile Innovation to life in consumer goods products.

So, to avoid you going through this same discovery process we had to, the remainder of this chapter provides real examples of how to successfully navigate the Agile product development process from clients we have worked with. However, before we go through the examples, we need to highlight some basic statistical terms, in particular statistical significance, as these are necessary tools when deciding when & why to pivot

Statistics

Statistical significance gives the confidence needed that the result achieved in the test is not down to chance, and that when repeated the answer would be more or less the same. Sometimes statistical significance is expressed as a margin of error, where a result is ± X%. If the answer if within the margin of error, it means it is not statistically significant; if it lies outside the margin of error, it is significant.

There are several ways to calculate statistical significance. One example is the Excel function =*CONFIDENCE(5%,50%, 250)*, where 250 is the number of people in the test, 5% represents the confidence level (i.e. 95%) and 50% represents the standard deviation[57]. Alternatively, there are online confidence calculators such as https://www.surveysystem.com/sscalc.htm

The reason for introducing the concept of statistical significance here is to ensure that the interpretation of the results from your Agile lab is correct, so you know when to pivot or when to persevere. Similar to sailing, we need to understand what the instruments are telling us and what that data means before we make a decision.

---

57 https://support.microsoft.com/en-us/office/confidence-function-75ccc007-f77c-4343-bc14-673642091ad6

Here are two practical examples to illustrate statistical significance.

A survey of 500 people asks the question 'Did you buy a turkey for last Christmas?' There are 56% of respondents who answer 'Yes', and 44% who answer 'No'. The statistical significance of 500 people at a 95% confidence interval is 4.4%. A confidence internal is defined as;

"A confidence interval (CI) is a range of values that's likely to include a population value with a certain degree of confidence. It is often expressed as a % whereby a population mean lies between an upper and lower interval. "

Therefore in the turkey example we can say that the 'Yes' is significant because the difference between 'Yes' and 'No' exceeds the statistical significance of 4.4%.

A survey of 250 people asks them if they would buy a specific wine, and 76% of them answer 'Yes'. A further 250 people are asked if they would buy a slightly different bottle of wine, and 71% of respondents answer 'Yes'. Is it fair to say that the first bottle of wine is more popular than the slightly different bottle? The answer is that although 500 people took part in total, the statistical significance is measured on each individual question, therefore the statistical significance is 6.2% at 95% confidence, and since the difference between the two wine bottles is less than 6.2% it is not accurate to say that the difference is statistically significant.

New product concepts
A national multiple grocer challenged us to develop a winning product that would sell 20% more than the current products in the range and to do it with a 30% saving on traditional development costs. We also had to do it in less time than the normal development.

This information alone helps us immediately understand our overall targets, specifically to save time, generate more sales, and do it with less money.

We also spent time with the project leaders to ensure we all understood the 'action standard' in advance. The action standard helps to ensure the objectivity of the idea, and we make certain all involved in the project agree and are aligned with the common action standard. In this case, it was to achieve a minimum of 80% of the average test score of the current range. To ascertain what this meant in reality, we ran a selection of the current range through our agile testing tool. We then combined this with the EPOS sales data which highlighted how the average product performed, and also how it scored in the research. Again we took the time to gain advance agreement and alignment to not just the measure itself, but also to the interpretation of the measure, specifically that any new ideas had to be better than this specific product. We also agreed on how we would measure the metrics, and what profile the 500 respondents would have. With our targets and measures agreed, we were able to commence.

We ran a workshop with twelve subject matter experts and developed approximately 180 concepts, which we tested with 500 shoppers who regularly shop in the given multiple grocer. Using this data, we whittled down 180 concepts to 40, excluding any which didn't hit the pre-agreed action standard. Having this pre-agreed pays dividends at this point as the process becomes smooth and avoids any moments of dispute. We have seen numerous times in workshops where people argue the case for their idea, despite the data suggesting it is performing some way below the required action standard. With a pre-agreed action standard, people stay humble and focus on developing great ideas. To use our sailing metaphor, whena boat wants to change tack and go in a different direction, the skipper calls out 'going about' with the crew in advance, so everyone knows their roles and what the commands will be, rather than having the crew react to the boat turning and then executing their processes.

Back to the workshop. 40 ideas would normally be sufficient output for a workshop, but we were confident we could improve upon them. We then developed 20 individual flavour variants of each of the 40 concepts, using inspiration from various sources, including current ranges of competitors and cookbooks. In total, we developed more than 800 concepts, testing them all against the benchmark of the current range. It may seem excessive to develop hundreds of variations, but this gave us more confidence that we were developing a strong product that motivated consumers. Again each of these concepts was tested with consumers in the same manner as previously agreed. The final result was more than a dozen products, all of which achieved our consumer benchmark. When the new products came to be launched, we easily achieved the targets of 20% rate of sale and 30% cost saving.

This inspiration for product development of existing and seemingly successful concepts can come from multiple sources. At its heart is the pursuit of perfection or constant improvement, as in Kanban (aka lean engineering). We have used as inspiration the following: new product launches from adjacent categories; competitors' products; products from other countries; online recipes; social media posts; and consumer complaint data. Having this inspiration helps in making the course correction easier to manage and execute.

Design elimination – cows on the pack

To give a different example of how course correction can work, here's what we found from the dairy industry. Common wisdom in the dairy industry is that cows sell products, and most dairy products will have a Friesian or Jersey cow emblazoned on the pack design. By eliminating different elements on the pack of dairy products, we were able to identify the value of each element, including the value of the cow on the packaging. We course corrected dozens of times to explore different pack elements, both with and without a cow, different types of cows. In fact cows add less value than the colour of the font and add little to no value versus a simpler plain pack design. It's a good example of how entrenched assumptions about a product or category can restrict innovation.

Milkshake flavours

We subsequently did some further work in the diary sector looking at milkshake flavours. The previous approach to product development in this business has been to test 15 flavours in research and pick the products to launch from those 15. To move things forward ee decided to develop a database of flavours to allow for quicker product development when necessary rather than during a frantic rush for new product ideas. We helped the business build up this database over time and it now holds several thousand flavours. We started off gaining inspiration from products within the category and pretty quickly exhausted those sources. We then went to adjacent categories with similar motivation, such as ice cream and desserts. Again we quickly exhausted those sources. We looked at sweets/candy. We looked at international markets. We looked at online and social media suggestions, and every week we added and tested more flavours. As each test went on, we developed a bigger and bigger list, which was our goal.

However, we also wanted to be efficient with our generation and measuring. Every three months, we would take a step back and look at what the data was telling us, both in the new data we had collected in the last three months, but also overall. Stepping back would be similar to reviewing our navigation in sailing, in particular looking to see if we were still on track to our destination with our current heading and speed, and ensuring that tides, currents or wind change were not taking us off course. What we found from these quarterly flavour reviews helped us massively.

The first finding was a correlation between what ideas were motivating and those that weren't motivating, assessed against the action standard; – just as in sailing, we could work out what sails were best for which conditions. We found that milkshake flavours that were more motivating to consumers tended to be more sweet, fun, comforting and indulgent. Milkshake flavours being sweet, comforting and indulgent is not really rocket science; it's mostly common sense. However, the degree of comfort fun, and indulgence was immense. We saw little opportunity for savoury flavours, as trend reports had previously predicted. We saw a limited opportunity for health flavours, kicking the trend of the last 20 years. Using this, we were able to dramatically alter the scores of flavours by over 20 percentage points. For example, mango and raspberry milkshake was a middle-order result that did not pass our action standard. But by adding a more indulgent phrase such as cheesecake to mango and raspberry made a terrific impact. A yachting analogy might be that the weather reports before setting off on the voyage indicate the wind may come from a certain direction and certain speed, just as the trend reports said that healthy and savoury flavours would be the ones to look out for in the future.

Second, we found by reviewing regularly that there was a much higher degree of seasonality than anticipated. In the summer, more indulgent fruit flavours worked, whereas in winter, more chocolate and thick flavours scored higher, such as fudge and marshmallow. Understanding seasonality allowed us to change course, so we could start to target specific flavours at specific times of the year we were launching, thus helping us both avoid a mistake in launching a summer product in winter, and maximise our sales at different times of the year with a more focused offering. In sailing terms we were using the correct tide charts for the right location, to ensure we didn't go aground in the middle of the night.

Colour of liquid

We can take this approach to deep levels of granularity. In this example, we were inspired by a famous test that Google performed and added more than $200m of incremental profit every year. Google wanted to optimise its advertising revenue and looked at what shade of blue was the most motivating to consumers. They tested 41 shades of blue and measured the difference amongst the variations of blue. As Google is able to AB test with millions of users in just a few minutes, they can have a very precise margin of error in their results. They had a clear action standard which was the current performance of the hyperlink.

We wanted to find out if we could improve our product by subtly changing the colour of the liquid. We tested over 70 changes in the colour of the liquid by changing the hue in Photoshop. We found that the vast majority of the tests were worse than the original, with only seven being within the margin of error of the original colour of the liquid. However, we did find one colour, a hue of green, that was better than the original to a statistically significant degree.

Protein shake ingredients

When developing a new protein shake we wanted to ensure that during the development stage of the process we were not diluting the original concept that was highly motivating to consumers. We tested every single element of the development stage with 500 UK consumers, including the claim benefits phrasing: 'Reduced sugar' or 'Sugar-free'; '100 calories' or '98 calories'. We tested the pack format, including can, PET bottle, HDPE bottle with sleeve, and TetraPak carton. We tested the serving size of 300ml, 330ml, 380ml, or 500ml. We tested the hierarchy of messaging on the pack design to understand what messages were more motivating. We tested the colours on the label and the font style and font size. Without detailing what we found as it's confidential for the client, we were able to give a very prescriptive brief to the Product Development team that is in essence, a detailed course for the yacht to follow.

Reframing a desk

Desks are desks, right? Wrong. A client wanted to introduce a new range of products into his portfolio, and since he had identified that there was a growth in PC gaming, he had sourced a 'Gaming desk', with a very modern and stark design. He initially was going to market it as a gaming desk. We demonstrated by testing with 500 UK-based consumers that reframing the desk as a 'modern, contemporary desk' rather than as a 'Gaming desk' was a statistically significant improvement, and therefore more motivating.

Pepperoni pieces

In times of increased pressure on product costs and value for money, we need to walk the thin line of reducing costs without aggravating shoppers and customers. We see plenty of news stories about brands reducing their size so they don't have to increase their price from a familiar price point, the notion of 'sizeflation' or 'shrinkflation'. We wanted to find out what the optimum product cost was for pepperoni pizza. We started with the existing pack design, and using different pack formats, found a cheaper pack format that was just as motivating for shoppers, and also had a positive environmental impact. We then tested the number of pepperoni pieces on the pizza, as this was the major add-on cost in the product. We started with an image of eight large pepperoni pieces, and tested this with 500 consumers. We subsequently tested different numbers of pepperoni pieces up to 15, and using an AB testing methodology, always tested versus the original eight pieces. The most motivating number of pepperoni pieces was nine, which was statistically significant over the current number of pepperoni pieces, giving a massive product cost saving.

Governance

Our last point in charting your course is a practical point about governance. We need to ensure that our propositions are delivering against the objectives set whilst at the same time allowing for the creativity in the process. By its nature creativity will develop products that do not meet the scope of the project but may meet the metrics of consumers. We advocate having a regular governance meeting to ensure that the organisation values the project's outputs. This governance needs to be frequent enough to not waste time on projects that won't fit the organisation but also infrequent enough not to kill off the creative process of developing products. The governance committee is, in effect, there to make sure you are on course, and to support you in changing or continuing on your course.

We have previously had a 3:1 cycle of three Sprints followed by one governance review. A 3:1 cycle allows for several cycles before checking on the progress of the project and ensuring the organisation wants to progress.

One example we have of this is where we developed an app to overcome a very real problem in how people used our product. The opportunity for the app was several million pounds, and bigger than any other product development ideas we had ever had. We tested it against our category benchmarks as well as against other app benchmarks, and in every case it was higher than the benchmarks. At our regular governance meetings, we presented the idea along with the others, and the governance committee rejected the idea. On the face of it, it seems ridiculous to reject a product idea that was something that consumers wanted, that would potentially boost sales in the category we operated in, and also potentially generate significant cash. However, the capability of developing the app, even financing the app, was not within the organisation's purview, so the governance committee correctly decided to curtail it.

We hope these practical examples have helped bring Agile practise to life, enabling you to visualise how the data from testing can help take product thinking in new directions.

 ### Key takeaways from this chapter
- Just like sailing, don't expect to have everything nailed down before you start. Be prepared to adapt and change as projects evolve
- You can and should be testing everything, not just the idea at the start, but every decision, from pack type, to name, ingredients, graphics and product claim.
- Ensure a balance of good governance of projects versus autonomy to ensure the project is adding value to the organisation. We recommend a 3:1 Sprints-to-governance ratio to keep projects on track.

Summary
and Close

Chapter 12 - Time to act

Yesterday is gone. Tomorrow has not yet come.
We have only today.
Let us begin. (Mother Teresa)

In the past, the CPG industry mired innovation in failure, and that failure was not only accepted as a cost of innovation but viewed as a prerequisite for generating profitable growth from innovation. A cynical view could hold that the supporting 'ecosystem' of innovation embedded that failure, as it supported research and insight agencies, design and graphic agencies, marketing agencies, packaging companies, legal departments, and even some retailers. It also supported the careers of innovators in CPG manufacturers, who with a slightly better than 90% failure rate could claim to be the best innovators ever; however, in any other field of work, having even a 70% failure rate in their job would mean they would never work again. Each stakeholder in the innovation process, except the shareholder, wanted the innovation process to remain static, to continue to fail; to not evolve, as it generated value for them in some sense. But at the heart of that failure was one consumer truth, that consumers are motivated to buy new products and see value in newness. And that value helped drive the ROI of 185%, even with such a staggering failure rate for launched products .

Today, we are able to see opportunities to improve and evolve innovation from other industries, in particular from tech. Tech businesses have adopted not just new processes, but a mindset change that moves away from 'make it then sell it', to 'sell it then make it'. They have endorsed bold new structures for their teams that enhance the working lives of their colleagues whilst at the same time reducing cost and improving quality by moving from 'pyramids' to 'pods'. They follow 'discover then deliver' with autonomy and alignment to a shared company purpose and vision. Their pace to adapt and then take advantage of the ever-changing landscape has shown the path for other industries to follow.

Our collective future for CPG innovation can be one where we continue to delight shoppers and consumers with unique new products, but are able to do so more efficiently both in terms of time and money by reducing the failure of launched products to zero. It will be a future where companies adopt new ways of working that demand more alignment and autonomy, giving colleagues more motivating and fulfilling roles, as well as generating better products quicker. As products develop quicker than before, the costs of development will plummet as we get it right the first time, rather than going back and forth through changes. It will be a future where a virtuous engine of innovation will generate more success for colleagues, managers, executives and shareholders.

Agile innovation is coming. Just as technology is disrupting all aspects of our daily lives, it is already disrupting the world of market research, with near-instantaneous results at prices that are orders of magnitude lower than 20 years ago. As those new technologies enter into the CPG world, the rate of change in innovation will only accelerate, and with that rate of innovation change, the rewards from innovation will multiply. Conversely, the costs of not taking action on innovation will increase, as market share is gifted to those willing to engage in the new world of innovation. Innovation will go through the same change that advertising went through in the last 15 years, as it became more measurable and therefore more effective. Thanks to the disruption of technology, innovation in FMCG will become more effective, and your choice is whether to be at the forefront of that change to drive profitable growth or to be following behind, working with ineffective agencies, in ineffective ways, developing ineffective products that are doomed from the start.

Agile Innovation presents a positive change for your business. It will mean better products that delight consumers and shoppers. It will engage teams and organisations as a whole. It will be an engine for growth for shareholders, employees, and leaders. It will change innovation forever.

We leave you with this closing thought.

As the business world tries to make sense of what has happened in 2020, both of us feel that we're witnessing five to ten years of change in just a few months. The crutch of yesterday's 'this is how we've always done it, and these are the costs of doing it the way we've always done it' has gone, with a need now to discover what the 'new' normal is. As businesses retrench and begin to look forwards at a radically changed landscape, the need to innovate successfully feels more relevant than ever before. A planet full of nervous, uncertain consumers means that consumer attitudes are shifting every week, so innovation needs to be done at a higher pace, with consumers at the front and centre of development all the way through the process, not just with a glancing view at the start.

If, as authors, we believed in Agile Innovation when we first started this project back in 2019, the events of the last six months have turned us into Agile evangelists.

FURTHER READING

Books

Brick by Brick: How LEGO Rewrote the Rules of Innovation and Conquered the Global Toy Industry by Bill Breen and David Robertson
ISBN-13 : 978-1847941176

Innovator's Dilemma: When New Technologies Cause Great Firms to Fail (Management of Innovation and Change) by Clayton M Christensen
ISBN-13 : 978-1422196021

The Choice Factory: 25 behavioural biases that influence what we buy by Richard Shotton
ISBN-13 : 978-0857196095

Predictably Irrational: The Hidden Forces That Shape Our Decisions by Dan Ariely
ISBN-13 : 978-0007256532

Consumerology: The Truth about Consumers and the Psychology of Shopping by Philip Graves
ISBN-13 : 978-1857885767

The Lean Startup: How Today's Entrepreneurs Use Continuous Innovation to Create Radically Successful Businesses by Eric Ries
ISBN-13 : 978-0307887894

REPORTS AND RESEARCH PAPERS

https://papers.ssrn.com/sol3/papers.cfm?abstract_id=3684428

https://www.iriworldwide.com/IRI/media/IRI-Clients/International/uk/new_product_study_wp_july16-Final.pdf

www.nielsen.com/wp-content/uploads/sites/3/2019/04/setting-the-record-straight-common-causes-of-innovation-failure-1.pdf

Mintel Attitudes Towards Innovation in the Food Market – UK – July 2015
https://reports.mintel.com/display/716155/

www.iriworldwide.com/IRI/media/IRI-Clients/International/uk/IRI-The-Big-Question-Range-and-NPD-May-2017-Client-Deck-Final_1.pdf

https://vyprclients.com/science/

RESOURCES – TEMPLATES

For the latest Agile Innovation Templates visit
https://www.agileinnovationplaybook.uk

Index

CPSIA information can be obtained
at www.ICGtesting.com
Printed in the USA
BVHW030027230321
603191BV00004B/126

WALLS OF SILENCE

*Ireland's Policy Towards People
with a Mental Disability*

by
ANNIE RYAN

Published
by
Red Lion Press

CONTENTS

First Edition 1999

© 1999 Annie Ryan

ISBN   0 9535769 0 6

Edited by: James A. McAuley

Published by: **Red Lion Press**
                  "Woodpark",
                  Great Oak,
                  Callan,
                  Co. Kilkenny.   Ireland.
                  Telephone: 056 - 25162

The publisher gratefully acknowledges the professional assistance and advice of Nicholas Harte, solicitor, Kilkenny.

Printed by: **Modern Printers**
                  Walkin Street,
                  Kilkenny. Ireland.
                  Telephone: 056 - 21739/212303

Cover Photograph by: Kevin Ryan. A.I.P.F.

Dedication

For Tom who endures a difficult life with great courage and dignity.

Acknowledgements

Any adequate expression of thanks to those who helped me in the preparation of this book would have to include the titles of all the books and reports which touched on the subject however obliquely.

In the course of preparation I disturbed the peace of many people, usually by means of 'phone calls. The unfailing courtesy of all amazed me. It would be impossible for me to list everybody's name but I thank them all. I thank all those who answered my questions and who sent me written information. I am especially grateful to all those who provided me with photographs and permission to reproduce them.

I owe a great deal to Gerry Ryan and Deirdre Carroll of the National Association for Mentally Handicapped of Ireland who gave me the full run of their library and to Loretta Gallagher who could locate anything in it.

I am deeply appreciative of the facilities provided at the National Archives, at the National Library and at Trinity College Library as well as the libraries of the Institute of Public Administration and the Department of Health.

Finally I thank my husband, Brendan Ryan who supported me with admirable patience in every way possible throughout the whole process.

Introduction

There is no doubt in my mind that if my eldest son had not been mentally handicapped, I would never have written a book about mental disability. And if my son had been provided with a service, the book would have been very different.

When he was younger our son kept our family very busy but not so busy that we did not notice that there were huge inequalities and anomalies in the way certain people with a mental handicap were treated. Where our family lives and have done since we had to move in search of a school which would accept our son, there was a large residential school for slow learners. These could, with a little organisation, have been catered for in a day school in their own community. For five years we passed that school at least twelve times a year on our way to and from Belfast where we found a school which would accept our son. He was not the only child who had to travel to Belfast to avail of his constitutional right. Why?

These and other questions came to mind over the years. When Tom went to St. Ita's Hospital, Portrane, Co. Dublin, in 1976 we stumbled on a scandal which had been going on for a long time. The conditions in many of the mental hospitals were appalling and were known to quite a few. Yet one never heard a word about them. Why?

The most puzzling question of all was one to which I found only partial answers. I found no villains anywhere. On the contrary one could not be but impressed by the hard work and dedication of those in charge of the services. How could so many honourable people who were undoubtedly charitable and competent, allow such a situation to develop?

One answer might be that our political system, even our constitution, does not adequately protect the helpless, certainly if they are less than visible. And that prompts the most likely explanation of all. The reticence with which the issue of mental disability has been approached does not help. When people have no voice, silence is not always golden. Neither is it sufficient simply to break the silence. Revelations do not guarantee reform although they are an important step in ensuring improvement.

Annie Ryan. (May 1999)

1

A GOVERNMENT IN BREACH

On the 23 October 1979, soon after the Dail had settled down to work for the day, Mr. Barry Desmond, a Labour Party T.D. for the Dunlaoire-Rathdown constituency put a question to the Minister for Health[1]. The Minister was Mr Charles Haughey. Mr. Desmond wanted to know when was the last time an Inspector of Mental Hospitals had made an annual report. It was a strange question. What Mr. Desmond was really asking was whether the Minister, or the Inspector of Mental Hospitals, or the Department of Health, or all three had broken the law - a law passed in that same chamber in 1945. No other law had replaced it. Its intention was to protect perhaps the most helpless group of citizens in the state.

Towards Transparency

According to the Mental Treatment Act 1945 the Inspector of Mental Hospitals was required to inspect every mental hospital in the country once a year. If the hospital was being run privately, he was required to inspect it twice a year. Furthermore, according to section 247 of the Mental Treatment Act 1945, the report should be laid before both Houses of the Oireachtas and a copy should be sent to the President of the High Court. The purpose of this requirement was to ensure that what happened to a group of people, most of whom were in the direct care of the state - out of sight and totally helpless - could not be kept secret. The framers of the act invoked not only the legislators but also the judiciary. It is highly disturbing that this precautionary measure failed dismally.

The importance of the Inspector of Mental Hospitals and the responsibilities of the office are clearly indicated in the 1945 Act. The whole of Part Two is given over to the protocol of his appointment and that of Assistant Inspectors. The status of this official is reflected in the remuneration of his office. Next to the

Secretary, the Inspector of Mental Hospitals was the most highly paid official in the Department of Health.

The Missing Reports

Now in the Dail Chamber in 1959 it was coming to light that Section 247 of the Mental Treatment Act[2] had been breached - not in just one year but in every year for the past thirteen years. In all that time nobody saw a report. Not the Minister, no T.D. or Senator, not even the President of the High Court. Nobody noticed. No member of the Dáil or the Senate had noticed a gap on the bookshelves. The President of the High Court, whose inclusion in the statutory requirement must have been meant as a protective back-up, never once as far as we know, inquired about his copy. In thirteen years not one of the Presidents of the High Court noticed anything amiss. For thirteen years, as far as the general public was concerned, the Inspector of Mental Hospitals or his reports might not have existed.

On that October afternoon the debate continued. Mr. Horgan T.D. asked two more questions. He wanted to know when the Oireachtas would receive a report and secondly who was the Inspector of Mental Hospitals. Mr Haughey answered the second question. Dr. Vincent J Dolphin was, he assured Deputy Horgan, Inspector of Mental Hospitals. A strange answer indeed, for Dr. Dolphin had retired in June 1979 and now it was October. Stranger still is the fact that Dr. Dolphin was still signing letters in 1983 four years after his retirement[3]. Perhaps Dr. Dolphin was making up for all those annual reports which he had not written while he had held office ! Mr. Haughey, the Minister for Health, made valiant attempts to explain the extraordinary non-existence of reports which by law should have been made by the Inspector .

This was not one of Mr. Haughey's finest hours. There was not the same need to make these reports, the Minister said, "now that the mental hospitals were no longer closed institutions". This information must have surprised any T. D. present who had ever tried to get into one of these institutions. Most of the wards in all the mental hospitals were locked and it was a serious disciplinary offence for a psychiatric nurse if he or she were to mislay the keys which were normally worn dangling from his or her waist. The Minister was not the only one to confuse the razing of perimeter walls with the opening up of institutions. It is arguable that patients in the mental institutions might have found it less confining if the walls had been left alone and the wards were unlocked instead.

However the Minister was quite adamant that the Inspector actually did inspect every single mental hospital in the country at least once a year, as well as every private institution every six months. Furthermore the reports were made available to Mr. Haughey so that the Department could take any action required by the inspection. In spite of this Mr. Haughey intended to change the whole system of inspections and reports as soon as ever he could. Fortunately, he told the House, he was about to introduce new mental treatment legislation before the end of the session[4].

Deputy Horgan still looked for the missing reports. "Why had the reports not been tabled?" he asked. Mr. Haughey gave him the answer that the Department of Health gives to-day when such questions are asked. "The practice fell into disuse over many years", the Minister said. Unfortunately Deputy Horgan did not ask how this had happened. It must be fairly unusual for a Department of State or for an Officer of that Department to fail to carry out a statutory requirement, not just on one occasion but repeatedly for a period of thirteen years.

Floundering

Mr. Haughey did not think that he or his department needed to do anything about the non-existent reports. He proposed to leave well enough alone. Valiantly he tried to persuade the Dail that they could all get over this awkward business when he brought in the new legislation later on in the session. Deputy Horgan did not agree with him. He did not think that this was on. He pointed out a few of the major implications of the inexcusable laxity of the Department of Health and a number of Governments in carrying out their duties to a defenceless group of citizens. The reports, he said, had to do with conditions in the hospitals. They had to do with the civil rights of persons who might be detained

3

in those hospitals against their will. The Minister, he thought, should have taken major steps to rectify the situation as soon as he had assumed office. Mr. Haughey did not agree. Then everyone spoke at once and Dr. Garret Fitzgerald, a leading member of the opposition, intervened.

"Is the Minister suggesting that where there is a statutory obligation he does not intend complying with it because he intends changing the law ?"
That is exactly what the Minister had intended. Everyone else had done it . Why couldn't he?

"The statutory obligation has not been adhered to in my time, in the time of my immediate predecessor, and in the time of a number of my predecessors before that," said Mr .Haughey.

Reasonable enough. Dr. FitzGerald grew soothing. It was basically an oversight on all their parts. He asked if the Minister could not now immediately comply with the law?

"I cannot", said Mr Haughey.

"What does the Minister mean? Is the Minister telling us that he cannot comply with the law?"
That is exactly what Mr. Haughey was saying. Not immediately, he couldn't comply. "We will have this new legislation this term", he desperately pleaded.

Dr. FitzGerald was beginning to understand. There might not be any reports. Nevertheless, hoping against hope, he expressed an opinion. "There are many existing reports", he stated tentatively. Mr Haughey grew prickly. He did not wish to be lectured. But Dr. FitzGerald was as worried as the Minister. No matter how competent they might be, the backroom boys who were the higher civil servants in the Department of Health, could not cobble anything together out of fresh air. There were no reports. There might not have been any inspections either.

Mr. Haughey made the matter clear: "The Deputy knows that this is not the only statutory obligation in regard to the preparation of those reports which has fallen into disuse. If my predecessor, who was a Cabinet colleague of Deputy FitzGerald, had not been remiss, he might have a stronger case for berating me about the matter". Deputy FitzGerald was conciliatory. He was not berating the Minister. "The failure", he said, "is

4

apparently due to a number of Ministers who have all in some way overlooked the matter".

Papering The Cracks

Indeed. But what to do now? Surprisingly the solution came from Mr. Barry Desmond who had raised the question in the first place. "Would it be possible", he asked, "in relation to 1977, 1978 and 1979 to have the data published? Forget the years from 1962". That was it. That was the solution to a most embarrassing situation for both Government and opposition. Mr. Haughey accepted Mr. Desmond's suggestion with relief.

Mr Jim Mitchell was still worried however. Representing, as he did, a Dublin constituency, he knew a bit about conditions in the two large mental hospitals in the greater Dublin area. Did the Minister not agree that the state of their mental hospitals was something that all parties should be ashamed of? Mr. Haughey did not think that the laying of reports before each House of the Oireachtas could improve the conditions. Mr. Mitchell had the last word in this little bi-partisan cover-up. He thought that "if the matter came before the House at least the condition of them would be reviewed."

The whole little difficulty passed over. Mr. Desmond's suggestion was followed by the Department and in due course a slim volume appeared quite unlike the annual reports which Dr. Dolphin had been used to produce twenty years before. The reports for the three years were combined into one, so strictly speaking it was not an annual report at all.

Limited though it was, an effort had been made. One might expect a certain contrition on the part of all concerned in the production of the Inspector's reports as well as a firm purpose of amendment. They had got away with the breach for a long time. Surely now that it had come to light they would be most careful to carry out the statutory requirements "which had fallen into disuse". But no. Astonishingly, publication of the reports ceased again for another nine years. Publication did not resume until 1988. By that time a new Inspector of Mental Hospitals had been appointed. The office has been much attenuated and I doubt if the remuneration approaches that of the Secretary of the

Department. But the reports are now published regularly, if a little late. They are almost as interesting as the early ones brought out in the 1920s, 30s, 40s and 50s although they lack, in my opinion, the immediacy of the earlier ones.

Dilution of Powers

It is unlikely that Dr. Vincent J Dolphin himself decided to allow the practice of writing reports "to fall into disuse". I am reliably informed that for some years in the early 1960s Dr. Dolphin was quite troubled by the downgrading to which he and his office were subjected. He would remind his listeners of the significance attached to his reports. Dr. Dolphin had no doubt about the importance of the office. The decision to dilute its powers was not his. As to how the decision was taken and how it was possible to take it without reference to the legislature is somewhat of a mystery. For as long as there have been mental hospitals and legislation to regulate them the Office of Inspector of Mental Hospitals had considerable autonomous powers in the supervision of the service.

It is possible to trace the thinking in the Department which lay behind the desire to curtail, if not to abolish, the Inspectors' reports. According to a Department of Health Memorandum, the matter of the Inspector's reports was discussed as early as 1959[5]. The problem for the Department was that the law, as laid down in the 1945 Act and which Mr. Haughey was to find so embarrassing almost exactly twenty years later, was hard to get round but in a memorandum addressed to the Assistant Secretary we read:

"The Assistant Legal Adviser was consulted informally in 1959 as to whether publication of the Inspector's report as part of the Department's Annual Report would meet the statutory requirements imposed by the Mental Treatment Act, 1945. He saw no legal objection to such a procedure - particularly if the title of the Department's Annual Report was amplified e.g. Annual Report of the Department of Health (including the Report of the Inspector of Mental Hospitals)".

The intention was that in future the report of the Inspector of Mental Hospitals would form part of a general report on health, a copy of which would be presented to the Houses of the Oireachtas each year. There would be no more separate reports. On 2nd. March 1965 the then Minister, Mr. McEntee, told the Dáil that he did not see much use in annual reports from the Department of Health and wondered if they were worth the effort. The Department was very busy preparing memoranda for the Select Committee on Health Services. "I am inclined to the view that a report covering five years would be more appropriate". And indeed work on such a report was begun. (March 31, 1965)[6].

One could not take exception to such an arrangement, especially as in 1960 it was planned to integrate services for the mentally disabled with general medical services. Such a tidying-up operation was already in place in Northern Ireland which had inherited an identical system of inspections and reports. But the amalgamation of the two reports did not happen. Instead they were dropped. We are earnestly assured that the statutory inspections did continue and although the traditional and statutory report might not have been made, some special reports on some hospitals were made. The content of these reports would be sufficient to explain the reluctance to publish. Successive Ministers had read them and were ashamed. Almost nothing was done. Not only was there little or nothing provided in the way of extra funding to improve degrading accommodation but the time and the resources required to prepare reports on them was begrudged. The preparation of the Inspector's reports tended to take up a lot of time and became rather a nuisance. The Department and successive ministers knew well the situation in the mental hospitals, but nobody wished to be reminded of this part of the hidden Ireland. Annual reports regularly published could be an awkward and tactless reminder. They had always been late. When they didn't appear at all nobody missed them. The Mental Hospitals and the condition they were in fell out of the public consciousness[7].

The Losers

The harrowing consequences bore most heavily on the long-stay patients. The long-stay patients consisted of two main groups. The first group was made up of the mentally ill patients who did not get better. Some mental illnesses resisted all treatment no matter how modern. The second group was made up of mentally handicapped people. People with a mental handicap in mental hospitals were almost by definition long-stay patients. Twenty per cent of all patients in the mental hospitals in 1980 were mentally handicapped.

The distinction between mental illness and mental handicap should be clearly understood. Mental handicap involves a greater than average difficulty in learning. This results in a delayed or incomplete development of a person's mind and presents difficulties in the person's ability to adapt to the cultural demands of society. The term has been used to cover a whole range of people with few common characteristics. At one extreme it may include people who appear no different from any other citizen but it also includes those whose disabilities are so severe that they will need a great deal of help and care throughout their lives. There are a number of known causes of mental handicap. These can be the result of genetic disorders, brain damage during pregnancy or at birth or at any point after birth, as well as from biological metabolic diseases. Mental handicap may also result from complex social and psychological causes.

People with a mental illness on the other hand are people who acquire, for whatever reason, a disorder of the mind quite unconnected with their intelligence. Unfortunately the disorder is sometimes permanent or more commonly recurrent. Mental illness is a general term to cover a variety of disturbances affecting emotional and social behaviour. It is characterised by inappropriate emotional reactions, by distortion of experience rather than lack of understanding and communication.

Another Effort

The new legislation which Mr. Haughey had promised in October 1979 was introduced in 1980 - not by Mr. Haughey but by Dr. Woods, the new Minister for Health. Mr Haughey had become Taoiseach in December 1979. As we might have guessed from Mr. Haughey's earnest pleadings with the opposition regarding the Inspector of Mental Hospitals and the missing reports, the new legislation proposed to get rid of the office altogether. A medical officer assigned by the Department would visit the hospitals instead. There were to be no reports. Most of the other duties were to go as well. However, interesting as the Bill was, the Department and the Minister were not successful in abolishing the Inspector, for although the Bill was passed by the Dail and the Senate, it was never implemented. By 1992 however, when the Department of Health issued its discussion document preparatory to preparing new legislation on mental health (yet again!) the office had been almost completely rehabilitated. On page 49 of the Green Paper[8] published by the Department of Health we read the following:

" The role of the Inspector of Mental Hospitals in relation to standards in these hospitals is of great importance. The inspector is required under the Mental Treatment Act, 1945 to visit each public psychiatric hospital once a year. A detailed report of each inspection is forwarded by the Department of Health to the Chief Executive of the responsible health board, initially for verification of information in the report and secondly for a response to the recommendations of the Inspector. In some cases, meetings are held between the Department, the Inspectorate and the health board to discuss improvements in the hospital and associated services".

On page 50 of the same document the Department makes a reference to the missing reports. They write:

"During the mid-1980s the practice of making annual reports lapsed due to the priority attached by the Department of Health to the implementation of Planning for the Future".

They make no mention of the thirteen years immediately prior to 1979 when Planning for the Future hadn't yet been mentioned by anyone in the Department. All was silence on the Mental Hospital front during those dismal years.

We can look forward to further developments in the new Mental Health Bill which has not yet seen the light of day[9].

Notes on Chapter One

1. The question might never have been asked if Mr. Donal Nevin, I.C.T.U., had not noticed a gap in his bookshelves and mentioned the matter to Mr. Desmond.
2. Parliamentary Debates, columns 387 - 392. (Questions 32 and 33) October 23, 1979.
3. Letter from the Department of Health to Mr. David Andrews, dated 1st. November, 1983. (in the writer's possession).
4. The Minister was referring to a new Mental Health Bill, introduced in 1980, enacted but never implemented.
5. Department of Health files L106/17. (National Archives). The issue of the publication of the reports of the Inspector of Mental Hospitals is set out very clearly in a submission initialled *JD* in the L division of the Department of Health for consideration by F division.
6. Parliamentary Debates. Dáil Éireann Questions. March 2, 1965.
7. In contrast to the services for the mentally handicapped, the mental hospitals were barely alluded to in the Dáil during the 1960s and early and mid 1970s.
8. Green Paper on Mental Health, Department of Health, June 1992.
9. At the time of publication the long awaited new Mental Health Bill has not yet been published. The Mental Treatment Act 1945 has long since been overtaken by changes in psychiatry and developments in international law. In 1980 the Health (Mental Services) Act was enacted but never implemented.

2

GOOD INTENTIONS

With one exception we inherited all our mental hospitals from the British. All were built in early to middle Victorian times, with the exception of Ardee which was built in 1933. The building of the mental hospitals in the last century was part of a reform movement which in time affected the whole of Britain and Ireland.

The British Legacy

The Irish mental hospitals were the outcome of the special attention given to the situation of the mentally ill in Ireland by various Select Committees of the House of Commons in Westminster. The first of these was set up in 1804. At that time there were in the whole of Ireland only two institutions devoted to the mentally ill apart from a few private asylums near Dublin. Those mentally disabled people who were not accommodated in these institutions found themselves in jails or houses of industry scattered in country towns all over the island. Although the Committee recommended that four provincial asylums should be established and a bill was introduced to that effect, it was never enacted.

In 1817 another Select Committee was set up. This Committee proposed the establishment of district asylums dedicated exclusively to the shelter of the insane. The proposal was accepted and eventually the Lunacy (Ireland) Act was passed in 1821. It was under this act that most of our mental hospitals were built. Their contribution to Irish history has been somewhat under-rated to say the least. Whilst not going quite so far as to view them as part of a penal system, commentators have been on the whole unsympathetic to these institutions and the people who worked in them. No doubt, some of this bad press has been due to a natural desire to get rid of institutions which are now outmoded. Often the distaste extends to the people who lived,

11

and still live, in them. Even today there are still traces of a less than respectful attitude to the nurses who looked after the mentally disabled in the hospitals - an attitude which frequently extended to the doctors in charge. This lack of status was in marked contrast to the esteem in which the members of Religious Orders, who were doing similar work, were held. Like the workhouses, the mental hospitals were looked on as relics of old unhappy far-off things. They stood - and stand - outside the main towns like fortresses .

Places of Refuge

Looked at from the standpoint of our "normalised" society where we are fast approaching the proliferation of single-person households and where even single sex religious communities living in large numbers in large buildings, are a rarity, life in a mental hospital must be unthinkable. There were, however, certain aspects of life in a mental home in immediate pre-famine and post-famine Ireland which must have been a comfort, the obvious one being the regularity and certainty of the next meal. A headline had been set in the regulations laid down by the first governors of Grangegorman in 1815[1]. The patients there were entitled to :

Breakfast:	*1/2 pint of milk, a quart of stirabout made with 6 ozs. of Meal.*
Dinner:	*On two days weekly: 3lbs.of Potatoes or colcannon, and a quart of broth or a pint of beer .*
	On the other days : 1/2 lb of bread or 2 lb of potatoes, 1/2 lb of boiled beef without bone and a pint of beer.
Supper:	*1 pint of beer and 1/2 lb of bread.*

The 'dietary' has always been important in Mental hospitals and its quality and quantity feature regularly in the reports submitted by the Inspector of Mental Hospitals. Times were hard in 19th. Century Ireland. For many they were not too easy in the early part of this century either.

The overriding disaster of the last century was the famine and the consequent stampede of emigration from a demoralised countryside. Social upheaval was followed by social re-adjustment which frequently did not accommodate the kind of people who were "guided" into the large mental institutions throughout the last century and most of the 20th. It must have made a pleasant change for many an unfortunate who was admitted, to find a place where strange behaviour passed unnoticed. For, whatever about the attitudes towards the Mental Hospitals and its patients on the part of people outside the walls, the acceptance within was total. In 1923 the Inspector of Mental Hospitals was disapproving. He wrote of his inspection of Portrane Hospital:

"The erection of attendants' cottages on the site overlooking the Chronic block has been unfortunate. The site appears most unsuitable. The attendants' children wander on the grounds amongst the patients. When the fire alarm was given a troop of children arrived with the Brigade."[2]

Throughout the two centuries each calamity added to the numbers seeking refuge from a society which could not cope with their disabilities. War, poverty, evictions, parental deaths, desertions, addiction, old age and emigration all created the complex set of circumstances where the only life available was that provided within the confines of one or other of the District Mental Hospitals strategically sited all over the country, north and south. When the country was partitioned the Northern six counties took their hospitals with them and got their own Inspector of Mental Hospitals.

A Degree of Openness

Apart from anecdotal evidence the best indication we have of what kind of life was available to the patient in the hospital are the little hints and clues which may be gleaned in the Inspector's reports. The Inspector had a very clear brief. He had to report on the admissions of patients and on their discharges or departures. Not only were the numbers of deaths reported but there was a special report on the numbers who died from Pulmonary Tuberculosis. The reports gave details of suicides and fatal accidents. Sworn Inquiries were reported and the hospitals where they had taken place were named. It was fairly difficult to hide any embarrassing events in the 1920s, 30s, 40s and 50s. Each report indicated the financial position of the mental hospitals generally, the receipts and expenditure, the average cost and the capital indebtedness. Any additional accommodation or improvements in a particular hospital were reported. Farms received special attention and the area of land held by each hospital was returned in an appendix.

The legal obligation to publish these reports was the mechanism whereby alarm bells were set ringing if things went badly wrong in the mental hospitals. Sometimes the Inspectors had to ring the bells very loudly indeed before they were heard but our Inspectors were a persistent lot and not easy to silence in the years when the reports were published.

Dr. Daniel Kelly was the first Inspector of Mental Hospitals to be appointed by an independent government in 1923. He set his face to his task almost without breaking step. A spot-check of his work load is impressive[3]. In January he was in Ennis where he found the condition of the patients "favourable". There was no serious overcrowding "and there was an absence of excitement and complaint."

In June Dr. Kelly devoted two days each to the mental hospitals at Grangegorman in Dublin and at Portrane in County Dublin. He found parts of Grangegorman old and difficult to adapt "to modern requirements". This was particularly true of the part of the hospital which had been a prison. The patients were well cared for and he was glad to see that the use of aluminium ware was being abandoned. Delph was "being gradually introduced".

In December Dr. Kelly visited Enniscorthy, Kilkenny and Killarney. In Killarney there was vacant accommodation on the female side. Everywhere he went Dr. Kelly noted what was good and what was bad and suggested improvements where he could. He approved of the provision of "Cinematograph exhibitions " in Portrane. The condition of the patients and their clothes was his first priority. The state of the buildings and the floors concerned him. "The wasteful escape of steam at several joints should have received the attention of the Engineer".

Job Commitment

All in all, the Inspector of Mental Hospitals had an awesome work load. In addition to the public mental hospitals, some of which were the size of villages, he was responsible for inspecting the private institutions at least twice a year, and a special inspection had to be made of the Criminal Lunatic Asylum at Dundrum.

Dr. Kelly was not afraid to criticise where he felt that the interests of the patients warranted his attention. For example, in 1924 he commented on the untidy appearance of patients in a well-known private hospital in Dublin. He was critical also of "the refractory ward which was unattractive and little calculated to ameliorate a patient's mental condition". He was pleased to note a "decided improvement in these matters" when he visited the hospital six months later[4]. Improvements like this took somewhat longer in the public sector but there is no doubt that the publishing of the reports had great value in bringing about improvements and in safeguarding the patients. It is manifest that the Inspector used them in this way. One of the best examples of this use is the matter of the fire-fighting arrangements in Kilkenny. In 1923 Dr. Kelly noticed that although there were internal hydrants in the hospital there were no hose pipes. "The hydrants had not been tested recently and the metal doors intended for use in the case of fire sagged a great deal". He was obliged to repeat his criticisms in 1924. And again in 1925. In 1926, although other aspects of the hospital had improved, the arrangements in the event of a fire were not yet up to standard. At last in his 1927 report we read: "The arrangements to cope with an outbreak of fire appear to be satisfactory. Chemical extinguishers are supplied to each ward as well as hydrants and fire hose. A staff of twenty attendants sleep in the institution and a fire extinguisher is fitted in each of their rooms"[5].

Consider what the week before Christmas in 1943 held for Dr. Kearney. On the 21st. December he was examining the overcrowded wards in Monaghan, noticing that some painting was in progress. Certain bathing facilities were not adequate. But the central heating system seemed to be running all right -

on turf¹. The patients were comfortably clad but he was a bit worried about the fire arrangements and the farm was satisfactory. The next day, on the 22nd. December, Dr. Kearney was in Mullingar, expressing his pleasure at the high recovery rate in the new unit. In Mullingar some of the male patients helped save the turf. The main building had no central heating and on that December day the dampness on the walls was recorded by Dr. Kearney. On the 23rd. December, the day before Christmas Eve, Dr. Kearney was in Portlaoise inspecting the hospital there. One hopes he got home for Christmas[6].

Everywhere the Inspector went he examined and reported on the farms and how efficiently or not they were managed. Astonishingly in those difficult years he managed to take in every hospital. To put it mildly, travel was not easy. I don't know if the Department of Health provided the Inspector with a car but I imagine he travelled by train. It was fortunate that the British had thoughtfully placed all the mental hospitals near railway stations.

A New Anxiety

It is in a report on Letterkenny that we first hear of Tuberculosis which was to be such a cause for anxiety in the following decades. In 1926 Dr. Kelly recommended that a small detached sanatorium for the accommodation of patients with T.B. be provided. Four years later, in 1930, he draws attention to the problem again. "The provision of verandas for tubercular patients is again recommended". In Limerick in that year too the death rate from tuberculosis was "still high" and Dr. Kelly urged the provision of separate wards or verandahs for tubercular patients. Throughout the 1930s and 40s Dr. Kelly and his successor, Dr. Kearney, chart the progress of the scourge of T. B. in the mental hospitals. The provision of separate accommodation was slow in coming, adding to the mortality rates as well as spreading infection. The deaths from Tuberculosis began to be returned as a separate statistic.

Already in the 1930s every difficulty which faced a mental hospital began to be compounded by the over-riding concern of the later decades - overcrowding. But before we consider the impact of this growing concern which became almost overwhelming in the late 1950ís, we must give some consideration to one of the great achievements of the mental hospitals which could easily escape attention.

Self-support

Almost from inception mental hospitals were self-sufficient to a degree, not only with regard to food but often also clothing and footwear as well. Women patients were employed in the laundry and in sewing and knitting and in what the Inspector described as "ordinary housework". Almost all the hospitals had farms attached where large numbers of men worked. Grangegorman did not have as much land as Portrane, which, to begin with, had 604 acres around the hospital, later extended to 991 acres, in addition to 220 acres at Santry Court. In Grangegorman the men worked in the gardens and the grounds. The lands around Grangegorman have been noted for fruit production since Norman times. Most of the institutions had their own bakeries and baked all the bread required. In addition, Portrane produced all the tweed used in the making of clothes for the patients and large numbers of dresses and other garments were turned out annually (1935). Patients assisted the tailors, shoemakers, carpenters and other tradesmen who contributed to making an alternative life for the people at Portrane. The cinema shows were run by a patient and the well-stocked library was run by two more. Milk, meat, potatoes, fruit, vegetables and cereals were produced in such quantities that Portrane was able to supply not only their own considerable population but were able to sell on their surplus to Grangegorman and the Richmond hospitals as well. At Christmas in Portrane they had so many chrysanthemums in their glasshouses that the nurses were able to decorate all the wards with the richly-coloured blooms.

For the people in the mental hospitals the years of the second world war, from 1939-1945, were well named the 'Emergency'. One wonders what would have happened to 20,000 or so inhabitants of the Big Houses if they hadn't been so self-sufficient. If the tardiness with which the necessary separate accommodation for T. B. patients was tackled is anything to go by, one shudders to think of the possibilities.

The Farming Dimension

It is no wonder then that the Inspector of Mental Hospitals devoted so much attention to the farms. He was delighted that Portrane had built up a T.B. free herd[7]. The piggeries in Castlebar were not up to standard[8]. In Enniscorthy additional land was urgently required. Mullingar had recently acquired land in 1943 and "there was a considerable reduction in the purchase of feeding stuffs". Happily the milk yield was up. The purchase of additional land at Monaghan was advisable (1943)[9]. The farms may have been considered a suitable means of providing therapy for a patient population coming mainly from a rural background, but during the war years and the years of scarcity which followed, these farms were the means of survival. In some hospitals the close involvement of very senior staff surprises us. It was not only the Inspectors of Mental Hospitals who were deeply interested in food production. The legendary Chief R.M.S. Dr. John Dunne who was in charge of the two Dublin mental hospitals, Grangegorman and Portrane, during the war years and after, thought it important enough to make a special recommendation in his report in 1940[10], regarding the vegetable situation:

" The supply up to now has been practically entirely composed of cabbage and swede turnips. There is no point in paying two highly-skilled gardeners merely to produce this class of vegetable. With the amount of land and labour at our disposal we should be able to have much greater variety".

He goes on to specify the variety:

"fresh peas, beans, cauliflowers, parsnips, carrots and onions." He even suggested what acreage should be allocated to each vegetable. Thereafter the gardener sent "a good supply of vegetables to the kitchen daily including scallions and lettuce to patients and staff twice a week" just as Edwardian gardeners did to the kitchens of other big houses just thirty years before. The supply of bread was more important and by 1942 that was seriously reduced by 9,500 lbs per week, and what flour they got had 12% potato flour so that the scarce wheat flour would go further.

But the really big worry was not the food but the fuel situation. Patients who lived out their lives in those large day rooms and dormitories with their high ceilings were in real danger. In Portrane, for example, on the 21st. May 1942 the Board was told that "the present supply of turf is altogether inadequate. The outlook for the future is extremely grave"[11]. Apart from the quality of some of the turf there were prodigious problems with transporting it from the midlands because of the poor roads. Fortunately, on that particular occasion, by permission of the Department of Supplies, they were allowed to purchase some coal.

Credit Due

The war ended. The crisis passed and as far as I know nobody has ever thanked the people who worked so hard to preserve the lives of all those who could so easily have starved or frozen to death during those long years of scarcity. The members of the Boards spent hours discussing familiar problems like the problem of hoose in the calves in Turvey[12] or unfamiliar ones like what to do with the ration books of the staff :

" We are at a complete loss to know what to do with the ration books of the staff. Some get meals at the institution on their on days and at home on their off days or when absent or on sick leave"[13]. And as for their clothes ration, their allocation of clothing coupons would allow each nurse one uniform and one shirt annually with nothing left for socks or collars!

Due credit has never been given to the work of staff and patients, R.M.S.s and Mental Hospital Boards, in those war years, unknown and hidden from the view of all, apart from the anxious concern of their Inspector. In particular, the work of Dr. Kearney and earlier that of Dr. Kelly has gone almost unrecognised. This country owes them a large debt. If it were not for them and their work the history of the mental hospitals and what we did with them and their occupants would be far worse.

Notes on Chapter Two

1. The District of Grangegorman by Thos King Moylan (Dublin Historical Record Vol. VII No. 1. December 1944 - January 1945).
2. Report of the Inspector of Mental Hospitals 1923.
3. Ibid
4. Report of the Inspector of Mental Hospitals 1924 (page 20).
5. Inspector of Mental Hospitals Report. 1927.
6. Report of the Inspector of Mental Hospitals 1943
7. Report of the Inspector of Mental Hospitals (Portrane 11th. December 1942).
8. Report of the Inspector of Mental Hospitals 1946.
9. Report of the Inspector of Mental Hospitals 1943.
10. Annual Report of Resident Medical Superintendent to the Mental Hospital Board 1940.
11. Grangegorman Mental Hospital. (Minutes of Meetings of Joint Committee of Management 1942)
12. Part of the vast farm attached to Portrane lay in the townland of Turvey, near Turvey House.
13. Grangegorman Mental Hospital. (Minutes of Meetings of Joint Committee of Management 1942)

3

THE NIGHTMARE YEARS

As soon as the Mental Hospitals began to lose their small measure of self-sufficiency they were in trouble. Much of this self-sufficiency was based on the working of the farms which were attached to every mental hospital when first established. The farms in some cases were very large. Portrane in North County Dublin, for instance, held 991 acres and Ballinasloe in County Galway had over 600 acres[1]. The patients, most of whom came from a rural background, worked in every branch of farming, some in dairying, some in tillage and some in the rearing and keeping of pigs and poultry. Many hospitals went on to process this produce within the hospital complexes. They were busy places and highly labour intensive. Fortunately medical opinion held the therapeutic value of work and particularly of farm work in high regard.

The Winds of Change
By the end of the 1950s farming had changed all over Ireland. Farmers had got through the war years as best they could mainly with the help of large numbers of workers. Soon after the war ended, farming became much more mechanised. The new machinery which now became necessary required investment decisions which few Mental Hospital Authorities were prepared to make. The therapeutic value of farm work became doubtful and Health Authorities were urged to rid themselves of their farms as soon as possible. They were strangely reluctant to do so, and by 1966 very few had. But in any case the farms and the work therapy which they provided, were becoming irrelevant to the needs of the kind of patient who was coming in to the hospitals in increasing numbers since the end of the Second World War in 1945. Two groups were particularly awkward - the "difficult" old and the mentally handicapped. Almost by definition both groups were going to be "long-stay" patients. Most of the old could be expected to die soon but there was no shortage of

replacements. In 1959 the number of patients aged over 65 who were admitted into mental hospitals was 1,666. In 1960 the number was 1,779.

For years Dr. Dolphin who had been appointed Inspector of Mental Hospitals in 1953, had worried about the likely effects of the apparent acceptance of the mental hospital as a convenient solution to purely social problems. In 1956 he identified overcrowding as one of the main problems in the year under review. All City and County Managers were advised to, examine the possibility of organising a suitable psychiatric consultant service and to ensure that, except in cases of urgency, an elderly patient would not be referred to a mental hospital until he had bee seen by a psychiatrist[2]. In 1957 he was forced to repeat this recommendation but he added that "the number of elderly patients received continues to increase and each mental hospital authority should re-examine its arrangements for the provision of a consultant psychiatric service and where possible, for the examination of the elderly patient and the assessment of home conditions before he is received into a mental hospital"[3]. He clearly thought that too many elderly people were in mental hospitals because of their home conditions rather than an illness.

A Group Adrift

Mentally handicapped people had always found a refuge in the mental hospitals as well as people with epileptic conditions. There was little distinction between the different mental disorders. But increasingly they were not welcome, particularly children. It was generally agreed that mental hospitals were not suitable places for "mental defectives"[4]. The hospitals became increasingly less suitable as they changed from being places of busy outdoor activity to locked day rooms with little or no stimulation of any kind. People with mental handicap, like so many of us, like to watch other people at work even when not able to work themselves.

Up to the late 40s many "mental defectives" were accommodated in the County Homes. In 1949 the acting R.M.S. in Waterford was indignant that he was forced to take in a boy with mental handicap "there was always an idiot ward in the

County Home" and he was extremely annoyed that they seemed to have dispensed with it without telling him. People with a mental handicap came instead to the mental hospital. They had nowhere else to go. But the acting R.M.S. had a point and he made it in the last paragraph. "It appears to me," he wrote, "that since we cannot admit such cases, not being insane persons, suitable provision should be made available in the County Home"[5]. There was little hope of that in 1949 for already in February an Interdepartmental Committee had been set up by the Government consisting of representatives of the Departments of Health, Finance, Social Welfare and Local Government to examine the question of the Reconstruction and Replacement of the County Homes and to submit a report to the Minister for Health. On the 31st. March 1950 there were 595 mental defectives in the County Homes. The Committee decided that the "mental defectives" would have to go. "They were a source of trouble and discomfort to other patients in the Homes"[6].

A 'Cassandra' of His Time

It was highly frustrating that just at the time when mental illness was being generally accepted as treatable and in most cases curable and when there was a chance at last of turning the district mental hospitals into "real" hospitals, every unit and every day room was full to the gills. Over and over again Dr. Dolphin referred to the appalling problem. Of all the Inspectors we have had since 1923 Dr. Dolphin deserves most sympathy. He was a Cassandra who lived to see his worst fears realised. He was helpless and ignored and in the end he was silenced. His last report (for the year 1962) was published in 1965.

Some of the horror can be glimpsed through the restrained prose of Dr. Dolphin's reports. In 1955 he wrote of Grangegorman: "The main refractory division was extremely overcrowded and the atmosphere generally was uncomfortable". In Killarney the overcrowding was very noticeable and they were forced to accommodate patients in rooms which "were gloomy and lacked proper ventilation and heating". In 1956 there was little improvement. There was marked overcrowding in almost every hospital. In addition many were cold, dark and poorly ventilated.

It was very difficult to establish any kind of modern service for the mentally ill in these circumstances. The best they could do was to separate new patients from the crowds of "chronic" mentally ill, the mentally handicapped and the old. Special admission units made it possible to treat the new mentally ill away from the hidden realities of life for the long-stay patients. Understandably in most hospitals resources were concentrated in these areas. Without the detailed reports of the Inspector it is harder to find out what happened to the long-stay patients, be they the old, the mentally handicapped, or the mentally ill who did not get better. Some inspections were made, however, and some reports were written. They give a very clear account of a horrifying story. We can do no better than to give in some detail what Dr. Ramsay, the Assistant Inspector of Mental Hospitals, wrote in his account of a special inspection of Clonmel in 1958. This report was never published.[7]

In 1958, Clonmel District Mental Hospital catered for the North and South Ridings of Tipperary. It was - and still is - situated about a mile from the town. At that time it contained about 850 patients. The hospital consisted of divisions of patients who were accommodated in an assortment of buildings scattered over a substantial area ranging from the main building, in which the majority of female patients were accommodated, down to a "temporary" structure occupied for years by a further 81 women. This building was known as the 'Red House' because it had a red galvanised roof.

A Damning Report

What Dr. Ramsay had to report was shocking in the extreme. He started with Division 1 where 58 women were living. His report reads as follows:

"Division 1 (female). Division 1 accommodates 58 patients. Eighteen patients sleep in single rooms. These rooms have windows placed high in the wall with shutters which when closed allow in a very small amount of air. The lighting is inadequate, even if left on, so that the patients are in darkness or in semi-darkness most of the time they are in these rooms. Neither for the single rooms nor for the dormitories is there any provision for the storage of patients' clothes so that the clothes have to be left on corridors or passages - sometimes on chairs and sometimes on the bare floor. The only sanitary accommodation for the patients at night is an outside closet which in practice is not used. There is only one bath for these 58 patients. Formerly white but it is now a blackish green colour. I was informed by the R.M.S. that it takes approximately 15 minutes to fill and 10 minutes to empty. The result is that patients cannot be bathed in clean water and three or four patients are bathed in the one lot of water. The bathroom is located at the end of a corridor and is a particularly cold and draughty place. There are four doors to the room and two windows. One door leads to the yard and is badly fitted. The floor is tiled.

"In the day-room there are only 17 square feet per patient. Heat is provided by an old stove. The outlook is most depressing . The windows on one side overlook a triangular yard. The centre of this yard contains dirt and rubble and is occupied by a number of hens - I understand these are the property of the Matron. The windows on the other side also look on to a yard. This yard which is in the centre of the building, is the only place provided for the exercise of the patients. An occasional walk to the farmyard in the Summer provides the patients with their glimpse of the outside world".

The Inspector sent an explanatory memorandum to the Principal Officer in the section of the Department dealing with mental health and mental handicap.[8] In his paragraph on the overcrowding he writes that in one large dormitory in "the Union Building, a number of patients sleep on the floor". He left the Department - and us - in no doubt as to what 17 square feet per patient meant:

"It is generally accepted that 40 to 50 square feet per person is necessary for day room accommodation. In Clonmel the space available is often less than 20 square feet - in one instance the space is 17 square feet per patient. The inadequacy of this accommodation can be appreciated when it is remembered that 17 square feet is little more than the size of an ordinary office table. On the basis of 17 square feet between 58 patients, the Minister's room which most of us have seen at some time, would accommodate 27 patients. It should be remembered that in wet or cold weather the patients may spend all their time out of bed in this accommodation."

But it is when Dr. Ramsay attempts to convey the full horror of the kitchen arrangements in Clonmel that his report begins to read like some grotesque Swiftian satire:

"In the kitchen, cabbage is taken out of the boiler by means of an ordinary farm-yard fork. It is then placed in a large iron colander which resembles a night watchman's brazier or a weedburner. The cabbage is then chopped up with a garden edging tool. The potatoes for patients are mashed and distributed in ordinary zinc buckets. I saw a meal being served in the female admission and infirmary unit. By the time the potatoes arrived there, they were practically cold and had turned slightly black. They were placed on cold chipped enamel plates and left on the tables before the patients were brought in to dine, so that they were almost certainly stone cold before the patients touched them. Owing to lack of cooking facilities vegetables were only served twice a week".

In Clonmel Mental Hospital, degradation, discomfort and boredom whiled away each day, but bed time was early. The patients were put to bed at 6.30 in the evening. Lights were put out in many places and even where they were left on they were, generally speaking, inadequate to permit the patients to read in bed.

"In the Union Building", we read, "....patients undress in the day-room downstairs. They then make their way up a stone staircase to the dormitories on the first and second floors. They have no clothing on them except their day shirts and in several cases they are naked".

An Equality of Contempt

There was a rough equality of contempt in the way staff - including the temporary Assistant Medical Doctors - were treated. For example, one of the temporary doctors occupied a bed-sitting cum dining room. This room was situated at the end of a corridor in a part of the main building occupied by patients. The patients, when passing, frequently kicked the door. There were no curtains on the windows and the furniture consisted of a few dilapidated pieces which were torn and dirty. The only washing facilities provided were a jug and basin. The toilet was located down a dark and dismal corridor and there was no bath. The contempt with which nursing staff was treated in Clonmel, and presumably in the majority of mental hospitals at this time, helps to explain the depth to which industrial relations, as well as discipline, sank in the decades which followed.

"The provision for nursing staff", Dr. Ramsay wrote, "is equally bad e.g. in the Male Nurses' dining room near the Union building there is no provision for keeping potatoes hot. They are brought at the same time as the patients' meal and as the patients are fed before the staff dine, an hour or more may elapse between the time the potatoes arrive and the time they are eaten. ......In many cases the nursing staff draw their rations and do all cooking on the divisions".

It is no wonder that Doctor Ramsay was of the opinion that the nursing staff had almost reached "the explosion stage." He describes arrangements in the female observation ward:

"There is a single lavatory without any window or other opening to the exterior of the building. The only place where the nurse can keep her cooking utensils is in this lavatory. She cooks at night on a dilapidated smoky heating stove in a corner of the ward".

Reactions

In 1959 and in the 1950s generally the country was not well off. But they were not famine times. Standards were rising. Rural electrification was completed at the beginning of the decade and by the early sixties most towns seemed to be looking for a swimming pool. All over the country people were building themselves comfortable houses some of which scandalised Dublin-based journalists. The poverty of our country is no justification. There can be no justification - only partial explanations. What strikes one today on reading these reports and memoranda on this hospital is the anger with which they were written. Not only was the Assistant Inspector of Mental hospitals angry but so were the higher civil servants who read the report. The conditions in Clonmel were no more acceptable in 1959 than they would be now.

In all likelihood the report was precipitated by Dr. Egan, the R.M.S. who had recently come from England. In fact when he began to make demands on the Mental Hospital Board, he was accused of bringing over "English" standards to Clonmel. The members of the board seemed to be totally ignorant of the true conditions in the hospital for which they were responsible. Dr. Egan resorted to a technique used by the victorious allies after the second world war, when they found it difficult to convince the neighbouring townsmen that anything untoward had happened in the Concentration Camps which had been located near their towns for years, - he took some of the Board on a conducted tour of the hospital

Dr. Ramsay's report of his inspection of Clonmel District Hospital of the 8th. November 1958 was considered so important by the Department of Health that a Conference regarding his inspection was arranged for December 29th. at the Department at 11.30 a.m[9]. It was attended by two senior civil servants from the section dealing with the mental services, two senior civil servants from the section dealing with the capital allocations, the Inspector of Mental Hospitals, Dr. Dolphin, and the Assistant Inspector of Mental Hospitals, Dr. Ramsay. Representing the Clonmel Mental Hospital Authority were the County Manager, Mr. J.P. Flynn, the Resident Medical Superindent, Dr. Egan, and the chief clerk, Mr. Murphy.

Departmental Prevarication

This was a high-powered meeting. All present had been fully briefed on the conditions. Mr. Brady, Assistant Secretary at the Department, opened the discussion. Referring to the appalling conditions which Dr. Ramsay had revealed in his report, Mr. Brady said that unfortunately Clonmel was not the only District Mental hospital where conditions were abysmal for patients. Mr. Jack Darby in his memorandum prepared for the information of the Assistant Secretary, had used terms like "abysmally low standards". Mr Darby had written:

"We are keeping patients at a low level of animal existence

and actively destroying any little bit of individuality, confidence or self-respect they may have left." But the meeting could hardly have got properly underway when Mr. Brady as Assistant Secretary was establishing the boundaries. He referred to the financial position, "which although it had improved somewhat in recent months was still pretty acute". He added that "while the Minister could not afford to be generous in regard to financial matters, the Board could be assured of his sympathy and his understanding in relation to any additional expenditure which might be necessitated in bringing conditions in the hospital up to a reasonable standard".

One suspects that the meeting was being told not to expect much. When Mr. Brady told the meeting that "it was the Secretary's desire that steps should be taken to make it known to the staff in the Mental Hospital that drastic improvements are contemplated, not alone in relation to their own living conditions but also concerning their relations with the patients", Dr. Egan certainly did not agree. To talk to the nurses about "relations with patients" in the kind of conditions which had to be endured in Clonmel would be not only stupid but downright dangerous. The nurses were at the end of their tether. Obviously the Secretary had no conception of the pitch of unrest which the staff at Clonmel had reached. Dr. Egan was certainly not going to go back to tell his exasperated staff about "contemplated" improvements in conditions. They needed more than promises. But it seemed that Mr. Brady intended that the meeting would make "concrete" proposals, but their implementation would take time. These planned improvements would take a couple of years to complete. For the present a plan of campaign should be drawn up. Luckily for everyone, but particularly for Mr. Brady, the staff in Clonmel did not hear his comments on the deficiencies in the service given to patients at Clonmel Mental Hospital:

"...that the question of physical improvements was only one aspect of the change which it was desired should be implemented in the hospital - a proper attitude and approach to the job on the part of all the staff was very important".

This was not the first time that the attitudes of nurses in the mental hospitals were invoked as being in some way responsible for scandalous conditions. In every sense of the word it was a cheap option. Mr. J. Darby the Principal Officer had emphasised in the briefing document which he had prepared for the Assistant Secretary, that finance was "the crux of the problem". It was a fact that was very well known to everyone who worked in the hospital. Mr. Darby had accompanied Dr. Ramsay on his inspection and although accustomed to very bad conditions in several other mental hospitals he was "thoroughly shocked". Mr. Darby, Dr. Dolphin, the Inspector of Mental Hospitals, and Dr. Ramsay, the Assistant Inspector of Mental Hospitals, all felt that despite the often expressed desire of the Minister for economy "in the present instance increased expenditure is absolutely essential".

The 'Cover-up'

The Conference went on to discuss the Inspector's report in detail. By far the most important decision taken at that meeting held on that winter's day at the very end of 1958 was the decision not to tell anyone of what the Inspector had found in the hospital at Clonmel. Outside of that group of nine men who attended the meeting, - and the Minister and the Secretary - no-one was told. Most significantly, Mr. Darby recommended that even the members of the mental hospital authority were not to get a copy of Dr. Ramsay's report - the very authority which was meant to take action. Mr. Darby wrote:

"If the deficiencies in the hospital were not so great we would send the mental hospital authority a copy..... If we issue the report in the present case it will probably become public, which is very undesirable".

The County Manager, Mr. J.P. Flynn, turned this amazing decision to good advantage for the finances of his County and the rates. "It could be accepted", he said, "that he would lend his wholehearted support". His problem would be to get as much money as possible out of the Joint Board. But how could he do this if the Board could not be told ? The County Manager, as he said himself, was: "on the one hand, restricted in the amount of work that could be carried out by the amount of money which his Board made available to him". On the other hand he was restricted in going to the Board and putting the full facts before them because if he were to do so and quote from Dr. Ramsay's report, "great distress would be caused to relatives of patients who were in the hospital".

On these spurious grounds the whole affair was kept secret. At the conference every one was in agreement on three points: Firstly, conditions in Clonmel and in many other hospitals were a disgrace; secondly, it would be impossible to do much about them unless the Board made more money available; thirdly, the members of the Board must not be told. If the Board were to get a copy of the Inspector's report the whole situation would become public. On no account must the public know about these conditions ostensibly because of the distress which might be caused to relatives of patients in the hospital.

Motives are always mixed but the real motive, I suspect, for not passing on the report to the Clonmel Board was the likely reaction of the public, not only in Clonmel, but all over the country. Already the few members of the Board, who had taken Dr. Egan's tour, and consequently knew something of the situation in the hospital wanted the whole of the capital sums available through the Hospitals' Trust Fund to be spent on the Mental Hospitals, for the next several years. This was not a reaction that the Department wanted to encourage and neither did the Minister. Whilst expressing his sympathy through the Secretary and the Assistant Secretary he had no wish to be too generous financially. We can deduce that neither the Department nor the Minister nor, indeed, the Government wanted to be bounced into spending large amounts of money on the mental hospitals by revelations of the truth.

There were many more mental hospitals in the country where conditions were similar. It is Clonmel's misfortune today that the Inspector's report of their particular hospital has survived. The publication of the Reports of the Inspector of Mental Hospitals had ceased in 1962 but the individual reports for each hospital had been dropped some years before. The last report written in any detail was for 1956. What was happening in the mental hospitals was not known to the vast majority of the people including the members of the mental hospital boards.

Futile Measures

But the Department of Health and the small band of officials who knew about Clonmel did try to do something. It is reasonable to assume that Dr. Ramsay's report had influenced to some degree the Minister's decision about the Mental Hospitals in the following year. The Minister, Mr. MacEntee, and others in the Department clearly felt that something would have to be done. But the troubled consciences of a few were not sufficient to repair the foul outrage of life in the mental hospitals. At a meeting held in Mr. Brady's office on the 22nd October, 1959[10], almost an exact year since the long Christmas meeting about Clonmel, Mr. Brady, who was Assistant Secretary in the Department of Health, was almost excited.

"Mr. Brady said that from the point of view of the mental patient the position was better now than ever it was inasmuch as we had the express sanction to go out and press local authorities to implement improvements and it was up to us to make the most of this opportunity".

He thought that "The effect of recent decisions was to give approval for the implementation of improvements in mental hospitals on a fairly extensive scale".

Mr. Brady's approach to the problem of the mental hospitals was very different to what it was at the Clonmel meeting. A conference for all the Resident Medical Superintendents in the state had been held in the previous February and it seems that the Minister at that conference had exhorted each of the assembled heads of all the mental hospitals to remedy the deficiencies in his hospital.

"The Minister was well aware that the exhortations to the Resident Medical Superintendents would have the effect of increased expenditure on mental hospitals and this excuse by the local people should no longer be accepted as a justification for sub-standard conditions".

No wonder Mr. Brady was confident. The Minister was fully behind the little group of officials and the Inspector, Dr. Dolphin and Dr.Ramsay in the Mental Hospitals Section of the Department of Health. Why was so little accomplished in the following years with backing such as this? In an address to people in the service in 1962[11] the Minister, who was still Mr. MacEntee was still exhorting:

"We must all, ministers and their staffs, and mental hospital authorities and theirs, together with the community as a whole, carry a share of responsibility for the conditions to which I have referred. If I have laid heavy emphasis on existing defects, I have done so only in order to bring home to us all the magnitude of the task which is before us and to impress ourselves with the urgency of the need to attack it".

In spite of the Minister's efforts the situation did not improve in the 1960s despite an undoubted period of prosperity throughout the decade. Sadly in 1966 the Minister's successor, Mr. Donagh O'Malley, in a speech in Grangegorman was to be heard describing how badly neglected the mental hospitals were. He was asked in the Dáil how he proposed to remedy the legacy of neglect. It was a taunt which could have been directed towards every Minister and every Government since Mr. MacEntee.

Mr. Donagh O'Malley did not remedy the legacy no more than succeeding Ministers did. The situation was not remedied. It simply was not mentioned. Mr. Donagh O'Malley moved to the Department of Education soon afterwards and introduced free secondary education for everyone. Life for the long-stay patients in the back wards of our mental hospitals continued as before. Hardly a word was heard about them. They died in those same conditions at the rate of approximately 1500 a year.

No Improvement

Twenty years later in 1978 when the population in our mental hospitals had dropped from 20,000 or thereabouts to 14,000 approximately, up to two hundred people lived in six huts in St. Ita's Portrane. Conditions there approached those of Clonmel in 1958. The visiting committee which had been established by relatives of the mentally handicapped at St. Ita's wrote in their first report[12] as follows:

"Units 9A, 9B, 8A, 8B, 11 and 11A are what is known as temporary structures, that is they were built in approximately 1890 as huts for the workmen who were building the hospital.

They are wooden, barn-like and they would constitute a grave fire-hazard. We visited two of these and were assured by the staff that they were typical of the others.

"In 9A there are 35 male patients, most of whom are mentally handicapped. They sleep in a long bare dormitory. The beds are old, mattresses sagging and the bedclothes did not look clean. Next to the dormitory there is a day room, bare of furniture except for forms arranged along the walls. The floors were very dirty, particularly near the walls where we noticed that the floor boards were rotting. This room measured approximately 40' x 20'. The roof is not sound. We were told that it leaks. The dining hall was a similar room. Rat holes were clearly in evidence and in fact the charge nurse had just got rid of rats. He expects them back. Several birds were gathered in a corner of the room. They were quite tame. The staff found them unhygienic, particularly at mealtimes when they hop onto the plates of the patients. The stench of ancient urine-soaked floors was palpable. Next to the dining hall were the toilets. We noticed no bath. There were four toilets and a urinal. The urinal regularly overflows and floods onto the floor."

In another part of the hospital which was not a temporary structure the Committee reported:

" We visited 7 East where 29 disturbed adolescents and young adults are accommodated. About 25 of these are grossly disturbed. There was a strong smell of urine and disinfectant. There was at least one hole in the ceiling and it was peeling in several places. The rooms were bare and overcrowded at the same time. The bedclothes were dirty. .....When parents and others visit their handicapped relatives here, nurses have been known to put their own jackets on the handicapped out of pity for the feelings of the visitors...... We noticed a plastic trolley full of an extraordinary assortment of unusable old shoes. .....17 of the mentally handicapped here are incontinent both daily and nightly..... Usually there are five nurses on duty, often four".

An Independent View

In the absence of reports by the Inspector of Mental Hospitals on the conditions of the long-stay patients for the whole period from1960 up to 1989, it is fortunate that sections of the media began to take an interest. In 1980 Magill magazine published a wide-ranging account of conditions in the mental hospitals generally. Their reporter Helen Connolly had spent several months visiting the various institutions accompanied by a photographer. In the course of her research for the article Helen Connolly found that mental hospitals were in a disgraceful condition. Our Lady's in Cork, St. Brigid's in Ballinasloe, St. Mary's in Castlebar and St. Loman's in Mullingar were all in an appalling state of dilapidation. In April 1980, a ceiling collapsed on a sleeping patient in St. Brendan's, Grangegorman in the heart of Dublin. Slates and bricks regularly fell off the roofs at Grangegorman. This should have surprised no-one. For many years little or no effort had been made to maintain them.

But what she found even worse was the state of the patients. "A pervading stench of urine, excrement and sweat confronts the visitor," she wrote. Patients suffered from pressure sores and urine rashes which went undetected for long periods. Almost all the patients were appallingly dressed. Dresses and suits were often worn for years on end. According to one nurse in Cork "Conditions there were barely above lice level and difficult to maintain at that". Patients slept in beds which were broken, covered by torn dirty sheets and bedspreads. Mounds of soiled linen accumulated in the washrooms which added to the general stench. The provision of adequate amounts of hot water was "a problem in many hospitals".

Worst of all, according to Helen Connolly, was the dreary boredom of life in these hospitals. "Eating is the sole diversion of many psychiatric patients" she wrote. Patients could be seen in all hospitals wandering aimlessly about, sitting in day-rooms and staring into space. Many of the hospitals were overcrowded. According to one of the nurses in St. Loman's, patients often wandered around the hospital at night looking for a bed.

In the twenty years since the Department of Health had held its special meeting to discuss Dr. Ramsay's report on Clonmel, little had changed. The hopeful meeting held just a year later had little result. The kind of impetus which a situation in Clonmel and other mental hospitals like it required, if it is to result in action is not produced at Departmental meetings or by Ministerial speeches. People would have to have seen Clonmel or places like it, or at least be able to read about it, if that impetus was to last.

The Malaise of Apathy

The obstacles to reforming the hospitals were immense. Most of them were referred to in the report of the meeting on Improvements in Mental Hospitals held in Mr. Brady's office in October, 1959[13].

The attitudes of Resident Medical Superintendents featured prominently in the report. They had been urged, for example, by the Minister at their conference to draw up plans and proposals which could in their opinion bring about improvements in their hospitals. By the date of the meeting six hospitals had not bothered to reply. Dr. Dolphin feared that the Superintendents generally hadn't taken advantage of the Minister's offer.

"He said that such of the replies as had been received were in the main in very general terms and were also rather woolly. He gave several instances of what he meant. He said that the general impression he had was that the Resident Medical Superintendents' reports tended to be in the nature of apologias for the shortcomings in the hospitals and were very largely defensive in tone. Summing up, he said there was virtually no acceptance on the part of the Superintendents of the Minister's offer".

This is an amazing revelation. The very people who were most directly charged with the welfare of the patients simply refused to co-operate with the efforts of the executive function of the state. Was this because, as Dr. Dolphin thought, that "many of the Resident Medical Superintendents were much too economy conscious"? What did Dr.Dolphin mean? Is it possible that in 1959 the Resident Medical Superintendents thought that money spent on their helpless patients was money wasted? In a memorandum[14] written by Mr J.Darby on 18th. November, soon after Dr. Ramsay had submitted his report on Clonmel District Mental Hospital to the Assistant Secretary, he made an interesting observation regarding the County Manager's embarrassment regarding the conditions in the hospital:

"..... the Manager is very keen to improve the hospital - he feels that he is to a certain extent culpable in having tolerated such conditions, but he told us that the previous R.M.S. made no complaints and assured him that mental patients are neither happy nor unhappy, they are withdrawn and oblivious of their surroundings leading little more than a vegetable existence".

It is a relief to read Mr. Darby's comment on the doctor's opinion of his patients:

" This, I understand, is nonsense as far as the vast majority of patients are concerned, or would be nonsense if they had not been reduced to a vegetable existence by the environment in which they are forced to live".

The implications of attitude of Resident Medical Superintendents were alarming. How would they feel about heating, for instance? Would some of the patients be in danger of hypothermia? Could such an R.M.S. be relied on to alert the County Manager if more money needed to be spent on the patients? Putting the patients to bed at 6 or 7 p.m. might not be enough. It was going to be difficult to convince some Superintendents that "the most important consideration for them was that the care and treatment of the patients entrusted to them should be up to a reasonable civilised standard". The R.M. S. had the primary responsibility for the care and treatment of the patients. These Superintendents were the key people. They must be worked on if anything was to change. The man who must do this was the Inspector of Mental Hospitals. "The pressure must be kept up and in this regard the Inspectors are our main link" (Mr.Brady).

Managers too were somewhat of a problem. According to Dr. Dolphin[15] they were too ready to accept things as they were in the mental hospitals. It was his impression that they simply didn't want to see what could be done to bring the standards in mental hospitals up to a reasonably civilised level. I think Dr. Dolphin was expecting rather too much of the Managers. People whose job it was to spread their resources over a wide range of demands, and when these resources were in part provided by the rates, were unlikely to "come to the R.M.S. looking for ways of spending money".

It was necessary to start with the Resident Medical Superintendents. They were not even looking for their minimum needs in staff and amenities. If they did not bother even to list the improvements they thought necessary, there was little the Department or the Minister could do to remedy the situation.

"It was agreed that the R.M.S.s in many cases had thrown in the towel before the fight had started. Both Dr.Dolphin and Dr. Ramsay said that that they had great hopes about the younger of the R.M.S.s but felt that it would be a waste of time trying to do anything with some of the older men who were due to retire in a few years anyway".

A Shameful Scenario

If the laying down of minimum standards and their enforcement had been successful there would have been great changes in the mental hospitals. It was a subject dear to Dr. Dolphin's heart. The enforcement of the standards would have required very strong support for the Inspector of Mental Hospitals and the office of Inspector.

"Matters to be investigated under this head would include cleanliness and hygienic conditions in relation to the preparation and service of food; adequate bathing, washing and sanitary facilities; suitable heating arrangements; suitable bedding; adequate and comfortable seats in day-rooms; adequate supply of books and newspapers, together with facilities for occupation, recreation, exercise and general cleanliness. In this connection the Inspectors should, as it were, put the R.M.S. in the dock and question him as to what steps he had taken to remedy any or all deficiencies in his hospital".

As it turned out no-one was put in the dock for what happened to the patients in the mental hospitals. The Department continued to worry about the mental hospitals in 1960 and in subsequent years and within the constraints of secrecy, they worked on them. Resident Medical Superintendents were called to conferences and invited to put forward plans. Some of them submitted some very interesting suggestions and one has sympathy for these men who were battling for very basic improvements. But the pace of change is bound up with public attitudes. Rather than increase the power of the Inspector's office it was greatly diminished. Resources were moved from the reform of the mental hospitals. The mental hospital section in the Department of Health threw in the towel. Significantly, it was at this time in 1959, that all the hospitals were renamed with saints' names.

The solution to the question which so exercised the minds of the Minister of Health and the Departmental Officials in the late fifties and the early sixties was eventually provided by quiet and merciful deaths in countless wards throughout the country. It took a long time. Whatever way we look at it, it was a shameful way to solve a problem and to plead poverty simply doesn't stand up as an excuse. We don't help matters now, by indulging in a collective act of amnesia.

The information, particularly at local level, which would have fuelled a change of attitudes in 1959 was denied. At the meeting on Clonmel great importance was attached to the concealment of the truth lest it would distress the relatives of the patients. The same excuse would have applied to other hospitals in other towns. But things could have been changed quietly. The leaders of Church and State in each town could have been mobilised if the will had been there. Who were the authorities afraid of offending? Or was it that they shared the opinion of the old R.M.S - the patients were really vegetables, not human, not worth spending money on. It is a sad and shameful story.

In the Health (Mental Services) Bill 1980, there was no provision for "specific standards of care" and as for the Inspector of Mental Hospitals, he was to go altogether. The temptation to close the door on the long-stay patients in the mental hospitals and to tiptoe into the future, had at last become too much for the Departmental officials and their political masters.

Up to a quarter of long-stay patients were mentally handicapped. It is arguable that many mentally handicapped people, perhaps even the majority, would not have been in the mental hospitals at all if it had not been for the ill-advised approach taken by the Department and particular Ministers to the establishment and the expansion of the services for the mentally handicapped. Both policies - the policy of silent concealment of the mental hospitals modulated by minor improvements, and the policy of total delegation of responsibility for the mentally handicapped to certain voluntary agencies, had their origin in the culture of the 1950s. The wonder is, the dogged persistence with which these policies have been followed ever since.

Notes on Chapter Three

1. See Appendix.
2. Report of the Inspector of Mental Hospitals 1956.
3. Report of the Inspector of Mental Hospitals 1957.
4. Letter dated 2nd. December, 1947 to Dr. Kearney (Inspector) requesting directions on the accommodation of children under the age of sixteen years in mental hospitals. The Inspector replied (letter dated 28th. January, 1948) "Mental Hospitals are not suitable places for mental defectives". National Archives L50/2.
5. Letter to the Inspector of Mental Hospitals signed by the acting R.M.S. Waterford, and dated 8th. February, 1949. National Archives L50/2.
6. Reconstruction and Improvement of County Homes. Department of Taoiseach files. National Archives Dublin. s14472A/
7. Report on Clonmel District Hospital 1958. Department of Health files. National Archives, Dublin. L5/134.
8. Letter from Dr. Ramsay to Mr. Darby. Department of Health files. National Archives, Dublin. L5/134.
9. Conference regarding Clonmel District Mental Hospital. Department of Health files. National Archives, Dublin. L5/134.
10. Report: Improvements in District Mental Hospitals, 22nd. October, 1959. Department of Health files. National Archives L107/18.
11. Report of Conference 1961. Department of Health files. National Archives L2/147.
12. Unpublished Report. St. Joseph's Association for the Mentally Handicapped. Portrane. (Visiting Committee).
13. Report of Conference 22nd. October, 1959. Department of Health files. National Archives L107/18, Dublin.
14. Memo addressed to the Assistant Secretary. Department of Health files. National Archives L5/134.
15. Improvements in District Mental Hospitals (meeting 22nd. October, 1959. Department of Health files. National Archives L107/18.

4

SEEKING SOFT OPTIONS

Mentally handicapped people had made up part of the intake of mental hospitals from their inception. Some would have come to the mental hospital when their parents grew too old to look after them, some would have come far earlier if their parents had died or if they never had parents. Non-marital children, if mentally handicapped, were at serious risk. Handicapped children were not put up for adoption. But by the late forties the presence of children in mental hospitals was no longer acceptable whatever about adult mentally handicapped. A special unit for children was built in Portrane in the mid fifties.

Where To Place 'Mental Defectives'?
Back in the 1940s Dr. Kearney had noticed a little boy in Killarney and recommended that a place be found for him in a special institution for the mentally handicapped. In 1946, the R.M.S. at Limerick Mental Hospital wrote to the Minister for Health about a little boy called Gerard, aged seven[1]. Gerard was "mute and had been sent back to the City Home in Limerick from St. Vincent's, Cabra, because of his mischievous behaviour". He was committed to the Mental Hospital immediately by the Home as "he was violent and bites and spits when restrained and attempted to get through the windows". Strange to say the staff at the mental hospital did not find him difficult. The R.M.S. wrote:

"While resident here he has been quite harmless and amenable and easily managed. I have tried to have him admitted to the Stuart Institute and also to St. Augustine's Colony Blackrock, but both were unable to receive him. I will be glad to receive any suggestion from the Minister as to any Institution to which this young boy may be transferred".

The R.M.S. was advised to try Lota in Cork, which was run by the Brothers of Charity. Other letters arrived at the Department from Resident Medical Superintendents during the 1950s sometimes addressed to the Minister, sometimes to the Inspector. "I would be obliged if you could let me have any information as to when an Institution for dealing with this type of case is likely to be opened"[2]. The Inspector replied that the Department was considering it and added that "mental hospitals were not suitable places for mental defectives"[3].

Some mental hospital boards were becoming more specific in their demands, none more so than Mullingar who had 5 or 6 "mental defectives" in their hospital under the age of sixteen[4]. There were already some privately run institutions which catered for mentally handicapped children for whom health authorities paid capitation fees if their parents were unable to afford them. It was becoming increasingly difficult, however, to find places at these institutions. The demand far exceeded supply. In 1957, the board began to talk of legislation to deal with the numbers of mentally handicapped children for whom no places could be found except in the mental hospital. They knew that legislation had been recently enacted in Britain. A resolution was passed by the Board requesting legislation to deal with the care and treatment of mentally defective children and was duly submitted to the Department. It read as follows:

Care and Treatment of mentally defective children:

"On the proposal of Mr. James Finn, seconded by Mr. Thomas Kilbride, the Joint Board resolved to request the Government to introduce legislation to deal with the care and treatment of mentally defective children and to provide suitable institutions in which they could be maintained and provided with accessible training. That as a matter of urgency and in order to provide immediate additional accommodation that the question should be examined of converting to this purpose some of the hospitals at present allocated to the treatment of tuberculosis and which may not now be required due to alterations in the method of treatment".

The 'Mental Deficiency Bill' That Never Was

By this time also, other Boards were thinking along the same lines. They were not to know it, but ten years before, in 1947, the Government had already prepared legislation, when Fianna Fail had been in power[5]. It was in 1947 that the Department of Health had been established, staffed by a forward-looking group of able young men under the leadership of a most talented and forward thinking Minister, Dr. Jim Ryan. It is not surprising that the Department turned its attention to the question of mental handicap as they had already done with plans for a greatly expanded public health scheme.

So: "Following consideration of a memorandum dated 13th. August 1947, submitted by the Minister for Health, together with the general scheme of the proposed Mental Deficiency Bill, authority was granted to have a bill drafted on the lines of the general scheme".

This was signed by the Secretaries of Health, Finance, Justice, and Education. But the Fianna Fáil Government fell in 1948 and the first Inter Party Government came to power. In 1951 that first Inter Party Government foundered on a health related issue, when Dr. Noel Browne's Mother and Child Scheme caused such reverberations in Church State relations that no politician could ever forget them. However in 1953, when Fianna Fáil returned to power, the Department of Health set to again. The Cabinet minutes tell us that[6]

"Following consideration of a memorandum dated the 4th. December 1953, submitted by the Minister for Health with the general scheme of a bill to provide for the care, supervision, and training of mentally defective persons, the Minister was authorised to have a bill drafted on the lines of the general scheme accompanying the memorandum".

Between 1953 and 1957 the idea of specific legislation was abandoned. It is possible to pinpoint almost to the day when that decision was taken. In November 1955 the Department of Health drafted a letter[7] to the Secretary of Westmeath County Council in which it is clearly stated "that legislation to deal with the care, training and supervision of such children is being prepared as a matter of urgency". The letter was never sent. Instead, a new letter was drafted which made no mention of legislation whatever. It is reasonable to pinpoint the date of the change in policy regarding legislation within the Department to that month and that year viz. November 1955. The Minister in 1955 was Mr. T.F. O'Higgins.

"Constitutional" Paralysis

In her book *"Health, Medicine and Politics"*, Dr. Ruth Barrington describes a certain shift towards what might be described as orthodox Catholic sociology, during the years immediately after the passing of the 1953 Health Act. In spite of the previous Minister's best efforts to safeguard his Act, he was beaten by the General Election in that year. Mr. T. F. O'Higgins did in fact succeed in modifying the 1953 Act and if he was able to do that with an Act he would have had no difficulty with legislation which was only at the draft stage. It should not surprise us that "constitutional obstacles" were identified. The Attorney General, Mr. Cecil Lavery, some years before, when the first coalition was in power, similarly identified constitutional obstacles in regard to school medical inspections, where a previous Attorney General had observed no such difficulties

The request for special legislation surfaced in the Dáil on the 28th May 1957[8], in a question asked by Deputy Griffin. Mr. Griffin asked the Minister for Health, Mr. Sean McEntee, "if in view of the absence of legislation for the treatment and training of mentally handicapped children and of the inadequate facilities available.... he will introduce legislation to deal with this matter....". But the moment for legislation had passed and the Minister's answer made that clear. He understood "that there are formidable constitutional difficulties in the way of the enactment of effective legislation". What these difficulties might have been was not mentioned and nobody asked. Whatever these "constitutional difficulties" were, they were enough to frighten off the Department and successive ministers for ever more. No special legislation for the establishment and regulation of services for the mentally handicapped was ever enacted in this state.

It is however somewhat surprising to find that Mr. McEntee, when he became Minister, made no effort to revisit the decision on legislation which had been agreed in Cabinet in 1953. But Mr. MacEntee was not Dr. Ryan. In the years since 1947 the alternative policy had been well established. Considerable investment had taken place. The old radical Fianna Fáil was running out of steam. The party which had decided to introduce legislation for the mentally handicapped in 1947 and again in 1953, felt that they had gone as far as they could, especially as the expense entailed in the expansion of the general health services was beginning to be a real problem. In 1957, it is probable that Mr. MacEntee was quite glad of some constitutional obstacles.

The "Religious" Solution

Meanwhile the demand for places for mentally handicapped persons went on increasing relentlessly, until it became almost overwhelming. The Department of Health was forced to look around for solutions. Already in the 1950s there were some privately-run residential institutions which looked after people with a mental handicap. The oldest of these was Stewarts Hospital which dated back to the last century. The rest were run by a few religious orders. There were many religious orders in Ireland in the 1950s and it was tempting to look on them as a handy resource for solving social problems. There was no scarcity of vocations. All over the country there were convents and religious houses full of young idealistic and talented young men and women. But this did not mean that there were all that many religious free to devote themselves to the care and training of the mentally handicapped. From the beginning of the state, the main focus of the Church had been on education. Accordingly there were many religious orders whose primary occupation was teaching. As the century went on, more and more religious devoted themselves to education, not merely to education of the rich but even more devotedly to education of the poor. Irish Orders expanded and others came in from abroad to fulfil their mission here.

When the Department looked around for ways to expand the mental handicap services it was the scarcity of religious orders, willing to expand into this field, which was their main problem. There were only two orders for men - the Hospitaller Order of St. John of God and the Brothers of Charity - interested in this work. The number of Congregations for women religious engaged in the field was not nearly enough either. At a meeting[9] held in

November 1953, three possible "methods...for providing accommodation for mental defectives" are ranked in the following order:
1. by institutions run wholly by religious orders,
2. by Institutions controlled by religious orders with a lay staff,
3. by Institutions operated by local authorities.

The meeting held on the 12th. November 1953 was the last of a series of meetings held with the representatives of the Religious Orders who were already engaged in the work of looking after the mentally handicapped. In July 1953 the Minister had sanctioned the expansion of the programme for the provision of accommodation for the mentally handicapped by at least 1,000 beds[10]. The November meeting had set out the options. There is no doubt that the preferred option was to create the extra 1000 places in institutions wholly run by religious orders. As well as sanctioning the expansion, the Minister agreed that if necessary, "new voluntary agencies be induced to enter this field". There would be no question of involving the local authorities.

A Carte Blanche

It should not surprise us that this was the option taken. It may have been that in the absence of legislation it was their only one. Certainly the third one namely, institutions operated by local authorities, would very likely require legislation. It would be unthinkable that a service which would require considerable funding from whatever source could be established without legislation. An even more important consideration was the vulnerable nature of the mentally handicapped. Only people such as the religious could be trusted to carry out this task without legislation of any kind. The decision at that meeting was that Dr. Dolphin the Inspector of Mental Hospitals "should get in touch with the La Sagesse Order and the Augustinian Nuns at Rathoath concerning females and with Brother Stanislaus of the Brothers of St. John of God concerning males "with a view to expanding whatever service was already provided". This would have been an excellent idea if this expanded service was to form part of a fully comprehensive service designed to work in tandem with the statutory bodies, but this is not what happened. It was at this point that virtually the entire service for the mentally handicapped was ceded to a few religious orders. As for the terms and conditions of the service, these were settled between them - in private. As far as the state was concerned it was a distinctly hands-off approach with the minimum of state involvement except that of funding. It was no substitute for the legislation that never was.

The arguments for specific legislation which the Department of Health officials presented in the memorandum prepared for the 1953 Cabinet meeting were compelling. They had succeeded in convincing the Department of Finance to accept their proposals. The arguments on grounds of equity alone were irrefutable. If the mentally handicapped were to be treated equally with others who were entitled to specific health services, legislation was necessary. By abandoning the policy of specific legislation for the regulation and funding of services for the mentally handicapped the State abandoned any possibility of equity for this section of its citizens. One of the arguments put forward by the Department in its Memorandum for the Government proposing the Mental Deficiency Bill in 1953, was that the legislation was "designed....to enable the best possible use to be made of the institutional accommodation which can be made available". Without legislation, no matter how much money the Department of Health was able to extract from the Exchequer, this was not possible. The Minister's decision to hand over the whole service to a very few voluntary bodies put the Department in a very bad bargaining position. The Department wanted the Religious far more than the Religious wanted them.

Acceptance a La Carte

Even in these early years, the Departmental officials were not totally starry-eyed about their relationship with voluntary bodies. The voluntary bodies which the Government proposed to use were totally autonomous and not necessarily interested in obliging the Department of Health. In 1957 there was an example of one of the snags which can arise when delegating a state-funded service informally. The Department became worried about the under-use of the facilities at Lota in Cork and at Clarenbridge in Galway, both residential institutions which were run by the Brothers of Charity and endowed by the Department. The average occupancy of the facilities was low. There were 280 places available in Lota of which only 192 were occupied. In Clarenbridge 100 places were available but only 69 people were admitted. This must have been galling for a Department which was inundated by letters from mental hospital boards and resident medical superintendents, not to mention the Parliamentary Questions in the Dáil. The problem became the subject of a very interesting exchange within the Department[11].

On the 14th. November 1957, the Assistant Inspector for Mental Hospitals had the Provincial of the Brothers of Charity into the office to discuss the matter. In the course of the discussion it turned out that the Provincial had great difficulty in accepting the kind of mentally handicapped people that the authorities expected him to take into his service. He needed time to make his decisions. One difficulty the Provincial described in more detail:

"One of the greatest difficulties has been that the people requesting places for children have returned completely unscrupulous information on their forms. This has necessitated extreme delay in filling the vacancies as one of the Brothers now has to travel and see every case in its own home before they will agree to receive it in hospital as they can not depend on the accuracy of the information furnished in the forms returned to them".

This certainly would delay things but it was an explanation which must have exasperated Dr. Ramsay, the same Inspector who was to make such a devastating report on the Clonmel Mental Hospital at the end of the following year. He writes at the end of this account of his interview with the Provincial:

"I can not see what action we can take as the whole matter of dealing with the mentally handicapped in this country is completely unorganised and uncoordinated".

The note is initialled and dated 15th. November 1957. It attracted some attention in the Department. The Assistant Inspector was asked to see "if there was any possibility of establishing some measure of co-ordination......by the establishment of some body similar to the Bed Bureau for Dublin Hospitals". Significantly the Memo went on:

"I know that it is not possible to compel any of the institutions for M.D.s (mental defectives) to take any patient but an arrangement whereunder there would be centralisation of records of bed occupancy of the various institutions (there are only twelve), might give a lead to the institutions themselves towards pooling their resources and possibly coming to an agreement between themselves as to the age groupings and classifications they would treat in their various institutions".

He goes on to say that as yet he was "not sure as to whether any scheme which might develop from this suggestion *would or would not require legislation. .....I will investigate that aspect of the matter*" (my italics). The memorandum is initialled and dated 2/12/'57.

However, a memorandum written on the 11/12/'57 reported a discussion with Dr. Ramsay, the Assistant Inspector for Mental Hospitals. Dr. Ramsay could see no "way of achieving co-ordination or organisation in the field of M. D. accommodation." As the Department officials tried hard to adapt their strategy to the agenda of different organisations in an effort to achieve some measure of equity and efficiency, one suspects that the Departmental officials still hankered after the legislation which they had so ably presented to the Cabinet four years before. But the climate of opinion was against them. Society in Ireland was already making extensive use of the Religious Orders in education, so that it was very natural to look to the brothers and the nuns to perform a like service for the mentally handicapped. But the two cases were quite dissimilar. No matter how dedicated and no matter how progressive the religious orders were, they had one enormous drawback - their geographical distribution.

Attitude of Indifference

Unlike the teaching Orders they were not to be found in every town. They were mainly concentrated in the larger cities of Dublin and Cork. In addition it was well known to the Department that Religious Orders were not always free agents. If they wished to extend or expand into another diocese other than the one in which they were located they first had to be accepted by the Bishop in that diocese. They were not always welcome.

There is no doubt that the services of the Religious Orders were in high demand all over the country. A whole meeting of the Ballinasloe Mental Hospital Board was spent in dreaming of the day when they would hand over Woodlands, a former orthopaedic hospital, to the St. John of God Brothers. The County Manager kept them enthralled as he outlined his plans. He would discuss it "with the order of St. John of God in Stillorgan to find out from them if it would suit them and if they would be prepared to take children or adults or both". They could only come to Galway with the permission of the Bishop of Galway[12] and the matter had not been discussed at all yet. He would have to find out the proposals first and he thought the first resolution should come from the Galway County Council who were the owners of the property. It was the opinion of one of the members of the Board, Mr. T. King, that "Galway County Council would have some trouble in finding use for Woodlands and this suggestion was the most practical suggestion he had heard so far". Mr. J. Geoghegan T.D. asked the plaintive question "If it came to pass, do you think that patients from here in other hospitals could be brought back?" The Manager thought they could "If there was accommodation available". (Roscommon Herald, February 2, 1958). As it turned out, the St. John of God Brothers never came to Galway.

But most important of all, the Religious had no wish to become the sole providers of a service which, quite rightly, they did not see as their responsibility. It might be thought rather late in the day when Brother Aloysius, Provincial of the St. John of God Brothers, made this clear at a Seminar on Comprehensive Care in 1977[13]. By 1977 the Brothers had received a not inconsiderable amount by way of capital grants. To be fair, they had made their position quite clear long before that date.

Back in 1953 when the Government found itself with some capital in the Hospital Trust Fund and was encouraging expansion of the services, they had the Superiors of two Orders in on separate occasions. They were anxious to sound out the Order of St. John of God in the person of Brother Quilligan on its plans for the future. Brother Quilligan told the Department that his Order was "being subjected to adverse comment from Rome on account of their having no activities in Ireland but the care of mental and mental defective patients"[14]. Lest there was any misunderstanding, on being questioned further on plans that his Order might have, Brother Quilligan left them in no doubt. He "would not", he said, "object to opening in Limerick, but it would not be for mental defectives. It is quite usual for our Order to operate general hospitals on the continent".

This pronouncement must have had a fairly deflating effect on the little group of civil servants charged with the burden of alleviating the problem of the mentally handicapped. Even when the Order came to them with what were undoubtedly welcome plans, there was something off-putting in the way it was offered. For example, on August the 23rd 1962, the Brothers were anxious to discuss the possibility of increased accommodation in Celbridge[15]. Brother Vincent was anxious to provide about seventy extra beds in St. Raphael's. Fifty of these would be for severely handicapped. "There are a number of young brothers at St. Raphael's", he said, "and they were anxious to give them experience in the care of the severely handicapped". Although such a double coincidence of wants was welcome I can not help thinking that the members of the Ballinasloe Mental Hospital Board and the County Manager would have been shocked.

No State Control

It was in the mid sixties that the effects of an "all eggs in one basket" policy produced some very embarrassing moments for unfortunate Ministers for Health on numerous Question Times in the Dáil. Not only did they put the eggs in one basket but the Department handed the basket over, quite out of its control[16]. Considerable grants of land and buildings were made to Religious Orders and other Institutes who conducted Homes for the Mentally Handicapped at this time. Dr. Dolphin, the Inspector who had been entrusted with the task of contacting the Order, was successful in persuading La Sagesse in Liverpool to come to Ireland. In due course the Order was settled in Cregg House in County Sligo at a cost of £230,439 - a sum which bought a lot of land and building in those days.

The cases which were drawn to the attention of the T.D.s were, in the nature of things bound to be the most harrowing. Normally most people don't bother their T.D.s unless they are desperate. According to Deputy Mark Clinton, a respected Fine Gael T.D., "every deputy is plagued by people all over the country"[17]. T.D.s became familiar with mental handicap terms, like 'severe' and 'profound'. They heard about Autistic children and more importantly what it meant for their families.

"Could you guarantee a place for a boy of nine who was injuring his little brothers and sisters?", a deputy from Donegal wanted to know[18].

"Could the Deputy let the Minister have the details and he'd see what he could do?"

The truth was that the Minister could make representations to one of the Institutions like any T.D. or Parish Priest or friend, no more and no less. The Department had no control over who got a service and neither had the Dáil.

Some of the exchanges in the Dáil would have been comic if one were not aware of the misery which lay behind the questions. On the 1st. June 1965, when asked where beds were provided for severely mentally handicapped persons, the Minister, Mr. Donagh O'Malley, read out a list of institutions and the number of beds supposedly available. Included in the list was Stewart's Hospital where the Minister maintained that there were 60 beds, soon to be available, for severely mentally handicapped people. Mr. Clinton did not accept the Minister's answer. He happened to be on the Board of Stewart's Hospital. Even so the Minister persisted with his answer:

"I am telling the Deputy - Stewarts has 40 beds ready which only await kitchen and laundry arrangements".

Mr. Clinton: "I am saying they are not for severely handicapped".

The Minister: "A further 20 beds will make 60".

Mr. Clinton: "The Board says 'No'".

The Minister: "I say 'Yes'".

Mr. Clinton: "Is the Minister aware that Stewart's is a voluntary hospital?"

The Minister: "The Deputy asked me. That is my information".

Mr. Clinton: "It is inaccurate".
And so the pantomime ended for that day. The Dáil moved on to other business.

The number and nature of the questions put by deputies from every political party and from all over the country leads one to wonder at the kind of answers which the Departmental officials thought appropriate to prepare for their minister. Nobody knew the situation better than they did. Somebody somewhere was misleading the Minister.

No Service Where Most Needed

As the questioning T.D.s were beginning to find out, the Voluntary Institutions did not necessarily wish to provide a service for the kind of cases which turned up as a last resort in a T.D.'s clinic. The common experience of parents and families was that the more severe the mental handicap and the more disruptive of family life the more difficult it was to find a place at a residential institution. In 1957 the Chief Medical Officer in County Kilkenny, Dr. K.G. McColgan-Barry, had written in her report that whereas higher grade mentally defective children are admitted into residential centres, the lower grade are not catered for at all and they eventually "drift into the Mental Hospitals. The Resident Medical Superintendents of these institutions only take them as there is no where else to send them"[19]. The situation had not changed a decade later. At this time there were at least three institutions devoted solely to the residential care of mildly handicapped children so that they could attend the special schools all located in these centres. The schools were not provided locally. Instead residential schools were provided by a few religious orders. The inevitable consequence was that there was no institution in the country which was willing to answer the desperate need which so many despairing parents poured out to their local T.D.s. The severely handicapped, the autistic, those mentally handicapped with behavioural difficulties, and the adult mentally handicapped, were excluded from any service, except for what could be provided in the mental hospitals.

A Cut-Off Policy

The department was well aware of the autonomy of each voluntary institution but the implications of certain esoteric policies regarding the care and treatment of the mentally handicapped were far more serious than they realised. There was some evidence of these policies and their effects in a supplementary question which Mr. James Dillon put to the Minister for Health on 6th June 1968[20]. He put the problem:

".......As we provide the new accommodation, these institutions prefer to take children at an early age, when they can be adapted to institutional treatment, with the result that children who have been waiting for admission for four and five and six years are now finding it virtually impossible to get vacancies because the institutions feel they can best serve afflicted children by getting them at four or five years of age, and so recoil from the responsibility of accepting children at the age of eight, nine, ten or eleven. Would the Minister consider giving local authorities, who are faced with the responsibilities of accommodating children aged from eight to twelve, special facilities, or otherwise these children will not be provided for at all".

The Minister tried to argue that the number of places was rising steadily but Mr. Dillon persisted:

".......The homes prefer infants. In those circumstances perhaps the Minister would give local authorities some kind of special facilities so that these children will be got into homes. It will be a non-recurring problem we hope".

Mr. Brennan who was standing in for the Minister, said that he would bring the matter to the attention of the Minister. Nobody mentioned legislation or equity or rights.

Throughout the 1960s, the distress of the families of mentally handicapped children and adolescents continued to surface in the Dáil during question time. Time after time the questions were fended off by listing off the new places which were planned or being built at centres run by voluntary bodies. In 1967 the Minister said that "there would be a great easing of the problem" in the next two years. Autistic children[21] who were at first denied the status of mentally handicapped would appear to be included in 1967 in the severely handicapped group. A special new place was to be established in Cork. Like Mr. Dillon, deputies demanded that old fever hospitals or sanatoria be taken over and new services established. Mr. Gilhawley wanted to take over the old County Hospital in Sligo. But the Minister refused to entertain the idea and reminded him that some years before, Cregg House had been established a short distance from the town. The La Sagesse Sisters, he told the Deputy, were shortly to get a new 60 bed unit.

Towards the end of the 1970s the question of the dismissal of the adult mentally handicapped began to be an issue. In 1968, some deputies were worried that centres "sent back the mentally handicapped when he reaches 16 and the only available place then is the mental hospital or the County Home". On the 4th July Dr. O'Connell inquired about facilities for people who have been discharged from the residential schools when they have reached 16 years of age[22]. The Minister told him that they could have recourse to the special centres. When Dr. O'Connell asked him where these centres were, the Minister listed them off:

Saint Augustine's, Blackrock; Holy Angels, Glenmaroon; Stewarts Hospital, Palmerstown; Saint Vincent's, Navan Road; Saint Michael's House.

"Are there vacancies?" asked Dr. O'Connell.

"There are no vacancies", said the Minister.

Presumably the good Doctor gave up in disgust. He asked no more questions that day.

Breaking of Bonds

Other deficiencies became apparent. "Accommodation was not provided on a County basis" the Minister informed the Dáil, thus making the breaking of family bonds inevitable. People whose children were accepted into centres run by the Religious Orders sometimes had to make very long journeys indeed if they wished to see their children. The consequences of broken family ties and sundered relationships were in the end far more destructive for some people with mental handicap than any absence of services could be. But the Department and successive ministers never faltered in their dedication to a policy which was obviously flawed. Throughout the sixties and seventies they continued to expand the service according to decisions taken in the 1950s. Dangers which they saw then, they now doggedly refused to acknowledge. Their plans became more expensive but as the Minister on more than one occasion said in the Dail "money was not the problem". Any capital which the section responsible could lay their hands on in the Department of Health was spent in establishing these centres. In contrast, very little went towards maintaining even basic decency in the mental hospitals.

. **Notes on Chapter Four**

1. Letter from R.M.S. Limerick dated 8/11/'46 to the Inspector of Mental Hospitals. Department of Health files L50/2 Vol.ii. National Archives.
2. Letter to Dr. Kearney, Inspector of Mental Hospitals dated 2nd December, 1947. Department of Health files L50/2 Vol.2.
3. Draft of letter in reply date 28th January, 1948. Department of Health files L50/2 Vol 2.
4. Letter to the Secretary, Department of Health, dated 11th May, 1957 from the Medical Superintendent. Department of Health files L25/2/57.
5. Cabinet Papers. Department of the Taoiseach. S14129. National Archives.
6. Cabinet Papers. Department of the Taoiseach. S12573B. National Archives.
7. Department of Health files. National Archives L50/2.
8. Parliamentary Debates. Dáil Éireann. Questions col. 1948 - 1949, May 28, 1957.
9. Provision of Extra Accommodation for Mental Defectives. Department of Health files H39/25. National Archives, Dublin.
10. Memorandum H39/25. Department of Health files. National Archives.
11. Series of Minutes arising from minute from Mr. Hargadon, dated 31/10/57. Department of Health files L50/2. National Archives.
12. Hand written note on H file reads: "The proposed use of the former Woodlands Sanatorium for the maintenance of mental defectives has had to be shelved because the Bishop will not allow another Order into the Diocese. That information is for the Department's use only and should not be released". Initialled and dated 24/7/59.
13. Report of Seminar NAMHI papers.
14. Report of Discussion September 1952. Department of Health files H. National Archives.
15. Report of Meeting. Department of Health files L50/73. National Archives Dublin.
16. Details of grants were given in answer to question put by Deputy L'Estrange Parliamentary Debates. March 2, 1966. Question 65. columns 1933 - 1937.
17. Parliamentary Debates. June1, 1965. Questions.
18. Parliamentary Debates. 27June, 1968. Questions 59.
19. Cutting from The Kilkenny People. Department of Health files H. National

Archives
20. Parliamentary Debates. Dáil Éireann. June 6, 1968. Questions 45 columns 707.
21. Autistic children feature prominently in Dáil question throughout the 1960s.
22. Parliamentary Debates. Dáil Éireann. July 4, 1968. Questions

5

REINFORCING THE ERROR

In 1961 the Minister set up two commissions, one in February and the other in July. These were the Commission of Inquiry on Mental Handicap in February, and the Commission of Inquiry on Mental Illness in July. They were twin commissions and their conclusions were meant to overlap and converge by the time they made their final reports. They turned out to be very separate in their deliberations and the implications of their conclusions, one for the other, seemed to elude them. But they were not unaware of the outstanding concerns in their respective sector.

Endorsement of Policy

Several years passed before either Commission made any report. The report on Mental Handicap was presented to the Minister in 1965, the report on mental illness a year later in 1966. It cannot be said that either influenced policy to any salient degree.

The Report of the Commission on Mental Handicap is a particularly puzzling document and not compelling in its logic. This Commission confirmed the policy of entrusting virtually the entire service for mentally handicapped people to the Voluntary Agencies already engaged in it. It recommended that as far as possible any additional accommodation should be based on voluntary agencies. Although the responsibility for providing diagnosis and assessment was to lie with the Health Authority, the assessment and, therefore, the placing was to be heavily influenced by the Voluntary Agencies. School assessments provided by Health Authorities would refer any cases in possible need of residential care to the assessment teams provided by the voluntary bodies. The policy of taking large numbers of mildly handicapped children into residential care continued although arguments to the contrary were discussed. There was a heavy emphasis on the desirability of the special, segregated school for the education of the mildly handicapped.(Page 76). In addition the Commission held that a special school must have at least

150 pupils for the most effective results. "If mildly handicapped pupils are to have the benefit of a wide, stimulating programme to help them overcome their intellectual and social disabilities, their teachers jointly must possess a considerable range of special qualifications and interests and have all the necessary facilities at their disposal.

"Only day schools in Dublin and Cork as well as residential schools are likely to reach the optimum size and very few are likely to exceed it".

The consequence of this was that the schools continued to be located at the Homes for the Mentally Handicapped. The category of mentally handicapped children most likely to be granted residential care was that of the mild, sometimes very mild indeed. By a kind of Gresham's law the mildly handicapped children drove out those whose need for residential care was dire. By the time the Commission had ceased its deliberations in 1965 it had endorsed every undesirable aspect of a misguided policy. Even as the Commission sat, the idea that special schools could only be established in large centres of population was being discredited as each year passed.

Well Meant Suggestions

There are grounds for believing that there were sharp divisions of opinion on sociological questions amongst members of the Commission. Even as the Commission sat efforts were made to modify the disastrous bias of a section of the members in favour of the existing practice of the Voluntary Bodies. There is small comfort in the fact that not everyone on the Commission agreed with everything in the final report. In addition to the two reservations which were published at the end of the main body of the report, there was also the Report of a Sub-committee. This Sub-committee had been appointed to consider the feasibility of submitting an interim report to recommend provisional measures for relieving parental strain, pending the completion of the Inquiry. Its Report presents a different emphasis on the needs of the mentally handicapped in Ireland in the early 1960s. The heavily annotated document and its accompanying minutes reveal a preoccupation with a question which even in 1962 some of the families of people with mental handicap might have considered ludicrously irrelevant. The question was stated by the Minister himself in a minute to his Secretary:[1]

"How far is it equitable and morally justifiable to relieve parents of responsibilities for the care and well-being of their offspring and to transfer these responsibilities to the community, many of whose members are hard-put to fulfil their responsibilities to their children?"

Mr. MacEntee should have known that it is usually the rich who object to giving a hand in raising other peoples' children. The idea that some parents of handicapped children would get off the hook - or avoid their cross ? - was provoked by a very few modest proposals made by the subcommittee who would appear to have been in touch with the true situation.

Because the final report was not going to be ready for a few years the members of the sub-committee were anxious to make some interim recommendations in order to relieve in some small way the acute shortage of places for mentally handicapped people. The report gives us the sense of a group of worried people who were in touch with worrying situations. They were anxious that children who needed residential care and were probably on the waiting lists of the residential institutions, should in the meantime be provided with day care centres, "as far as possible through voluntary effort, but with help and support from Local Authorities" where they could be given "some training, occupation and recreation, and that, above all, their parents will be relieved of their full-time care, and will have the comfort of knowing that the community accepts and shares their burden. We should like at this point, to stress our strong conviction of the desirability of community care for the mentally handicapped, both now and in the future, wherever and whenever possible".

These practical suggestions set alarm bells ringing and antennae twitching. It was the idea that any kind of community support could be used to relieve the parents which seemed to bother them more than anything else. The immediate reaction of the Chief Medical Adviser was to establish first principles. He writes:

"I believe that the parents of mentally handicapped children are responsible for their care and upbringing and nothing should be said or done which would suggest that they are not".

He conceded that the community could accept "a secondary responsibility". They could be given assistance in providing educational and care facilities which they could not provide for themselves. "There should be no question of the community taking over the care of mentally handicapped children..... Parent participation is essential in all activities"[2].

One wonders how many boarding schools, which were heavily used by the middle classes at the time, could have satisfied these conditions.

Cautious Response

The reaction of the Department and the Minister to the suggestions in the sub-committee's report would suggest that there were more than economic considerations at work here. In 1962 it should have been clear that taking children out of their own homes away from their families was an expensive way of educating or training them. It should have seemed like a good idea to give some financial aid to families the caring for mentally handicapped at home instead. Coupled with a network of day centres and special schools the necessity for residential care for many could have been avoided. But it was not well received. The senior medical inspector thought that other dependent members of a family, if they had a physical disability, might be equally deserving. The strong recommendation by the sub-committee that residential care should be avoided at all costs was ignored. The sub-committee had written:

"In the main, however, we are in agreement with the opinion expressed by the World Health Organisation that it is both more desirable and more economic for mentally handicapped to be looked after at home, provided that parents have financial, advisory and other help from the community".

Only where the retention of the child at home could seriously dislocate other aspects of family life would they recommend institutional care. The final report did indeed consider the undesirability of placing children with a mild or high moderate degree of mental handicap in residential institutions, but it argued that demographic factors made this placing necessary. By its total rejection of the use of special classes in the mainstream school and the numerical limits which it set as desirable in special schools which would be reserved for the mildly handicapped alone, it set the terms for the conclusion to this debate. The truth is that mildly mentally handicapped children were already receiving special education in residential schools, whether they lived in rural areas or not. That situation continued. It is hard to resist the conclusion that whatever the World Health Organisation or any other experts might say, Ireland would stick with what they had.

Although there is a formal recognition in the final report that care outside residential centres was therapeutically better for a handicapped person, there is a palpable distrust of the parents' role in the upbringing of their handicapped child:

"Parents will usually lack the knowledge required in order to give the skilled training, care and supervision which will help the mentally handicapped child to overcome or at least to minimise, his disability" (page 51).

The dominant thinking of the Commission is revealed, perhaps unconsciously, in the paragraph titled General on page 52 in Chapter Five of its Report:

"It will frequently be found that all or several of the services can suitably be made available by the same organisation - provided it can arrange for such segregation as is necessary on the basis of age, sex and type of defect".

Need for a Mother Figure

Neither the minister nor the Department accepted the recommendations of the sub-committee, and one of the recommendations had to be repeated in Mrs Kingsmill-Moores Reservation. The minute[3] initialled JD (probably Jack Darby) reads:

"That mentally handicapped boys up to the age of 10 should be cared for by women. The recommendations on this matter are not very clear but I think it is intended that all children should be cared for by persons of both sexes".

That, as JD remarks "was tantamount to condemning many

institutions which are run by religious bodies". JD thought that the recommendation was directed at Lota (an institution run by the Brothers of Charity in Cork). "there was no female staff at the time we visited. I understand that it was a rule of the Order that female staff could not be employed, but I am told that this has now changed and that females will probably be employed in the future. No particular action as far as the Minister is concerned, appears to be necessary".

That was as maybe, but Mrs Kingsmill-Moore was forced to write the following into her reservation some three years later:

"...... I recommend strongly that more women should be included on the staffs of all organisations dealing with children and young adults. Nothing can exceed the devotion and care shown by male religious orders, but the deprivation suffered by children and adolescents owing to the absence of a mother-figure is acute and lasting. This need is, happily, now being more widely recognised". (page 178 of the Report of the Commission of Inquiry on Mental Handicap)

The decisions taken on the recommendations of the sub-committee were not taken for economic reasons. They were political decisions taken because of the prevailing attitude to Church-State relations. The reluctance on the part of the State to take on its responsibilities to the weakest and the most vulnerable of its citizens may very well have had its roots in the thinking at this time when there was an ideological preoccupation with the possible encroachment of the State into territory which the Church regarded as its own. The strong antipathy to any involvement of the state in family affairs made mental handicap a very private affair, and the state was expected to act through the agency of a voluntary body preferably religious. The religious were the experts in a field where neither the family nor ordinary lay people were presumed to know anything. Things had changed a lot since the 1940's when Mr. MacEntee did not hesitate to defend the things of Caesar in open and unconciliatory debate with the Bishop of Clonfert.

Good Sense Prevails

In time all the recommendations of the sub-committee were adopted, but only when people all over the country began to put a service together themselves. There is a hint in the last paragraph of the report of the sub-committee that this had already begun.

"..... the sub-committee has taken into consideration the views of bodies and individuals throughout the country. Each member has made special enquiries and brought back to the sub-committee opinions supporting the need for the immediate amelioration of the plight of mentally handicapped children, adults and their parents and families .....".

The Commission's belief in the benefits of special education for the mildly mentally handicapped (which in the case of places outside Dublin or Cork would mean residential care) was so strong that they seriously considered compulsory treatment. "It has been found", they wrote, "that some parents, particularly parents of mildly mentally handicapped children, either through neglect, or because they will not concede the presence of mental handicap, will not voluntarily send their children for special care or treatment".

Happily the Commission did not recommend compulsion but the implication is clear. The good parent of a mildly handicapped child was the parent who expelled the child from family, brothers and sisters, and the neighbours.

The Terms of Reference of the Commission did not pay particular attention to the problems of those people with a mental handicap, who had severe disabilities and who were unlikely ever to become productive members of society. There were obvious attractions in plans and projects, even in theories, that promised some productivity at the end of the day. Hence the emphasis on education and training for employment.

Ambivalence on Long-term Care

It is when the Commission comes to consider how the accommodation for the adult mentally handicapped should be arranged that their arguments and the thinking behind them become positively murky. Their first conclusion was that County Homes were not suitable places for the care of adult mentally handicapped - unless they were already there, in which case it would serve no useful purpose to move them. The majority of mental hospitals were not suitable either. But in view of the very large numbers of places needed "it seems inevitable that a number of mentally handicapped must be accommodated in district mental hospitals". The Commission pointed out certain advantages "they are generally well sited in the principal county towns" (presumably in contrast to the siting of centres run by the voluntary bodies) "have adequate space for additional facilities such as workshops and have farms attached". All in all the Commission saw no objection in principle to the provision of long-term care for the mentally handicapped in conjunction with the long-term care of the mentally ill provided that the living accommodation would be suitable and separate for the mentally handicapped. The Commission also required the hospitals to develop into well-staffed and well-equipped centres.

One wonders then, why Mrs Kingsmill-Moore, a most experienced and knowledgeable member, found it necessary to write her reservation on the future use of mental hospitals. She considered them "highly unsuitable for the treatment of mental or any other handicap". The reservation was entitled "The Future Use of the Mental Hospitals" and Mrs Kingsmill-Moore was aghast at the recommendation that those mentally handicapped adults whom the Voluntary Agencies did not wish to retain in their institutions could be accommodated in the mental hospitals when "acute psychiatric cases are removed from mental hospitals and accommodated in units attached to general hospitals". One suspects that Mrs Kingsmill-Moore did not expect that there would be any great changes in the mental hospitals as they existed then. The least that could be done, she thought, was to establish a pilot-scheme, but her recommendations were not acceptable to the other members. Mrs Kingsmill-Moore was forced to write her reservation which was signed by three other members. It is unlikely that the other members of the Commission were not aware of conditions in the mental hospitals and certainly the Department of Health was. The Conference Regarding Clonmel Mental Hospital had been held at the end of December 1958, seven or eight years earlier. It was something that neither Dr. Ramsay, Assistant Inspector of Mental Hospitals, nor Mr. Jack Darby, Principal Officer of the mental services, was likely to forget. Both were members of the Commission of Inquiry on Mental Handicap.

The oddest feature of the Commission's recommendation was that they proposed to reserve about 2,500 adults for care by the voluntary bodies. According to the report, the reason for this was to enable the voluntary organisations, providing services for children, to be "in a position to evaluate the long- term results of the care, training and education provided by them" - almost as if the whole effort was a kind of experiment where the service providers would of course be the only people qualified to evaluate — a mildly fascist sentiment which should have rung alarm bells but didn't.

There was nothing new in the practice of dismissing people with a mental handicap from their Home for Mentally Handicapped back to their place of origin and straight into the local mental hospital. "No useful purpose would be served by retaining them in these homes", writes a Mr C. O'Clerihan in 1947 to the Clerk of Castlebar Mental Hospital[4] concerning some girls who were to be transferred from St. Vincent's Cabra and St. Joseph's Clonsilla by ambulance.

But some were selected to stay on. There was no mention in 1947 of any clear criteria for retaining some people and dismissing others except the rather vague one of "serving a useful purpose". We are given no clue in the report of the Commission either. Many parents of children in Homes for the Mentally Handicapped have spent sleepless nights worrying about this aspect of autonomy.

A Political 'Mantra'

Sad to say, the Minister for Health in 1968 when questioned about the considerable number of mentally handicapped adults in St. Brendan's at Grangegorman was able to shelter behind the Commission's recommendation. "The Commission did not rule it out", he said, "provided they were segregated".[5] Later, succeeding Ministers responded to similar questions by repeating like a mantra that the policy of successive governments was not to admit any people with mental handicap into the psychiatric hospitals as the mental hospitals began to be known. Whatever they were called, the mentally handicapped continued to go into them, and do so even at the present day.

"De-designation"

In 1966 Dr. Ivor Browne who had been appointed Chief Psychiatrist on the first day of the same year put forward a programme to the Dublin Health Authority, which effectively sealed the fate of many a person with a mental handicap. Like most psychiatrists, Dr. Browne's main interest lay in that section of the mentally ill whose condition was curable. Like everyone else he realised that there were very many people in the mental hospitals who could not be included in this category. The Dublin Health Authority alone had 500 people with a mental handicap in its care in psychiatric hospitals, namely St. Ita's at Portrane and St. Brendan's at Grangegorman. Dr. Browne wrote in his report to the Health Authority:

"We feel therefore that we should face this situation honestly, and that part of our hospital facilities must be turned over to the mentally handicapped, de-designated, creating an autonomous service with the appropriate trained staff and rehabilitation programme. As this will, by its very nature, be a long term institutional service it would seem appropriate that it should be associated with St. Ita's Hospital which is, because of its geographical location, essentially an institution".

Dr. Browne did not spell out what he meant by the term "de-designate" or what the implications might be for the people with mental handicap. The term acquired a significance for the Department of Health much later on which was not foreseen at the time. Under the Mental Treatment Act (1945) certain institutions were deemed to be provided by the mental hospital authorities for the discharge of their functions under the Act. The buildings, wards, lands etc. were *designated*. The people admitted to these institutions were entitled to the treatment, maintenance, services and advice, which was the duty of the Mental Hospital Authority to provide. It was never quite clear what the occupants of a hospital or part of a hospital were entitled to when their place of occupation became de-designated, but there is little doubt that the term "de-designate" was employed as a device to conceal the true figures of long-stay patients in the psychiatric hospitals including people with mental handicap. What certainly did change for the occupants of de-designated wards or hospitals or parts of hospitals was the loss of their entitlements under the Act.

Dr. Browne was not unfamiliar with St. Ita's Hospital. He had worked there at least for a short time. Its location, on a promontory in North County Dublin, could hardly have been more isolated. But Dr. Browne proposed that part of this vast hospital should be set aside not only for the 500 or so mentally handicapped already in the care of the Dublin Health Authority but it was to become the option of last resort for a further 200 who as children had been in the care of religious bodies and who were now discharged. These were the mentally handicapped who were not among the 2,500 adults chosen to live on in the Homes for the Mentally handicapped which the Department of Health was so energetically establishing at the time. Mrs Kingsmill-Moore's worst fears were justified and Dr. Browne's programme greatly facilitated the implementation of the scandalous policy already decided on by the Commission and policy makers within the Department of Health.

Dr. Browne did however express a pious hope which others had expressed before him and which many others would express after him:

"It is hoped that, once a proper service for the mentally handicapped has been set up in the Dublin Health Authority, close links can be formed with the services run by religious orders such as St. John of God, and the Sisters of Charity for mentally handicapped children so that a properly co-ordinated service for the mentally handicapped of all ages can be created".

What Dr. Browne and the Dublin Health Authority hoped to get out of this co-ordination it is hard to say. They certainly did not get the funding which was required to establish "a properly organised service" even on the modest terms outlined by the Chief Psychiatrist "which could be situated in the present farm buildings". Suffice to say that not one of the agencies for which he had such obvious respect would have tolerated a service in some old farm buildings. For understandable reasons Dr. Browne did not dwell on the accommodation which he envisaged for the extra numbers of mentally handicapped at St. Ita's.

Some Sensible Suggestions

If the report of the Commission of Inquiry on Mental Handicap was largely an endorsement of the status quo the report of the Commission on Mental Illness looked forward to a new order "where all manner of things will be well". They had good reason for optimism. In 1966, the year in which they made their report, the advent of the new psychotrophic drugs and the improved attitude of society to mental illness were major factors in the new outlook. Increasingly, mental illness began to be viewed as just another illness. Henceforth there would appear to be no logical reason to have special hospitals for the mentally ill. Psychiatry would be integrated with general medicine and psychiatric units for short term in-patient care would be established at general hospitals. A full range of treatments would be provided by, not only psychiatrists and psychiatric nurses, but also by occupational therapists, psychologists and social workers. Clearly the old horrific days were to end soon - at least for new patients.

The Commission made similar sensible suggestions for the long-stay patient. Programmes of rehabilitation should replace the old custodial methods. Sheltered workshops should be organised for those not capable of working in the community. Work habits should be re-established or established for the first time. Hospitals should establish industrial therapy projects. Every effort should be made to preserve the individuality of the patient. Above all, the aim must be to reduce the numbers in the hospital. Not much attention was paid to the mentally handicapped even though they already made up a significant proportion of the long-stay patients. The fact that one of the recommendations of the Commission on Mental Handicap would ensure that the numbers were bound to be replenished from year to year provoked no comment. One would be forgiven for thinking that the members of the Commission of Inquiry into Mental Illness were too polite to mention this shared piece of territory, although the Commission of Inquiry into Mental Handicap had published their report several months earlier. It was almost as if they had not read it and yet at least two members of the Commission of Inquiry on Mental Handicap also sat on the Commission dealing with mental illness. One of these was Dr. Ramsay, the Assistant Inspector of Mental Hospitals, who had been so horrified by the conditions which he had found when he had carried out a detailed inspection of the mental hospital in Clonmel in 1959. The other was Mr. Jack Darby who had accompanied Dr. Ramsay on that inspection.

Discrimination Acknowledged

The Commission of Inquiry into Mental Illness did refer to the awful conditions which the long-stay patients, including the mentally handicapped, had to endure. They recognised that many long-stay patients would live and die in these conditions. In the years that the Commission had examined the situation, the members had visited each of the mental hospitals. They were keenly aware of the discrimination which existed towards the mental hospitals. As little as possible was spent on furniture or furnishings, on maintenance, or on catering. Patients were living in primitive conditions because so little was spent on heating or sanitary facilities. They were conscious of the contrast in the way the General Hospitals were equipped and maintained.[6]

The report might have been written about Clonmel in 1958. Worse still it could have been written about Portrane or Grangegorman or indeed Ballinasloe in 1980. The Government of the day took scarcely any action. It is not easy to understand and it certainly was not because the section of the Department of Health responsible had no interest. Meeting after meeting was held. It is true that technically the mental hospitals were the direct responsibility of mental hospital boards (and after 1970 the Health Boards). It is true that where the mental hospital had an energetic and committed R.M.S., certain reforms did take place. Even when new and forward looking Resident Medical Superintendents were appointed, how could they succeed without the backing of the community in which the mental hospitals were located? If certain Resident Medical Superintendents could have been won over towards more humane attitudes, (or "indoctrinated" as Dr. Dolphin had put it)

70

and thereafter encouraged to involve the whole community, how different the story might have been!

Model Rejected

There is evidence of something of the kind when Dr. Power, the R.M.S in Ennis in 1962, had some success in involving people outside the mental hospital service in programmes for improving life for people in their local mental hospital. Ever since Dr. Power had been appointed as R.M.S at Ennis Mental hospital "it was accepted that big improvements have been made in Ennis". (note on Health Department file)[7]. The Department of Health was very impressed by the submission that he had made to the Conference of Resident Medical Superintendents and Managers which was held in the Department in December of 1961. Dr. Power had made wide-ranging recommendations which the County Manager was pleased to accept and recommend for adoption by his County Council. The improvements would involve an additional charge of one penny on the rates. Dr. Power's strategy included enlisting the expertise of the Vocational Education Committee and the Agricultural Committee. Both of these bodies had responded with enthusiasm. All in all, Dr. Power's project could have been a model for almost all the mental hospitals in the country. But Dr. Power's programme was not generally adopted.

"While the Minister welcomes these suggestions, it will be appreciated that some are matters which will probably be considered by the Commission which is at present examining problems relating to the mentally ill and it may be considered advisable to await the Commission's findings".

For people who put their trust in the efficacy of Commissions in establishing policies or in changing practices the two Commissions and their reports must have been disappointing. The existence of both Commissions was useful to the Minister for Health while the members were deliberating for the five years it took them to reach their conclusions. It was during those years that so many questions about the services began to be asked, particularly about the lack of services for the mentally handicapped. Routinely the Minister would remind the Dail of the two Commissions as he fended off questions concerning inadequacies in the services in the first half of the 1960s. But policy had been decided long before. It had not been decided in the Dáil and had not emerged from any kind of informed debate or consultation.

Notes on Chapter Five

1. Department of Health files L50/7
2. Ibid
3. Department of Health files L50/7
4. Department of Health files L50/2. National Archives.
5. Parliamentary Debates, Dáil Éireann. Questions July 4, 1968.
   Minister (Deputy Seán Flanagan): "there are considerable numbers in St. Brendan's. The Commission of Inquiry did not rule it out provided they were segregated. The adults in St. Brendan's are to go to Portrane......"
6. Commission of Inquiry on Mental Illness Report. Pages 50 - 53.
7. Department of Health files L7/147. National Archives.

6

PEOPLE POWER

The political system had failed the mentally disabled. The abdication of responsibility was complete. There were no Inspector of Mental Hospital reports to remind the public of the thousands who were 'forgotten' in the mental hospitals.

Filling The Gap

But as regards the mentally handicapped where the Government had failed the people took over. It began in Dublin where, although there were special schools for mentally handicapped children, they were all residential and even if they were able to take in all those children who required schooling, there would not have been room for them. As well as that, not all parents wished to send their children, particularly very young children, into boarding schools. By the 1960s the movement began to spread beyond Dublin. The mentally handicapped were becoming less invisible than they used to be. Families everywhere were becoming less secretive when a child of theirs was found to have a mental handicap. To their eternal credit in every part of Ireland there were people who responded to their need. This spontaneous response was something totally unexpected. The movement at the beginning was sporadic and slow and although it never could address the problems of the most severely afflicted, in time it had a powerful modifying effect on the worst effects of Government policy.

It began in 1946, with the birth of a boy called Brian. Brian was born with Down's Syndrome. Two years later his mother, Mrs Patricia Farrell, took Brian to a clinic in London where she learned to understand and cope with his syndrome. It was while she was in London that Mrs Farrell attended a support group for parents like herself. Mrs Farrell[1] saw the need for a similar group in Ireland and when she returned to Dublin she set about establishing such a group. She enlisted the help of her close friend, Mrs Madge Atcock a former fashion model, and together they planned their strategy. In 1955 they placed an advertisement in the Irish Times which read:

"Parents of mentally handicapped boy would like to get in touch with other similar parents with a view to starting some association".

Prototype Foundation

About twenty parents responded to the advertisement. A meeting was arranged to be held in the Savoy tea rooms. The assembled parents and friends appointed a committee and arranged to fundraise. Far more important, however, was what the people who founded the organisation wanted for their children. Up to that time people, if they could, sent their children away to residential care. This group of Dublin parents did not want to do this. There were enough of them at that first meeting and they were sufficiently resourceful in organising the means to enable them to establish the first day care centre in the country.

This was a momentous development not only for the Dublin children who did not have to leave home and family because St. Michael's had been founded, but for the many others throughout the country whose parents and friends followed Mrs Patricia Farrell's example, quite literally down to the letter in the paper, as a first step. The special National School founded by the Association of Parents and Friends in 1954, later called St. Michael's House, was the prototype of many throughout the country.

In the early sixties, the birth of a profoundly mentally handicapped child into the family of a near neighbour inspired Mrs Sylvia Dawson to take the first steps on the long road to establishing a service for mentally handicapped in County Longford.[2] She was aware that all over rural Ireland there were children and adults with a mental handicap with no services. The services which the Department of Health was trying to establish might as well have been on the moon for all the relevance they had to the situation in places like County Longford. Thirteen miles from Longford town, the only health services available to Sylvia Dawson's neighbour was the local dispensary, "with an overworked midwife and a G.P".

An Idea 'Gets Legs'

The first step Sylvia Dawson took was to consult the County Medical Officer. County Medical Officers were key figures in the early stages of all these County-based associations. Like the mental hospitals, County Medical Officers of Health were an inheritance from pre-independence days established on an *ad hoc* basis. They were finally and formally established by the Government in 1925. Unlike other doctors they were salaried state employees whose duties were strictly concerned with public health. The County Medical Officer was responsible for supervising the implementation of the sanitary laws; for the maternity and child welfare services, the medical inspection of school children, the welfare of the blind, the inspection of midwives and the eradication of Tuberculosis. It is most likely that had the Department of Health and the Minister succeeded in getting their proposed legislation through in 1953 and afterwards, it would have been the County Medical Officers of Health who would have been responsible for its implementation. In the 1960s they were undoubtedly the best informed people in the country on the numbers and the categories of the mentally handicapped in their respective counties.

Sylvia's next step was to have a letter published in the Longford Leader in February 1964 asking anyone interested to get in touch. At first the response was slow. There were a few offers of help and a phone-call from County Leitrim. Nevertheless the first meeting was set for September 8th, 1964. Sixteen people in all turned up, eight of them parents. That was the beginning of meetings and minutes of meetings, fund raising and financial records, journeys to Dublin and consultations with others who had gone down the same road. The National Association for the Mentally Handicapped had been formed recently and its early membership was very helpful.

In 1966 the infant association was successful in getting a major concession. Up to that time there had been no assessment service or indeed even the most rudimentary counselling services of any kind. But in that year the Department of Health granted them access to a psychologist from Dundalk in St. Loman's

Hospital, Mullingar once a fortnight. Sylvia herself drove two children over to Mullingar every fortnight. Meanwhile the first services for the mentally handicapped children in Longford began to take form in temporary premises with voluntary teachers and voluntary drivers. Shortly after, the association was encouraged by a sympathetic County Secretary, to acquire a permanent site just outside the town of Longford. On this site the association erected the first pre-fab ever seen in Longford.

The division of the county for the purposes of fund raising was a feature of the Longford association, as it was of all the county associations. Which association thought of this method of ensuring thorough coverage as well as a certain element of competitive generosity is a matter of some dispute but it was certainly effective. It became particularly effective as a means of educating the general public and was invaluable in reducing the stigma attached to mental handicap "in the family".

While The Minister Talked....

In 1968 the Minister for Health was still talking of extensions to existing institutions as a means of coping with the number of mentally handicapped children who had no services - not even schools. But he had no idea how many. "It is rather difficult to say", he explained, "because the projections in regard to number were all wrong because of the emergence of new drugs which have enabled children to be kept alive"[3]. While the Minister talked, almost in every county people simply got on with it.

In County Kildare it was the parents of a handicapped child who were the centre of the movement that resulted in the founding of Kare which today provides a range of facilities in Kildare, West Wicklow and East Offaly. Almost their first step was to speak to the County Medical Officer, Dr. Brendan O'Donnell. What County Medical Officers were able to do was to give the emerging organisations an idea of the numbers involved. This kind of information was invaluable to Mr. and Mrs. O'Donovan and all the people who had to argue their case strenuously with government departments. It strikes one as distinctly odd that the Minister seemed to be unable to get the same information, or to give it to the Dáil. This reticence

A view of St. Ita's, Portrane in 1995.

Photo by Derek Speirs

One of the many long corridors in St. Ita's, Portrane

Photo by Derek Speirs

St. Luke's Hospital, Clonmel

Dr. Ivor Browne.
Chief Psychiatrist of Eastern
Health Board

Dr. Thomas Egan.
R.M.S. at St. Luke's Clonmel
from 1957 to 1964

Mr. Seán McEntee, Minister for Health 1957 - 1965

courtesy of Irish Times

Boys in the care of St. John of God Brothers at a confirmation ceremony in the 1950s.

Obelisk Park. St. Augustine's Colony, Blackrock.

Dr. Kearney, Inspector of Mental Hospitals.

Mr. David Andrews T.D.   *Mr. Mark Clinton T.D.*

Opening of St. John of God Services in Drumcar, County Louth, by Dr. Noel Browne when he announced his plans for the Health Services.

Cheeverstown House

Mr. Michael Woods, Minister for Health, 'cuts the sod' at Cheeverstown.

Mr. Charles Haughey.
Minister for Health 1977 - 1979

Mr. Seán Flanagan.
Minister for Health 1966 - 1969

Dr. Jim Ryan, Minister for Health 1951 - 1954, (front row, third from right) at the opening of Kilcornan House in 1952

Mr. Barry Desmond, Minister for Health 1982 - 1987, 'cutting the sod' at Belcamp, St. Michael's House.

Mr. T.F. O'Higgins.
Minister for Health 1954 - 1957

Dr. Rory O'Hanlon.
Minister for Health 1987 - 1991

*Dr. Barbara Stokes (front right) at Cheeverstown House
with Dr. Michael Woods T.D. in background.*

Sylvia Dawson as a young nurse.
Founder of the County Longford
Association of the Mentally
Handicapped

*Dr. John O'Connell.
Minister for Health 1992 - 1993*

Mr. John Boland T.D.

Mrs. Patsy Farrell.
Founder of St. Michael's Parents
and Friends

Slow learners in the care of the Daughters of Charity, Glenmaroon.

Mr. Pat Moloney former Chief Executive Officer of St. Michael's House.

Kerry Parents and Friends at Killarney

frequently gave the impression of an insurmountable problem which a little country like ours could not possibly tackle.

The Offaly Mentally Handicapped Association had its beginnings in a Garda station in Shinrone. Thirty three years ago Garda Sergeant Pat O'Reilly and Mr. Peter Campion met there to organise a public meeting which duly took place on Tuesday March 22nd, 1966, in the Marian Hall in Birr. That first meeting included not only people from Shinrone like Dr. Brigid Taffe, Mr. Peter Campion, Mr. Eamon Stafford and Mr. Paddy O'Reilly, but word had spread and there was a large attendance from all over the County. Dean Quinn was there as well as Reverend E. Vaughan and the Reverend Canon Francis Burke, Church of Ireland. That first meeting was addressed by the County Medical Officer, Dr. Reeves.

The pattern of organisation was laid down. Like the County Longford association it was based on the formation of branches - Shinrone, Birr, Kinnity, Moneygall, Kilcormac, Clara, Edenderry, Ferbane, Banagher, Tullamore, Coolderry. The population in the midlands might have been sparse but whoever thought of this method of structuring the new associations knew that if one wishes to involve people one starts with communities like these. It was a highly successful method[4]. The claim to "inventing" the branch structure system has been made by the KARE organisation in County Kildare in their recent publication *"An Extraordinary Commitment"*. It may be true that the structure was based on the political branch system in County Kildare but the system was well established in Longford and Offaly several years before. The County Wexford association established voluntary committees in the four major towns which was a slightly different approach.

Apart from providing information which was essential for the small County organisations, the County Medical Officer "played a vital role in encouraging parents to have their children assessed. Through him alone names were put forward for assessment in a highly confidential manner". Thus the small associations showed how the barrier of confidentiality could be overcome.

The Help of The Media

In 1966, Castlebar, County Mayo had no services of any kind for any child with a mental handicap. Mr. Johnny Mee, who worked for the Connaught Telegraph, was beginning to be very worried[5]. His greatest fear, as his daughter was coming up to school age, was that his wife and himself would be forced to send their little girl to a residential institution far away in Dublin or Cork if she were to get the care and schooling to which she was entitled. At the same time he realised that the ordinary national school, at the time, did not provide the right environment for the education of his child.

It so happened that just as he was about to give up hope he saw a programme on RTE about St. Michael's House in Dublin. He saw that it was possible to provide special facilities in a special school which could be adapted to the needs of the mentally handicapped child. Perhaps, after all, his wife and himself need not part with their beloved offspring. Straightaway he wrote a letter to Connaught Telegraph setting out his ideas and concerns. He had two important phone-calls as a result - one from Mr. Michael J. Egan, the other from Mr. Tom Fallon. Together the three called a public meeting in the Imperial Hotel. They expected an attendance of about fifteen or twenty people. Approximately one hundred attended that first meting.

Like most of these County associations the main aim at first was to establish special schools for the mentally handicapped in the area. Most of their pupils were mildly handicapped. It took them two years to get their first school, built on land donated by the Sisters of Mercy in Castlebar. The enterprise which began at that public meeting in the Imperial Hotel became Western Care which provides a comprehensive range of services for people with mental handicap all over County Mayo to-day. They started with schools for the mildly handicapped. Later Western Care established schools for the moderately handicapped as well.

Long Term Planning

Almost from the day when they achieved the coveted status of recognised Special National School, each organisation was looking ahead to the future. Training facilities, hostels and workshops had to be planned for and in those early years fundraising was central to their development strategy. Whatever one thinks today about the rights of people with a mental handicap versus the necessity of fundraising, in 1967 it was not an issue. The money had to be got somewhere and quite often the only way was through sponsored walks, giant fetes, bed pushes, all-star football events, coffee mornings and cheese and wine evenings - all adding to the gaiety of the nation! Nevertheless once these voluntary agencies began to be serious providers of services in their areas they began to look for statutory support. However reluctantly, it was the health boards who were the main contributor.

It is at least arguable that the establishment of the health boards in 1970 was not the best development in the world for the small county-based associations. The health board areas were much bigger than the counties and did not command the same loyalties. It is much more difficult to persuade members of your local health board to part with money than it is to impress your own county men. Even before the establishment of the health boards it had been noticed that the "practice of dealing directly with the voluntary agencies has also tended to lessen the active interest of local authorities and to relieve them of their responsibility of making a direct contribution to the problem of accommodation". (Department of Health Memorandum 1951). When the larger voluntary agencies were able to obtain their funding directly from the Department of Health even after the health boards had been established by the 1970 Health Act, the health boards became even less helpful. The absence of specific legislation for the mentally handicapped was a further complication. When the new Health Act came into force in 1971 or thereabouts the new voluntary agencies for the mentally handicapped began to be funded under a section from an earlier Health Act which is as good evidence as any of the unforeseen and accidental nature of the whole county-based voluntary movement.

One unforeseen consequence of the small county-based voluntary organisation composed of parents and friends was the part they were enabled to play in bringing out the services of the large directly funded agencies from their rather isolated establishments. For the first time these institutions began to be involved in their immediate neighbourhood, especially when they were located outside Dublin. For example the Offaly Association forged close links with the Sisters of Jesus and Mary at Monasterevan. In the same way the County Roscommon Association was able to use the services of the Brothers of Charity in their area.

From Support to Service Provision

By 1973 when the Kerry Parents and Friends Association was founded, the Home for the Mentally Handicapped in Killarney was run by the Franciscan Sisters. It was deeply embedded in the local scene - a very different story from similar establishments ten or twenty years before. The Kerry Parents and Friends was started as a support group for the Sisters who were involved in fund raising for their residential home which had opened in 1968. Killarney was small enough to involve all the community.

The two people who first had the idea of establishing the organisation were two doctors - Dr. Norrie Buckley who was the visiting G.P. to the Home and, unusually, Dr. Jack O'Connor who held the post of R.M.S. at Killarney Psychiatric Hospital, St. Finnian's. Later other key figures became involved: Father (later Monsignor) Bobby Murphy, Dean of Tralee; Canon Enright, Church of Ireland, Waterville; Séamus and Eileen Keating, parents; Mrs Wall, Tralee, parent; Sister Fatima, Superior, St. Mary of the Angels. Two friends, Mary Doyle and Mrs Helen O'Connell were also active in their support as well as the two initiators of the whole project, Dr. Norrie Buckley and Dr. Jack O'Connor. They were able to enlist the organisational skills of the County Manager, Séamus Keating. Canon Enright happened to be an accountant as well as a clergyman, which was one of those strokes of good fortune which the Kerry Parents and Friends has always been able to put to good use.

The Kerry Parents and Friends which had started out as a support group went on to become service providers themselves, specialising in providing services for adults. At first these were young adults who had finished their training at St. Mary of the Angels.

The founding of Parents and Friends' associations which continued to be support groups for particular service agencies became commonplace. Their main activity was fund raising but not exclusively. One in particular, the County Cork Parents and Friends campaigned successfully for the people with mental handicap who were accommodated in their local psychiatric hospital, Our Lady's, Cork. The only voluntary association of parents and friends concerned exclusively with the mentally handicapped in a psychiatric hospital, was St. Joseph's Association for the Mentally Handicapped, St. Ita's, Portrane. It was founded in 1976 by Dr. Vincent Moloney, the Director of Mental Handicap at St. Ita's Portrane.

Notes on Chapter Six

1. Letter from St. Michael's House Interview with Mrs Patsy Farrell.
2. Letter and interview with Mrs Dawson 1998.
3. Parliamentary Debates. April 25, 1968, in answer to question by Deputy Dillon.
4. Interview with Mrs Gladys Johnston. Summer 1998.
5. Interview with Mr. Mee. Summer 1998.

7

PERPETUATING THE NONSENSE

By 1980 the effects of the arrangements which had been set in place in the 1950s had become glaringly obvious. After all the capital grants to the voluntary agencies, and after all the deliberations by the Commissions, and after all the Dáil questions over two decades, the Department had managed to produce a nonsense which was eminently foreseeable when the elements of the policy were being put in place.

Misplacement
Nobody put the situation better than the Working Party set up by the Department of Health itself[1]. This informal working group had been established with the purpose of deriving an estimate of the number of places needed in residential centres for the mentally handicapped. It reported its findings in 1980.

According to the Group there were 2000 people in residential care who should not be there. There were 2000 people with serious mental handicap living outside in the community, who needed residential care and there were 2,500 mentally handicapped people in psychiatric or geriatric institutions. There was no mention of the most glaring misplacement of all - the inclusion of 225 people with normal intelligence in services for the mentally handicapped, probably residential. This interesting aspect did not come to light until the report of a survey preparatory to the compiling of a data base in 1995.

If this kind of mess had occurred in any other area of life besides mental handicap there would have been uproar. The report of the working party tiptoed carefully round the question and there was scarcely a hint that anyone was to blame. There was no word as to how the 2000 people who should not be in residential care had got there. Yet the Department of Health would have known for years that they were there. According to the 1974 Census of the Mentally Handicapped 514 people of borderline intelligence were in residential care and in the same census 1,845 persons were returned as mildly handicapped. In 1981 there were 2,035 persons with a borderline/mild mental handicap in residential care. The department did not have to wait for the Census returns. They were kept up to date by the Voluntary Agenciesí annual figures.

Plucked from Family and Friends

Of all the people whose lives were destroyed by well-meaning people this last group of 2,035 mildly handicapped children and adults is the most deserving of our sympathy. As the Working Party pronounced (in paragraph 8.3, page 30) "There is also the fact that, for many of these persons, the link with family and friends has been broken and would be extremely difficult to re-establish".

Even when this particular group of the misplaced did return to their original neighbourhoods, a significant number were socially isolated. Deirdre Carroll, in her study of the fortunes of a section of people with a mild mental handicap after they had left the well known St. John of God centre at Blackrock, wrote:

"For many of these past pupils the opportunity to make friends in their own locality did not arise as they were away in school as boarders for most of the year. The friends they made at school were their only friends. Once they left school they lost contact with them"[2].

But many others did not return to their families or their extended families and neighbours from whom they had been plucked - fully funded by the State. The Working Party concluded that they must stay where they were. Moreover, the Working Party could not and did not give any guarantee that the practice of taking people with a mild mental handicap (or none at all) into residential care would cease. Arrangements were frequently made privately when neither the Department of Health nor the health board knew the identity of the person placed in the home or indeed the degree of disability. The Department might admonish and encourage, but no more than that. The arrangements which were set in place in the 1950s were sacrosanct. The capital grants had no strings attached and since

1974 the method of funding was by direct global grant from the Department to the main agencies who provided residential care. Allocations were not and are not based on the numbers of people being cared for or on their levels of handicap. The annual allocations were based solely on the previous year's outturn, on approvals to improve or expand the services, and on availability of finance generally. The working party did nothing to upset this delicate arrangement.

Death and The Passage of Time

Their approach to the people with mental handicap who were in the mental hospitals was not quite so benevolent. Thirty four per cent of all the moderately, severely or profoundly mentally handicapped were in the mental hospitals, but when it came to solutions for this group of mentally handicapped, the Department reached for its old ally - one which had served it well in the past. Death and the passage of time would eventually wipe out the numbers of mentally handicapped in the mental hospitals.

The Department no longer stood over the policy of admitting the adult mentally handicapped into the mental hospitals as a matter of course. In 1980 the policy was that no more mentally handicapped persons were to be admitted into mental hospitals (or 'psychiatric' hospitals, as they were now called). The policy was not always adhered to, but on the basis of the changed policy the working party was able to make some calculations for the future of the 2000 mentally handicapped in the mental hospitals. On page 24 of the report the Working Party, with the help of Irish Life, worked out how many would have survived by the year 1994. They set out their calculations in Table 7.4. Balancing one thing with another they expected that by 1994, no more than 1660 persons with a mental handicap would survive in the mental hospitals. Certainly the conditions in the mental hospitals in 1980 were not conducive to a long life.

"For the twenty years up to 1994", said the report, "the number should reduce by about 22% at least".

As for the 2000 people who were in need of residential care out in the community on waiting lists, the committee thought that the provision of extra places for this section "should be treated with caution". The real problem which the working party did not express, was that even if the Department did provide the extra places on the same terms as heretofore there was no guarantee that they would go to those most in need of them. And yet the Department and the policy makers doggedly stuck to a policy which was both ineffective and unjust. There was a quite noticeable increase in capital grants to the voluntary agencies in 1980.

Not Listening!!

In truth there was little pressure on the Department of Health to change its policy towards people with a mental disability. A motion which Dr. John O'Connell had put before the Dáil in 1977[3] and which called on the Minister for Health to "devise a system of differential grants for the mentally handicap which would take account of the different degrees of handicap", was ignored. In the same motion Dr. O'Connell urged that an approved points system be established to decide priorities for admission to residential and day centres for the handicapped. There is no evidence that the Department ever considered these suggestions for a minute despite Dr. O'Connell's strenuous efforts to put the true situation before the Dáil on that November day in 1977. In the course of putting the motion he said:

"These anomalies have resulted in 22.6 per cent of existing places being taken up by people who should not be there - cases of borderline or mild mental handicap. These are the cases that belong in the community and for whom adequate day care facilities should be provided.

"I shall elaborate a little further on this point. According to the census there are 8,652 places in residential homes of which 2,359 were taken up by borderline or mild cases, cases which those who compiled the census did not see fit to include in the final tabulation for the prevalence of mental handicap. Therefore we must ask how many of these borderline or mildly mentally handicapped persons belong in residential care and, if a substantial number can be excluded, how many actual places have we for the treatment of the moderate, severe and profound mentally handicapped who really need residential care".

The Minister's response in this debate sounds woefully inadequate today. Dr. O'Connell had emphasised the power of admittance and dismissal into residential care which the voluntary agencies held. The Minister, Mr. Haughey, was at pains to reassure the voluntary agencies. According to Mr. Haughey, parents and friends of the mentally handicapped were perfectly happy with things as they were. Moreover, none of the health board officers wished for any change. He went on to describe the system of admission:

"At present when a centre receives an application for admission either from a health board or direct from a family, the normal procedure is that the authorities of the centre will arrange for an assessment report. This assessment is usually carried out by an assessment team employed by the authorities of the centre. If on the basis of the assessment, authorities are satisfied that the patient is suitable for admission, his or her name is placed on a waiting list. Admissions are arranged as suitable vacancies occur. I understand that selections from the waiting lists are made on the basis of the greatest need........ I would not claim that in every instance the right decision is made".

A Council Not So 'Social'

As we have seen, when the Working Party came to make its report in 1980, one senses that they were not quite so happy with the system, but not unhappy enough to suggest any change.

In 1980 there was hardly anyone who thought there was anything odd about the way the State dealt with the mentally handicapped. Prestigious bodies like the National Economic and Social Council failed to see the connection between shortfalls in the mental handicap services for certain groups such as severely handicapped people who needed residential care, and the number of mildly handicapped who were occupying expensive places in the residential centres[4]. They were aware that places which the agencies intended for children were now being occupied by adults. They did not seem to know that shortly before this, as a matter of routine, adults in these centres were despatched to the mental hospitals. That is how many of them had got there in the first place and in 1980, thirty four per cent of all those in residential care were in the mental hospitals. The council thought it "highly unlikely" that they would ever leave.

It is not clear from the Council's publication *"Major Issues in Planning Services for Mentally Handicapped and Physically Handicapped Persons"* whether the authors had ever stood in a unit in a Psychiatric Hospital where mentally handicapped people spent their lives. There is a suspicion, however, that whoever briefed them on the characteristics of mentally handicapped residents in psychiatric hospitals may not have been a disinterested party. They base their reasons for the non-transfer of the mentally handicapped from the psychiatric hospitals on their age, their high incidence of mental illness, the length of time that they had been in the hospital and on their exclusion from society. The statistics which underlie their recommendations are not compelling, if one remembers the numbers of mentally handicapped people who were long-stay patients at the time.

The supposed incidence of a diagnosis of mental illness in the mentally handicapped was 45 per cent. This left 55 per cent who had no such diagnosis. If 55 per cent of the mentally handicapped had been in the psychiatric hospitals for longer than ten years, then 45 per cent had not been there that long. The fourth characteristic, that of social exclusion, which this prestigious council considered as imposing "considerable limitations on the possible options", is worth quoting :

"......30% of those in psychiatric hospitals were never visited or never went on holidays to relatives/friends compared to 13% of those in special residential centres".

Was it really a good reason to condemn them to continue to live out their lives in the mental hospitals because they never went on holiday? One might have thought that a council with the word "social" in its title would have been coming up with suggestions to end or alleviate their isolation. But the Council seemed to indicate that it was another reason for leaving the mentally handicapped where it found them. Certainly the average age of people with a mental handicap was much higher in the psychiatric hospitals than in the special residential centres. The reason for this was obvious. The special residential centres were running schools, seven of which were residential schools for mildly handicapped children. It is truly astonishing that in 1980 a Council called the National Economic and Social Council did not advert to the uneconomic aspects of residential schooling for mildly handicapped children, not to mention the disastrous effects socially. There might have been some excuse in the 1950s when special national schools were unusual but by 1980 they were quite commonplace. Any advice which might emerge from the Council was unlikely to upset old ways.

'Special' Arrangements

The relationship between the Department and the larger voluntary agencies had always been special but after the 1970 Health Act it positively flourished. When the Act was first passed it looked as if the Agencies might have to deal with the new Health Boards like everyone else. But this did not happen. Yet another special arrangement was put in place for the large voluntary agencies, on the spurious grounds that their existence predated the new Act. It was decided through a special derogation that the larger voluntary agencies were to be funded directly by the Department. It is doubtful if the Health Boards even knew of the extent of this funding or if the voluntary agencies thought that they had any right to know.

Under the new Act, the Health Boards did have certain ill-defined obligations towards the mentally handicapped, but they would have held that these obligations were discharged indirectly, by agreement with the mental handicap agencies who had already received their money from the Department of Health. The Health Board had little or no part in placing a person with a mental handicap with one of these agencies. Frequently it was an arrangement between the family of the person with the mental handicap and the mental handicap agency. There was no need for the Health Board to come into the matter at all. It would seem that the Department of Health was happy enough with this state of affairs. As far as the general public was concerned there were impressive centres coming on stream fairly regularly. The families of those unselected or dismissed from the voluntary agencies did not have a high profile.

In 1970 with the passing of the Health Act the psychiatric hospitals exchanged the old mental hospital boards for the new Health Boards. The new health boards continued to provide places in the psychiatric hospitals for those mentally handicapped whose case was desperate. The change-over was no help at all. The funding of the psychiatric hospitals was more constrained than ever. Even if the Health Boards wished to change the way in which the people in the Psychiatric Hospitals were treated, their ability to do so was extremely limited.

The 'Cinderella' Syndrome

Since 1970 the term "health service" had come to include a wide range of social services, income maintenance, and even some housing functions. When the health board met annually to decide how the money it had received from the Department of Health should be divided out between its many responsibilities, the old mental hospitals had little chance of attracting any funds which would enable change to take place. The money which of necessity had to be provided was grudged. The old buildings were uneconomic even when maintained at the disgraceful level of the 1980s and before. Serious inflation affected the costs of all public services in the late 1970s and 1980s and the mental hospitals, full of very dependent people, had increasingly high pay costs. The psychiatric hospitals did not even manage to hang on to the funding which they had.

In 1980 the Chief Executive Officer of the Southern Health Board, Mr. Denis Dudley, on March 26, wrote to the members of his board describing what "the difficult economic circumstances" would mean for the psychiatric hospitals:

"It will mean a reduction in spending on furniture, crockery, bedding, clothing, heating, lighting, medicines, medical appliances, x-ray, pathology, travelling expenses, stationery and telephones".

Our Lady's Hospital, Cork was one of the psychiatric hospitals in the Southern Health Board area and the Health Board had

had almost ten years to familiarise themselves with it. In 1980 Miss Helen Connolly wrote:

"Nurses in several hospitals report patients suffering from pressure sores and urine rashes...... Patients are expected to undertake much of the cleaning themselves and many of them are clearly incapable of such activity. Conditions are worst in Our Lady's Hospital, Cork where three quarters of the units have no full time cleaner".

There was no hope of establishing a new service in conditions like these, although brave attempts were made. The most noteworthy of these attempts was made at St. Ita's Portrane, Donabate, County Dublin.

Notes on Chapter Seven

1. Services for the Mentally Handicapped. Report of a Working Party. (Stationery Office 1980).
2. "Whatever Happened To Them". A study of post-school adjustment of past pupils of St Augustine's School, Blackrock, Co Dublin. Publishers: Hospitaller Order of St. John of God.
3. Parliamentary Debates, Dáil Éireann 1977.
4. "Major Issues in Planning Services for Mentally and Physically Handicapped Persons" (National Economic and Social Council). Published by the Stationery Office.

8

SUFFERING IN SILENCE

St. Ita's Hospital had started out its long life as 'Portrane Lunatic Asylum', built in the last years of the last century to relieve overcrowding at the other much older lunatic asylum at Grangegorman. The new Asylum was a vast undertaking. It was planned to accommodate some 1200 patients. It consisted of a large central block containing administrative offices, boardroom, kitchen, central dining hall and some accommodation for nurses and attendants. On each side of this central block were the patients' accommodation, four male blocks and four females with day rooms and dormitories for 600 patients on either side as well as a laundry, bakery, boiler-house, bathrooms, and workshops. The symmetry was preserved by the erection of a Catholic chapel and a Protestant chapel, one on either side of the central block. The whole edifice was connected internally by a network of corridors extending to more than half a mile long. Sited on the sea coast and commanding magnificent views it was a most impressive edifice. In the years since it had been built it changed little except its name. In 1925 it became known as 'Portrane Mental Hospital'. In 1958 it shared in the general sanctification of the fifties and was re-named St. Ita's.

Close to the hospital were the wooden huts which had been used by the workmen who had built the hospital. In 1903 it had been decided by the joint committee which ran the hospital that they would retain these wooden buildings in case they were ever needed again. By 1904 one of the wooden buildings had been put to use again. All six were in use when Dr. Ivor Browne's plan was adopted in 1966.

A Herculean Task

On the 4th July, 1968[1], in response to the concern expressed by Dr. John O'Connell about the "considerable" numbers of mentally handicapped people in St. Brendan's Hospital, Grangegorman, the Minister for Health announced the imminent appointment of a medical director. His function would be to co-ordinate and direct the services for the mentally handicapped at St. Ita's, Portrane, where the mentally handicapped already living there were to be joined by the adult mentally handicapped from St. Brendan's, in accordance with Dr. Ivor Browne's plan. It took eight years before the promised Director of Mental Handicap was appointed. In 1976, Dr.Vincent Moloney was appointed to St Ita's, Portrane as medical director for mental handicap. Two years earlier Mr. Ted Keyes had been appointed Programme Manager for the special hospitals by the Eastern Health Board.

These two men were expected to perform miracles. The task which faced them was Herculean. Mr Keyes was expected to straighten out the largest and possibly the most neglected hospital in the country. Dr. Moloney was expected to graft on a service for the mentally handicapped in a hospital whose only claim to suitability was that, of all the psychiatric hospitals in the country it had the largest population of mentally handicapped. Despite its size it was also overcrowded.

Sixteen years before, in June 1960, Male and Female Wards 1 and 2 at St.Ita's Hospital were subdivided. Some idea of what was meant by overcrowding can be inferred from an extract from a letter written by the Dublin Health Authority on the 14th September, 1962 to the Department of Health[2]. Before the subdivision Male 1 unit contained 160 men, and Male 2 unit accommodated 143. After the subdivision the numbers in Male 1 had reduced to 101. The newly created unit, Male 1A, held 102 men and in Male 2 unit the number of men was brought down to 95.

On the female side, before the subdivision Female Unit 1 accommodated 153 women, whilst Female Unit 2 held 128. After subdivision the figures stood at: Female 1—88 women, Female 1A—88 women, and Female 2—86 women.

In 1962 the numbers of mentally handicapped could not be known with certainty because the mentally ill and the mentally handicapped - to their mutual discomfort - shared the same wards. It was estimated that there were about 550 people with a mental handicap at the hospital. About the same number of mentally ill patients were in the care of St. Ita's, Portrane.

Low Staff Morale

The conditions of the wards and the patients were not any worse in Portrane than in many other psychiatric hospitals, but it was not alone the physical structure of the hospital which had been totally neglected in Portrane. Far more serious was the effect that this neglect had on some of the nurses. Many were cynical in the extreme. They had been listening for years to talk of new mental health services and the threat of hospital closure. All round them they had the evidence of their own eyes of the marked reluctance to spend any thing but the barest minimum on maintenance or repairs.

Theoretically the Resident Medical Superintendent was responsible for the hospital but the effectiveness of his authority depended on a hierarchy of command which had long since broken down. The days had gone when a junior nurse could be checked for gossiping on the job and have his time off docked. It would have taken a small police force to monitor the hospital which was bigger than most Irish villages. In 1959 Dr. Dolphin had said at a Departmental meeting[3] that "there was no denying the fact that the hospitals at Cork and Grangegorman were much too big for any one man to be able to exercise proper supervision over them and he was wondering whether an attempt shouldn't be made at this stage to lay down a maximum size for mental institutions".

But the Assistant Secretary who presided at this meeting told Dr. Dolphin and the rest of the meeting that "There were no large sums of money available for new buildings.....we would have to put up with what we had for the present and make the most of them". Several years later, everyone in Portrane, including the R.M.S., was still struggling with the harrowing conditions in which their patients were kept. No-one could be indifferent to the suffering of patients in overcrowded day rooms. An example of a common dilemma which a Resident Medical Superintendent faced was one told me in a letter by the widow of an R.M.S[4]. She wrote that, some years before, he had been successful in establishing an occupational therapy unit for a group of patients. This had taken a long time and a great deal of effort. "He felt, rightly it seems, that to wait for heating to be installed would be to wait for a long time. He used to worry on cold days about whether the patients should be allowed to continue working or stopped, which might upset them more for they loved the work". These were the kind of pitiful decisions which faced anyone who wished to bring about the smallest improvement.

Pioneering Work

It is against this background that we must view the assignment given to Dr.Moloney in 1976. His task was to graft on a service specifically geared to the needs of the mentally handicapped at first in the hospital, and eventually, as he was given every reason to expect, at Loughlinstown on the south side of Dublin. It was there that the Eastern Health Board proposed to build a large village-type complex modelled on the villages which had already been built for the Voluntary Agencies.

Dr. Moloney's approach was to build up a team of nurses who would be interested in specialising in mental handicap and, with their co-operation, to establish a few therapies in the disused farmyard, which had been ear-marked for the purpose by Dr. Ivor Browne ten years before. Of necessity the therapies were woefully sketchy with an air of impermanence about them. I don't know if Dr. Moloney had looked for exchequer funding for the very important pioneering work which he had undertaken. If he did, there is no evidence that he ever got it.

Without funding it is very difficult to establish any service. But Dr. Moloney tried everything. He founded St. Joseph's Association for the Mentally Handicapped, Portrane, an association for the parents and friends. The association has been consistently active for more than twenty two years. His first aim was to improve the image of Portrane. This was very difficult in the light of the reality which was Portrane. A Summer garden party was held in the grounds of one of the staff houses, well away from the unit. It was attended by President Hillery's wife, Dr. Maeve Hillery. An empty building in the farmyard was converted into a makeshift theatre and a Christmas concert was put on by the new little group of mental handicap staff and their more able residents. A Christmas raffle was arranged and the firm from which the hospital bought most of its supplies provided a bicycle as first prize. The National Indoor Games were also established at Portrane by Dr. Moloney's team.

A Shocking Discovery

And so it might have gone on if the association which Dr. Moloney had founded had not found out about the kind of conditions which the adult mentally handicapped had to endure as long-stay patients at St. Ita's. From the day in February 1978 when one of the parents accompanied by two "outside" parents[5] were given permission to visit the "huts" as well as certain other wards where mentally handicapped were accommodated, the whole character of the association changed. In a state of profound shock at what they saw they lobbied everyone they could, including the board which ran the hospital. They were able to persuade the members of the Eastern Health Board to grant them a semi-official status as a visiting committee with permission to visit any part of the hospital where the mentally handicapped were accommodated.

From that time on the visiting committee has, on a regular basis, visited different parts of the hospital where mentally handicapped people were accommodated. The association sent written reports of these visits to the Inspector of Mental Hospitals. In view of what has come to light since about the Inspector and his reports, I am not sure that he read them. However they were regularly acknowledged by one of the Departmental officials.

The association almost lost interest in Dr. Moloney's plans to establish the bare bones of a service for the mentally handicapped, in its efforts to force the authorities to get rid of the more obscene features of accommodation in Portrane, in particular the huts already described. Incidentally, the association was amazed that the statutory visiting committee of the Eastern Health Board had no idea that the huts were occupied. At the time this was almost unbelievable but the account of the inspection of Clonmel hospital in 1959 and the emphasis which the Departmental conference placed on keeping it secret, makes the protestations of those members much more credible.

95

Staff Opposition

The Association worked desperately hard in those early days of its existence but people who were not parents of anyone in Portrane worked even harder. Mrs Clare Kelly's contribution was particularly important. She was secretary of the association at a vital time and her courage and intelligence were an inspiration.

Efforts to establish the service for the mentally handicapped continued at Portrane in the face of some opposition from a section of the nursing staff. The reasons for this opposition had little to do with any views on modern methods of caring for the mentally handicapped or any marked lack of adaptability in the nursing force. It had far more to do with the conditions endured by psychiatric nurses down the years.

Psychiatric nurses had been treated abominably, particularly in large neglected hospitals like Portrane. (As late as 1962 the Dublin Health Authority was still discussing the *installation* of bathrooms in staff houses on the grounds of St. Ita's.) Psychiatric nurses knew that the job they did was undervalued by society. They were seldom treated with the respect that they deserved - not even by the Departmental officials whose attitude was different when they visited a mental hospital to that displayed when they attended the beautiful villages which they had helped to establish for the voluntary bodies. It is not easy to look after overcrowded wards, with difficult patients, many of them incontinent, but to be regarded as almost part of the problem by the authorities must have been almost intolerable.

As is the nature of these things the opposition coalesced around the structuring of the working day, the integration of male and female staff and promotion procedures. All of these were important to the staff, especially the time-honoured practice of working one day on and one day off.

But the real issue was hardly a routine Trade Union matter. This was the question of who really ran Portrane hospital. The issue came to the fore in 1979 in the matter of a new block known as the 72-bed unit. There is no doubt that the new unit - the first for a long time - was intended from the beginning for the mentally handicapped. The nurses disputed this and insisted

96

that the new unit should be given over to the care of the psycho-geriatric. They threatened to block the opening of the unit unless they got their way. As well as real fear for the future of their jobs and their conditions, many of the nurses genuinely could not see why the mentally handicapped should be singled out for special treatment. No doubt the patients in the old geriatric wards were in equal need of new quarters. Very few believed at the time that the motives of the nurses were totally altruistic.

The opening of the 72-bed unit became the subject of negotiations between the nurses and the Department of Health. Dr. Joseph Robins, the principal officer in the section of the Department responsible for mental services tried hard to negotiate the opening of the new unit for the mentally handicapped but his efforts were treated with derision. Blame for the years of neglect and disrespect was heaped on the unfortunate civil servant. He complained bitterly of the way he was treated in his attempts to negotiate some compromise in the deadlocked situation. He stuck it as long as he could and then reported to his Minister, Mr. Charles Haughey. Mr. Haughey decided to intervene personally.

Political Intervention

There is no reason to suspect that Mr. Haughey's personal intervention was not due to his concern for the mentally disabled in Portrane, but there was also the uniquely important position politically of the hospital in the constituency of Dublin North. Mental hospitals everywhere with their large staffs and their families were important electorally but Portrane was special. Portrane is situated in splendid isolation at the end of a promontory and its staff of nurses were not recruited locally. The nature of their job and their social isolation gave them a cohesiveness which was not usual. In addition, St. Ita's, Portrane, had their own T.D., Mr. Paddy Burke, who was elected in the mid 40s. Mr Paddy Burke had worked all his life at Portrane before he was elected. When he retired as T.D. he was succeeded by his son Mr. Raphael Burke. Both were members of the Fianna Fáil party. Naturally the party had come to rely on a consistently high vote at Portrane. Mr Raphael Burke had been thoroughly briefed on the nurses' point of view in relation to the new unit. When the Minister himself came out to the hospital in July of 1979 the outcome was a foregone conclusion. The nurses won.

The impact of this decision on the possibility of reforming the management at St. Ita's can only be guessed at. Certainly it did not make Mr. Keyes's position any easier. As for Dr. Moloney, he began to fix his sights more and more firmly on the prospect of the new facility at Loughlinstown[6]. Any enthusiasm there had been for establishing a dedicated and modern service at St. Ita's for the mentally handicapped evaporated. When the Eastern Health Board managed to lease part of a large seminary from the Augustinian Fathers in 1980 the attention of Dr. Moloney and his immediate team switched to Ballyboden and away somewhat from St. Ita's.

But Mr. Haughey's visit to Portrane had much more significant long-term effects which were on the whole beneficial. On his visit to Portrane the Minister could not fail to notice the more extraordinary features of the place. At a meeting with St. Joseph's Association soon after his visit, he described the hospital as an "independent republic". He proceeded to take some practical steps towards re-integrating it into the rest of the country. Soon after Mr. Haughey's visit to Portrane, one of the most effective civil servants of the Department practically took up residence at the hospital. In addition, in 1980 the Minister for Health lent his psychiatric nursing adviser to the Eastern Health Board to review nursing services at St. Ita's Hospital at Portrane. A programme for the refurbishment of the old Chronic Block was completed in the early 1980ís and the patients were finally moved out of the notorious huts in 1982.

A 'Running Sore'

The newly re-furbished units were an enormous improvement on the old festering eye-sores, but the old mental hospital lay-outs survived. Mentally handicapped people were still condemned to hour after hour in the large day rooms. They slept at night in the long dormitories. The numbers were still high. Long ago in 1959, on one of their exploratory visits to the continent Dr. Ramsay and

Mr. Darby, the Principal officer in the relevant section in the Department, had noticed that the largest dormitory in the largest units had no more than four beds[7]. Even in 1959 some hospitals in this country had managed to break down their large ward units, for example St. Dympna's at Carlow. Carlow was the exception. Not so the majority, including St. Ita's Hospital, Portrane.

Although the mentally handicapped were at last separated from the mentally ill, the prospect of establishing suitable care for them seemed to recede ever further into the distance. The physical layout of the hospital, the inadequate staffing levels, the increasing demands on the skills of this staff, exacerbated by the practice of "dumping" highly dependent and behaviourally disturbed mentally handicapped people into St. Ita's made for an extremely worrying situation. The attention of St. Joseph's Association became more and more focused on the necessity of eradicating the worst features of ward care with insufficient numbers of staff. They had valid grounds for disquiet as was to emerge a few years later when the nursing adviser made his report. The report - *"Report on a Nursing Survey at St. Ita's Hospital, Portrane, Donabate, County Dublin"*[8], confirmed the members' worst fears. What the nursing adviser found was an utterly neglected hospital long before identified as impossible to manage because of its size.

One of the terms of reference of the report was the identification of problems in the delivery of nursing services at Portrane. In the course of his review he confirmed what had been emerging in the reports of the visiting committee established by the Association. Exactly the same ward which the nursing adviser had described as "inhuman" and "a running sore", was the one which had worried the Association for some time. On the matter of the hygiene of the patients generally the nursing adviser wrote:

"<u>Hygiene of Patients</u>: To us this is a major scandal that so many patients are so dirty in appearance and a smell from their clothes that is all too indicative of nursing neglect. In this area much depends on the quality of your charge nurse."
And on

"Maintenance and Ward Conditions: ......The conditions and facilities are indeed shocking and a national disgrace, especially when compared with the standards of hygiene, cleanliness and facilities that prevail in general hospitals, and with the level of care provided by voluntary and religious bodies. St. Ita's Hospital is like a "cancer" when we make such comparisons."

The report referred to the resignation of a Matron who had resigned within months of her appointment some years before. Her resignation so soon after her appointment marked the apotheosis of the power of the small group of male nurses "who really ran Portrane". The nursing adviser wrote:

"Many of the staff are convinced that (the Matron) was diplomatically moved to her present position. This they believe was a great loss".

Inevitably the adviser found scandals in the hospital, but the wonder was that there were not many more. In Chapter 4 the report states:

"When we have witnessed at close range the conditions in which so many nurses and others have to carry out their daily work for patients - we can only come to one conclusion - their dedication is superb...."

The nursing adviser's last recommendation in a long list of recommendations reads as follows:

"We recommend a Public Inquiry. Is it really the only solution? Would it be counter productive ?

"Adverse publicity for a mental hospital so often sets in motion a cycle of demoralisation which is virtually impossible to stop. Yet we have heard and seen so much that is ugly during our survey - a public inquiry seems to be the last resort to raise standards from a nursing, administrative and medical point of view. We would all like to see this unfortunate hospital transformed for the sake of staff and patients".

Needless to say there never was a public inquiry. Just like the report on the mental hospital in Clonmel in the last days of 1958, it was all kept very quiet.

Worried Parents

The minute book, in which the monthly meetings of St. Joseph's Association were scrupulously recorded at this time, makes grim reading. It is full of worries and complaints. Parents complained about the state of clothing of their children on visits home. There were at least two incidents of children being burned on radiators. There were unexplained bruises and cuts, sometimes infected. There was the lack of therapy except for the very few. The minutes of January 14th 1980 record that:

"There was no proper laundry service and the condition of the patients' clothes was discussed. Tiles have lifted from the floor in 7 East and are dangerous. A patient was seen to trip and hit his face. Heat and light were off in therapy unit from 9 a.m. till 1 p.m. It only took the electrician five minutes to make the necessary repair. There has been a refusal to install fluorescent lighting and power points where necessary".

The reports of the visiting committee often provoked very fraught meetings. The meeting on the 18th March 1981 was one of these. This meeting had been specially called at the request of parents

"Because of their deep concern for their children in the conditions described of the 11th February 1981, it was felt that there is a complete fall down where maintenance is concerned. Other matters discussed were the scandal and danger of raw sewage on toilet floors, inadequate staffing, inadequate and dirty bedclothes, inadequate heating and laundry. It was the unanimous decision of the parents of the mentally handicapped in St. Ita's that they wanted their children out. They demanded that they be given conditions and care appropriate to their needs, as is given to the mentally handicapped in other residential centres".

Over-sedation

But dominating all were the constant complaints about over-sedation. Almost every parent at the meetings complained. They complained that their children were like zombies. A father described how, when his boy came home for the week-end, he had to be carried into the house. Another lay on the hall floor fast asleep. Parents threatened to take their over-sedated children to Jervis St. to be treated for overdose. But whether parents complained to the staff who worked at the units or whether they wrote to the medical authorities, all complaints on the over-sedation of their children were ignored.

Regular complaints were made to the Department of Health but these were also ignored. The situation came to a head in 1983 when one of the patients was so over-sedated that he fell into a coma and had to be removed into intensive care at the Richmond Hospital. There was no Sworn Inquiry and no satisfactory explanation was ever given. Curiously, Dr. Dolphin who had retired in June 1979, made a brief contribution. Mr. David Andrews had written to the Inspector of Mental Hospitals regarding the incident, and his letter was answered by Dr. Dolphin. Mr. Andrews passed on the letter to the Association. That was the first and last time that members of the Association ever saw Dr. Dolphin's signature.

The whole question of complaints and how they were dealt with came up for discussion at the meeting following this incident when a report was made on a meeting held at Ballyboden regarding injuries to patients and the over-sedation of patients. The meeting was attended by Dr. Moloney and Mr. Keyes, as well as the Chairman and Secretary of the Association. The secretary had written a list of all complaints as recorded in the minutes and sent them by registered post to Mr. Keyes. A copy was sent to Dr. Campbell, the Inspector of Mental Hospitals, and he was understood to have visited the hospital. Over drugging did not feature so strongly in the minutes of subsequent meetings.

Slow Progress

In February 1982 at the height of a snow blizzard the hospital was without electricity for a period of 31 hours. The generator at the hospital was inadequate and so there was no heat or light at the hospital. It is understood that the nurses put all the patients to bed and watched over them in their overcoats using torches for light. Not a word of this ever reached the papers, although up to a thousand patients were involved. The papers were full of news of the blizzard and were particularly concerned about the plight of the sheep in the Wicklow hills. Only then was the faulty generator replaced.

It was in this manner that almost any progress in Portrane was achieved. After each crisis, usually involving some exposure in the media, the particular aspect of abuse would be addressed. This is a slow way to improve a service. It was particularly slow in Portrane as the policy of emptying the hospitals, including St. Ita's, Portrane, gathered momentum. No effort was made to break up the over-large units. The minimum was spent on hospital maintenance. There was no attempt made to extend therapies to cover a larger number of mentally handicapped. Large numbers of people with a mental handicap never left the dreary day rooms except to go to bed, especially if the weather was bad. As the Eastern Health Board put it in their report on the services at St. Ita's Hospital :

"Since 1980 we have had an ongoing policy of transferring the less dependent residents from St. Ita's. However, the vacated places were immediately filled by highly dependent patients, mainly disturbed".

In spite of the scandal of the huts and in spite of all the hopes of establishing a service at St. Ita's, Portrane, the hospital had retained its function as a dumping ground for the rejected people from the other services. As the Eastern Health Board put it:

"This has been largely to do with the fact that the emphasis has been on devoting the limited resources available to the needs of the less disturbed mentally handicapped......... Most mentally handicapped persons with seriously disturbed behaviour invariably end up being admitted to St. Ita's and become long-stay residents".

The unacknowledged price of a selective and prestigious residential service in the Eastern Health Board area was Portrane.

Notes on Chapter 8

1. Parliamentary Debates, Dáil Éireann Questions. July 4, 1968.
2. Letter from J.F. Reynolds to E. Ó Caoimh, Chief Executive Officer, Dublin Health Authority. Dated 14th September, 1962.
3. Improvements in District Mental Hospitals, 1959. Department of Health files L107/18. National Archives.
4. Letter in possession of the writer.
5. Mr. Pat Campbell and Mrs. Clare Kelly, both members of the St. John of God Joint Parents Association accompanied Mrs Annie Ryan who was a member of St. Joseph's Association for the Mentally Handicapped, Portrane, on the first visit to certain wards in St. Ita's.
6. The Eastern Health Board had plans to build a special village type complex at Loughlinstown, intended to alleviate the problems of the mentally handicapped in the area. It was never built.
7. Meeting on 22nd October, 1959. National Archives. Department of Health files L107/18.

9

DASHING OF DREAMS

When Barry Desmond became Minister for Health in 1982 it was rumoured that the voluntary bodies in the mental handicap field were somewhat anxious. Mr. Desmond had been heard to comment rather critically on certain aspects of the voluntary bodies which he regarded as undesirable. He mentioned features such as "empire building" which he thought certain agencies engaged in to the detriment of the mentally handicapped generally. The voluntary agencies had no need to worry. Despite the hard times which were beginning to affect all branches of the health service in the 1980s, the favoured position of the voluntary bodies remained untouched.

A Health Board Venture

Nothing showed this better than the axing of a long cherished Eastern Health Board project - the development of a village type facility for the mentally handicapped at Loughlinstown in south County Dublin.

Loughlinstown had featured for years in the answers given to Dáil questions about shortfalls in residential places for the mentally handicapped. Mr. Desmond himself had asked about it by name in October 1976 at the same time as he inquired about Cheeverstown, a voluntary agency project. Loughlinstown was unusual in that it was to be a health board venture.

Health boards varied in their attitude to entering directly into the provision of residential services specifically for the mentally handicapped. The Western Health Board was unique amongst health boards in successfully establishing a residential centre at Swinford, County Mayo. The South Eastern Health Board had plans for building a facility for 200 mentally handicapped people at Enniscorthy, but like Loughlinstown it was never built.

Throughout the late 60s when the pressure for residential places was very great, over and over again the Minister for

Health and his department was asked to involve local authorities. The Minister resisted and in answer to the unceasing pressure at question time in the Dáil, the Minister or a spokesman would recite a list of new ventures like a mantra[1]. The health boards were not encouraged to participate and, generally speaking, had no wish to do so. No Health Board was more reluctant than the Eastern Health Board, particularly after 1974 when the voluntary agencies in their area began to be funded directly by the Department of Health by means of a global grant. The most important voluntary agencies were located in Dublin within lobbying distance of the nation's purse strings. The Health Boards had no wish to compete. But when the Department of Health and the Minister appointed a Director of Mental Handicap in that Health Board area, for the first time a change seemed possible. The intervention of the Minister in 1979, in the 72-bed unit fiasco at Portrane, showed the board where they fitted into things.

The Fall of the Ministerial Axe

The second blow was Loughlinstown, which was axed long before its demise was announced. The Department and its experts, particularly psychologists, began to profess a fervent conversion to the idea of community care and the suspicion grew that this might be the preliminary step in the abandonment of the Loughlinstown project. Nobody was quite clear on what was meant by community care but whatever was meant Loughlinstown was not it. The formal announcement was made by Mr. Barry Desmond in 1985. With the announcement went any chance of breaking up the huge concentration of mentally handicapped at Portrane. Not only would there be no Loughlinstown for some of them to move to, but because Loughlinstown was not built, the continuous replenishment of the numbers must continue. There was nowhere else for the non selected and the rejects to go.

The Loughlinstown project was to have provided places for 210 residents and 120 day attenders. It was to accommodate 160 residents in two storey structures, 40 in single storey chalets and the remaining ten places were intended as infirmary or crisis intervention places. The Health Board had thrown a little party for the launch of the plans, probably intended as an arm-twisting exercise. It was a lovely dream while it lasted especially for anyone familiar with Portrane.

'Coating' the Pill

In 1985 the Department of Health had to make cut-backs. At the same time the concept of community care was becoming increasingly accepted, particularly by psychologists. The Minister's speech[2] on the occasion of the axing of the Loughlinstown project was a masterly example of the hi-jacking of a concept of care in order to make an unpopular cutback more palatable. The idea of a large scale facility like Loughlinstown was represented as being now out of date and backward. Mentally handicapped people could now live in ordinary "residential settings", he told the assembled people. The mental handicap services had improved so much that the potential of the mentally handicapped had increased. Parents and friends and the community at large had also improved, he thought. They were now much better than they used to be - "more involved and more concerned". The ideal now was home care. He conceded that it was true that people who were severely or profoundly handicapped would continue to need residential care. But, he pointed out, there were fewer of these than there used to be. The 1981 census had shown that there were 50 per cent fewer with profound mental handicap and 20 per cent fewer with a severe mental handicap. The Minister did not advert to the cautionary qualification expressed in the Census Report that the "upward shift in the level of ability among the lower categories.... could be due simply to a change in the method of classification".

If the numbers of people with a severe or profound level of handicap had reduced to the point where Loughlinstown was no longer needed, the third objective for which the Loughlinstown project was designed still remained. The proposed building of Loughlinstown had been meant to assist in the "implementation of the Board's decision of long standing that the use of certain buildings at St.Ita's Hospital, Portrane for the accommodation of mentally handicapped patients should be discontinued with all possible speed and a centre of more manageable size established there". The axing of Loughlinstown threw that decision out the window.

We shall never know if Loughlinstown would have "re-create(d) the institutional environment which detracted from the services provided at St. Ita's" which worried the Minister so much. There was a lot more wrong with the service at St.Ita's besides the "institutional setting" which the Minister must have known about. The Minister's decision ensured that the mentally handicapped people who were there would remain there. That, after all, was the plan set out by the Department's policy document of 1980, as set out in the Working Party's report.

Hard To Swallow

It was hard for the parents and friends of the mentally handicapped in Portrane to relinquish any hope of ever acquiring a facility like Loughlinstown and it was difficult for them to listen to this news, but when the Minister went on with astonishing effrontery to tell the assembled officials and service providers what he intended to do with the capital saved it was almost unbearable. As far as we could gather from the rest of the address, we were meant to believe that Fashion had killed the Loughlinstown project. It had become an outdated concept. But the project just up the road run by the St. John of God Brothers at Dunmore House was bang up to date! The Brothers had convinced the Minister:

"I have been speaking in recent weeks to representatives of the Order", said the Minister. The Brothers wished to move a number of residents off the campus out of Dunbeg House into ordinary houses in the locality. And this is where some of the capital which might have been spent on Loughlinstown was going.

"I intend to provide immediate capital resources to facilitate the transfer. These developments are well advanced and I will be asking senior officers of my department to expand on the details of the Dunmore development proposal with your officers at Health Board level", said the Minister.

Pity the poor Health Board officials. They had come to hear

about the Loughlinstown project on which they had worked for seven years only to be told about the progressive non-statutory service provider in the neighbourhood who, the Minister decided, had first claim on any money that was going. When Mr. Desmond had been a member of the opposition he had a sound grasp of the basically flawed policy on mental handicap. It is more than likely that he understood it even better as a Minister. What every Minister for Health has understood about the services for the mentally handicapped since the 1950s is that when it comes to cutbacks it is easier to cut back on the weakest. When it came to a choice between the patients in Portrane and the St. John of God services there was no contest.

A Matter of Influence

On the 30th November 1983, Dr. McCarthy T.D. asked Mr Desmond, the Minister for Health, a significant question: "Why is it", he asked, "in this day and age that we still must have people who are physically disabled in psychiatric hospitals?" He might have asked why any one, whether physically or mentally disabled, should have to endure the conditions which existed in so many of these hospitals. But the answer that Mr. Desmond gave is even more interesting. The Minister replied:

"I suppose that the short answer to that is that they do not have the same political influence as the Deputy and I do".

A throw-away answer, I have no doubt, but nevertheless a disgraceful one. It expressed an acquiescence which was not confined to the Minister or his party.

But the Minister hadn't got it quite right. The truth was that the power to decide who should get which service, was not in the hands of the politicians. Ministers and T.D.s were not as important as they might think in ensuring that the people who needed the services most were the people who got them. Choices were made and continue to be made in the interests of those groups able to exercise most influence on how the resources available were allocated. They did not include politicians, mainly because they were neither interested nor informed in the fair allocation of state funding for this section of the population. The physically disabled, as a group, had little influence. Any group of long-stay patients in a psychiatric hospital had no influence. The people with influence in the field of disability were not the disabled themselves, whether inside or outside a psychiatric hospital. Not even well placed families were particularly influential. The people who ran the non- statutory services which in the main were established with state capital and kept going with annual grants from the exchequer, were the people who made the decisions. They were an effective lobby and it is possible that the politicians rather enjoyed the system, so that they could intervene and use their "influence" to bend things a little in favour óf a constituent. It certainly kept the constituency clinics full and probably did them no harm when the next election came round.

Priorities or Luck?

There is no denying that in 1985 when the Minister was making his address to the members of the Eastern Health Board[3] that the capital resources available were scarcer than usual but it is in times of scarcity that the priorities become really clear. The relocation of some mentally handicapped people from a perfectly acceptable facility to ordinary houses in the locality ranked ahead of the needs of people in Portrane or people without a service at all, for no other reason than the St. John of God Brothers had decided that that was the way to go. The Department had no function except to fund it and to put a good gloss on it. It was a pattern that was to become familiar.

The axing of the Enniscorthy project had even more serious implications for the South Eastern Health Board area. In 1975 the South Eastern Health Board appointed a Regional Mental Handicap Committee and in 1979 the Board asked this committee to examine generally the services for the mentally handicapped in the South Eastern Health Board area. The Committee carried out a survey, confining it to the moderately, severely and profoundly handicapped. They came to the conclusion that many of the more severely and profoundly mentally handicapped needed a residential setting with a wide range of accessible staff and facilities. More importantly, they concluded that any future residential development should form the nucleus of and a resource centre for the needs of a developing community service.

The categories for which the Committee intended the proposed project included people with a mental handicap who also had another handicapping condition such as autism, emotional disturbance or epilepsy. People in the Health Board's area who were under the age of twenty five and living at psychiatric hospitals, could be relocated at this new village-type centre. "Each unit of residential accommodation should be of domestic scale and reflect a 'family home' atmosphere".

But Enniscorthy went the way of Loughlinstown. The loss to the people of the South Eastern Health Board area has never been made up. The only purpose-built project initiated and planned by a Health Board for people with a mental handicap which succeeded in being built was the one at Swinford, County Mayo. It is no coincidence that it is also the Health Board area which has been the most successful in reducing the numbers of mentally handicapped persons living in Psychiatric Hospitals.

It could be said that both the Loughlinstown and the Enniscorthy projects were simply unlucky. They had missed the period of expansion enjoyed by the voluntary bodies in the sixties, seventies and the early years of the 1980s. There had been years before when cut-backs bit into plans for new hospitals and projects, notably in 1957. In that year project after project was axed or deferred. A significant exception was made in the case of Cregg House in County Sligo because of "promises made".

'Energetic' Lobbying

The truth is that projects like Loughlinstown needed both influential backing and energetic lobbying if they were to stand a chance. The Eastern Health Board had neither. Health Boards rarely had. The contrast between the fate of Loughlinstown and that of Cheeverstown is a case in point.

If the capital funding of projects depended on luck, then Cheeverstown was extremely lucky indeed. Cheeverstown was a project which used to be mentioned in the same breath as Loughlinstown. As we saw, the Minister himself had done so in 1976 when he asked about them both in the Dáil. It stands today on the road to Tallaght and the M50, and is fully operational. It provides residential services for 124 residents, in most enviable conditions. It provides 16 places in group homes outside the Cheeverstown campus. But the capital funding of projects does not depend on luck unless you count it as lucky to have prestigious sponsors.

The original Cheeverstown foundation, located at Templeogue on the outskirts of the city, was an old Dublin charity where the members of the board were drawn from the successful and relatively well-off members of society. It had been established in 1904 with the purpose of providing convalescent care for the sick children of the poor. Convalescent care was a real necessity in the early years of this century, particularly for the sick children of the crowded tenements in Dublin. As the century progressed the need for the service declined. Cheeverstown ceased to function as a Convalescent Home sometime in the early 1960s, leaving a fine old house and ten acres vacant. By this time St. Michael's House had a Board too, drawn from much the same section of society as Cheeverstown. They needed another centre for their rapidly expanding service. The Cheeverstown Board gave them the use of their property at Templeogue where they opened yet another day centre for mentally handicapped children. The two organisations grew close and the relationship was cemented by an exchange of board members - two from each board. This overlap of board membership had an important influence on the plans for the development of Cheeverstown. It was felt that better use could be made of the ten acres and the idea of a purpose built "village" for the mentally handicapped was floated. Dr. Barbara Stokes, Medical Director at St. Michael's House, was a key figure in the execution of the Cheeverstown plan. A well-known figure in mental handicap circles, she had made a wide study of different ways of providing care and accommodation for people with mental handicap, visiting not only the Scandinavian countries but going as far afield as Russia. The "Cheeverstown village" was to be her dream. The Minister for Health was lobbied and the advantage of a purpose built centre for the mentally handicapped in keeping with modern trends was quite attractive Eventually the Minister agreed and building began in 1980[4].

A Change in Funding

There was a long delay about the opening of Cheeverstown. As a large new facility the Board of Cheeverstown, which had close connections with St. Michael's House, the first large non-residential agency in the country, saw no reason why the new village should not be funded in the same manner as that agency and the other directly-funded voluntary bodies. But by now it was becoming clear to the Department of Health that the idiosyncratic method of funding voluntary agencies would have to come to a stop. There were other voluntary services throughout the country which might opt for the preferential treatment afforded by direct funding if Cheeverstown were given it. Cheeverstown must be made to agree to funding through the Health Board. The opening of Cheeverstown was delayed by at least two years but at last an agreement was hammered out. Cheeverstown would open on a phased basis with guaranteed funding more or less equal to that which they would have got if directly funded by the Department. The policy makers were beginning to see the necessity for change.

Notes On Chapter 9

1. From 1965 when the Commission of Inquiry on Mental Handicap made its report, the shortage of residential places in particular featured heavily in the Parliamentary Debates, Dáil Éireann, Questions.
2. Address by Barry Desmond T.D., Minister for Health and Social Welfare to members of the Eastern Health Board on Monday, 16th December, 1985.
3. N.A.M.H.I. papers.
4. Interview with Mr. Moloney, Chief Executive, Cheeverstown.

10

VALUE FOR MONEY

The trouble with change, particularly when the proposed rationalisation is not to one's advantage, is that no one wants to be the first. Cheeverstown hung out for funding comparable to the funding which the directly-funded agencies were receiving. There are only fourteen directly-funded agencies and there is no problem in finding out the funding for each agency. It is a matter of public record. Nevertheless, the Health Board was aghast at the kind of funding which Cheeverstown thought they should have. They had never spent anything like it on the mentally handicapped.

As always in these cases Cheeverstown held most of the cards, the trump card being the pressure for more places. In the end it was decided that Cheeverstown would not be directly funded by the Department of Health. It was the first large voluntary agency which was to be funded by the Health Board but to a standard acceptable to the Cheeverstown Board. It was an important point of principle for the Department and was essential if any further progress was ever to be made in the equitable allocation of resources to the mentally handicapped as distinct from their service providers. In addition Cheeverstown agreed to the transfer of 31 mentally handicapped residents from St.Ita's/St. Brendan's. According to the Eastern Health Board Cheeverstown, who had the choosing, selected the least dependent residents. It was no help at all to Portrane and, coming on top of the axing of Loughlinstown, helped to seal the fate of the mentally handicapped patients there.

Ongoing Anomalies

The payments by the state towards the services for mentally disabled people have never been consistent, even in the days when the voluntary bodies had been re-imbursed on a per capita basis. Back in 1966 a person with mental handicap in Stewarts Hospital had £9-10s paid weekly for his accommodation and care.

The St. John of God Brothers charged £7-7s weekly, whether in St. Augustine's boarding school for children with a mild or borderline handicap or in their other residential centres at Drumcar and Celbridge. Any one of the Brothers of Charity Homes cost less. Their weekly capitation fee worked out at £5-10s, whilst the Daughters of Charity were able to provide the service for £5-0s at any one of their five centres. The Sisters of Charity at Delvin and Moore Abbey cost a little more at £6. La Sagesse were almost bottom of the list at £4. Peamount, a relative newcomer to the field, received £5 weekly for each handicapped person and Cope, the only agency which had not received any capital funding up to this date, received £3-10s per week per person in their care.

That was in 1967. When the the Health Boards were established on the enactment of the 1970 Health Act, the voluntary agencies engaged in the delivery of services for the mentally handicapped were selected for direct funding by the Department of Health on very much the same terms as the voluntary hospitals. Allocations are made by means of a global grant to the directly-funded agencies on the basis of the previous year's outturn, the approvals to improve or expand services, and the availability of finance generally. There was little connection between the size of the grant and the numbers cared for, or the category of handicap or the degree of handicap. The grants are based on the previous year's outturn. The previous year was based in turn on the outturn of the year before that and so on. Additional monies have been added to that base sum according to "identified needs" about which the Department keeps itself informed "almost on a daily basis" (Dail Questions 17th October, 1995).

Between 1990 and 1995 the grants to homes for mentally handicapped persons directly funded by the Department of Health - fourteen in all - rose from £74,679 million in 1990 to £123,768 million in 1995. The global grant to one of the large agencies increased from £12.578 million in 1991 to £24.171 million in 1997. How this increase came about is hard to understand. The agency in question spends more than two thirds of the grant in the Eastern Health Board region. The number of residential places provided in that region by that particular agency has fallen from 606 in 1991 to 563 in 1997.

'Buying a Pig in a Poke'

The capital funding was equally eccentric and the criteria on which it was based were, to say the least, not well known - if there were any at all. Most of it reflected the desperate efforts of the Department of Health to buy a service for the mentally handicapped,again without specifying what category of handicap. The absence of any kind of regulatory legislation encouraged the development of a hit-or-miss service which was almost totally immune to criticism or even any kind of monitoring.

But even more important still was the reticence which surrounded the whole subject of mental disability and mental handicap. Certainly in the 1950s mental handicap was almost a taboo subject. Ordinary lay people knew very little about it. In this Ireland was no different from other countries. If a family member had a mental disability of any kind the family did not speak about it. When Joseph Kennedy, the father of John F. Kennedy, the President of the U.S.A., first spoke in public about his mentally handicapped daughter, he was considered very unusual.

The service providers were the experts and in Ireland, apart from Stewarts Hospital, there were no others except the religious orders. Religious Orders were held to be the most suitable not just because they could be relied on for their dedication, but even more significantly for their confidentiality. When the State decided to buy this service, the number of sellers was extremely limited. Moreover, it was a service more in the interests of the families of the mentally handicapped rather than the mentally handicapped themselves. The State, in the late 1950s and 1960s was in effect buying a pig in a poke and buying in a hurry.

Without any legislation, without any public debate either inside or outside the Oireachtas, the State handed over land and buildings to private agencies who, thirty years later are at perfect liberty to sell up and move - or move the money - out of the service or out of the country[1]. Horrible prospect though it might be, it is possible that Health Boards all over the country may have to buy again the service for the mentally handicapped which the Department of Health thought they had bought in the

1950s, 60s 70s and 80s (and the 90s?). The secrecy which surrounded these grants of land and capital meant that very few people knew that these agencies were not quite so dependent on fund raising as we were led to believe. Moreover, any questioning of financial endowments by the state was likely to be equated in the public mind with the dissolution of the monasteries in the sixteenth century. This made T.D.s in particular very careful.

The immediate effect of the capital contributions to the private agencies was to put these agencies in a more powerful position relative to the state whenever the State wished to change funding methods as in 1970, for example, on the passing of the new Health Act. This explains, at least partially, why these agencies retained their direct funding from the Department whilst other voluntary agencies, for example in the field of physical disability, had to go to their Health Board for their running costs. Whether - as the story went at the time - certain Provincials of certain Religious Orders threatened immediate emigration to New Zealand, taking their capital and facilities with them, is true or not, the point is that it would not have been necessary to articulate any threat, when one considers how much land and money had already been invested, not to mention the numbers of mentally handicapped people involved.

It is almost tasteless to mention the running costs of the mental hospitals in this context, considering what we know of the conditions in most of them. The costs at Youghal in or about the same time where only mentally handicapped people were accommodated and which therefore would be a closer basis for comparison, were £143-0s-5d per patient annually or a little less than £3 per week[2].

No Criteria

It is notoriously difficult for a Department of State to fund any branch of a health service equitably, the least important excuse being the scarcity of resources although without doubt it is the one most often cited as the excuse for quite grave injustices. It is not the scarcity of resources but their allocation that is the problem. If you want to know anyones's real values see how he/she spends his/her discretionary income. If someone professes to have a profound interest in the arts and at the same time spends all his discretionary income at the races then he ranks racing higher than the arts.

When it comes to the income of the State there are vast areas in every spending Department which are not discretionary and with the passage of time there are areas of spending which become so fixed that it is difficult to change them. An example of this might be the difficulty of dealing with the vested interests in maintaining a service which has lost its relevance. When people talk about the scarcity of resources as an excuse for shameful neglect what they are really saying is that their priorities do not include equitable spending. But whose priorities should decide the share-out of resources? And in this particular context whose priorities should decide the spending of that portion of the Health Budget available to services for people with a mental disability?

These services are all free at the point of delivery so the financial strength or otherwise of the consumer doesn't come into it. But to have a service vital for human dignity delivered on the basis of influence is, to say the least, unsavoury. We are all familiar with the unease we might feel with a health system which favoured the rich even when the rich paid for it themselves. We have not given sufficient thought to equality of access to services which are provided free of charge to everyone, particularly services for people with a disability whether physical or mental. No objective criterion such as the provision of basic human rights existed. It was - and is - the business of the legislature to ensure the existence of these criteria and then to arrange the provision of services according to those criteria, whether by contract with private agencies or directly through statutory agencies.

A Dream Come True

To illustrate what happens in our present system, consider the following situation which repeated, twenty years later, the basic method of capital funding used in the establishment of Cheeverstown:

A member of an agency - in this case a religious community - has a dream. The dream is an admirable one in itself. All she wants is the very best for the people in her care. She wants to establish an ideal service. The people in her care, although profoundly handicapped, will live in the very best of houses built of the very best materials. The houses will each have well appointed kitchens with cooker, microwave, dishwasher, liquidiser and food processor. The living areas will be provided with modern television, stereo and video equipment as well as teak china cabinets containing vases. She regards an attractive environment as important not just for its therapeutic effect on the residents but as an encouragement to relatives and friends to visit. Special chairs will be provided for some of the handicapped at a cost of £999 each. The bedrooms, three double and three single, will each be fitted with wash-hand basin, ordinary lights and dimmer lights with attractive fittings. Beds with orthopoedic mattresses, duvets and bedspreads will be provided. The windows throughout will be fitted with decorative curtains and tasseled blinds. All clothing worn by the mentally handicapped residents will be personal and marked and stored in separate compartments in the individual wardrobes which will be provided. Each person will be allocated £150 for the purchase of clothes and shoes. Underclothes will be provided from the stores. Twelve of these specially built bungalows will be built on the Campus near all the therapies which will include the use of a swimming pool, physiotherapy, the use of a multi-sensory room, a ball pool and beauty therapy. Frequent outings will be arranged like going out for a meal or going to a concert at the Point Depot.

This was the dream which the sister had - not for herself but for some ninety people with a mental handicap. So she wrote to the Secretary of the Department of Health outlining the elements of her dream. And lo! her dream became a reality. What wouldn't an ordinary Programme Manager in a statutory agency give for charisma such as this!

The building of the dream cost a lot of money and the costs of running the village type facility with its therapies is so expensive that we have never been told the amount. It might provide the explanation for the annual increase in the grant required by that same agency throughout the 1990s.

To criticise such an ideal facility for the care of some very severely mentally handicapped people is to sound mean minded and envious. This is not the point. What we should consider here is the best allocation of resources in the command of the Department of Health. Is it moral to attempt to fulfill the demands of the few whilst virtually no attempt is made to provide for the needs of a few others? What can be called needs? How do we define them? How do we rank them in order of priority so that the best use is made of the money available? I doubt if these considerations entered the head of the Secretary of the Department of Health. The temptation for the Department of Health was to put the money where one could see impressive results rather than spread it out in the interests of equity. There was not a single T.D. - and there were many - who attended the opening of that facility, who would have questioned the judgement of the Department.

Delivery on Grace and Favour

It is hard to believe that this method of allocating scarce resources to the needs of a publicly financed service should have taken place so recently. The message is quite clear to parents and service providers alike. The quality of life in so far as the state can ensure it, is delivered on the basis of grace and favour. It is an extraordinary way for the State to behave and has implications far beyond the field of disability.

The quasi religious reverence in which many voluntary agencies which were established by Religious Orders are held is a notable characteristic of social policy in Ireland. In recent years the attitude has become more critical. But the conviction that without the Religious Orders there would be no service for the mentally handicapped in Ireland is still strong. It is a belief held by parents of those mentally handicapped who enjoy the service. It is also widely held by the general public. The lives of saintly founders used to be told and retold so effectively as to become part of the common consciousness of the nation.

The intensive fund raising engaged in by many voluntary agencies encourages the belief that the Religious Orders are still providing the service out of their own resources with little or no help from the state. Add to this the attraction of practising "good works by proxy" which has always been a great temptation for Catholic laymen in positions of power, be they prince, politician, or civil servant, and it is easier to understand the blatant favouritism towards capital schemes planned, designed and submitted to the Department by the Religious Orders engaged in the mental handicap services. Superficially the thinking would appear to be that the heroic nuns and brothers of long ago, who dedicated their lives to the mentally handicapped with no hope of reward in this life, must now be compensated in some material way. The nuns and brothers of long ago are long since dead. So, one hopes, are most of the long-stay patients of mental hospitals like Clonmel or Ballinasloe. No one today would wish to deny the part the religious played in raising the standards of care for the mentally handicapped. What they achieved by raising these standards set valuable precedents for other voluntary organisations. It is certainly not their fault that those who were not lucky enough to be chosen have not yet been enabled to catch up just a little.

Departmental Inertia

But perhaps the explanation for inequitable distribution of funding is far simpler. I was once told by a Departmental official that large religious agencies (like the one who was able to charm the Secretary of the Department to such good effect) were the only agencies who were doing anything at all about mental handicap. This might very well be true but if the large directly-funded agencies were the only people doing anything about mental handicap services it was because they had been enabled to do so - on terms which the agencies themselves had decided. Nevertheless, it is certain that the Health Boards were not falling over themselves trying to establish services.

Even before the financial crisis which came to a head in the mid-eighties and which was the real explanation for the axing of the Loughlinstown and Enniscorthy projects, the Health Boards were not encouraged to enter into any adventurous schemes which would entail spending money. In effect their cheque books were taken from them, in the mid eighties. This situation has eased somewhat lately and it is now possible for Health Boards to initiate capital projects by paying half the capital cost from the sale of Health Board assets. The Department of Health would pay the other half. There are eight health boards and they have varying records, but not many of them come forward with new initiatives. It is not just a question of money. It is more often a question of sheer inertia. The kind of enthusiasm which starts new services and reforms old ones, is rarely to be found in the administrative offices of Health Boards, particularly if they are inundated already by other pressures. Sometimes it seems that their safest bet is to keep their heads down, eyes on their balance sheets and a glib explanation whenever the public want to know what is happening. The more figures they can put into these explanations the better. This approach has two merits: it either renders their critics speechless with rage or intimidates them. Either way the Health Board official stands a good chance of reaching pensionable age or of moving to another part of the service without actually changing anything of significance.

To be fair the health boards have less choice than one would think. Since the Health Boards were reined in during the 1980s the options open to health board members are either to spread the available resources more thinly over all the existing services, if they are to be able to scrape a bit for a new one, or to reduce the level of services in certain areas, for example in the mental hospitals. Whatever the explanation, plans and projects put forward by the statutory bodies rarely get off the ground. This is particularly hard on those professional people in the statutory services who work directly with the mentally disabled.

Need for Legislation

The absence of legislation in the 1950s, inevitably led to funding patterns which are with us to this day. They were cemented into the system by the arrangements for direct funding of the principal voluntary agencies subsequent to the 1970 Health Act. Legislation might have provided a rational structure for services for the mentally handicapped. Criteria for admission into residential services could have been agreed. Funding according to the needs of the person with the disability rather than the negotiating skills of particular agencies could have been established. The uncoordinated and inefficient service which an exasperated Dr. Ramsay had drawn attention to as early as 1957, was allowed to survive in spite of various attempts to change it.

It is manifest that this pattern of funding does not ensure value for money. The direct funding of the larger agencies by the Department of Health had the effect of pushing the health boards off the mental handicap scene whilst the ultimate responsibility for the most difficult and dependent people remained with the boards. The extent of that responsibility was deliberately vague. The health boards knew nothing of those people with a mental handicap who were in the care of the directly funded voluntary agencies. The Voluntary Agencies selected those they wished to care for. The rest were left.

The establishment of co-ordinating committees and central planning committees in the early 1990s were notable attempts to square the circle that had been created by the thought patterns of a bygone age. Efforts have been made by the Department of Health in recent years to alleviate the worst effects of direct funding, notably in the Health Strategy document[3] where it is proposed to channel all funding through the Health Boards. It will be a long time before it makes any great difference to the relative positions of say a mentally handicapped person in a psychiatric hospital and a mentally handicapped person in the care of one of the large voluntary agencies. The advantage will still lie with the person partaking of the service run by the voluntary agency. There will be more therapies, more outings, more holidays, more of everything - except security.

There are people who feel threatened by the aspiration to "equitable distribution". Some people, not least parents of those people who are enjoying a generously funded service at present, do not want change. In the absence of legislation there is a limit to what a Department of State can do through patient persuasion. Until we prepare for it by open debate and discussion through which we can all clarify our values, no matter how much money we spend we can never have a rational, efficient and equitable service for the mentally disabled, particularly that section of people with a mental disability who are the subject of this book - the unselected.

Legislation for the effective delivery of services for the mentally handicapped is long overdue. Who now would say that there are "formidable constitutional difficulties in the way of the enactment of effective legislation" as the Minister for Health said all those long years ago. Whose rights was he thinking of, I wonder? The rights of the little mildly mentally handicapped children who were sent away to distant institutions never to come home again? The rights of the mentally handicapped who rotted their lives away in the back wards of the mental hospitals? The rights of those mentally handicapped who are now living with infirm and elderly parents because they had no statutory right to a service? There was little debate on these questions in 1957 when the question was asked. In those days certain people were presumed to know better than the rest of us, and as long as the control of the services, of which they rarely had any personal experience themselves, was consistent with passionately held theories, there was no further discussion. It is significant that the same people never voiced the slightest criticism of the way the State treated the people in the mental hospitals.

Monuments to a Kindlier Age

There was never any question of direct funding for the mental hospitals. They took their chance with the County Councils before the 1970 Health Act, competing for some share of rates. This was a guarantee in itself that there would be no risk of overgenerous contributions to the mental hospitals. Rates were a very emotional subject at the time and ratepayers were strongly represented even on the mental hospital boards. People were fully informed and probably had personal experience of the problems of ratepayers. They knew little or nothing of the problems of the people in the mental hospitals, but they did know that they were a burden on the rates. Not all the funding was left in local hands. The Department of Health took on responsibility for fifty per cent of the expense, but the local involvement provided a welcome brake on budgetary expenditure. The meaner the boards were the less had to be provided from central funds.

When it came to providing capital from the Hospital Trust Funds over which the Department had discretionary powers the mental hospitals lost out every time not only to the general hospitals but also, as we have seen, to the voluntary agencies engaged in services for the mentally handicapped. Virtually all the capital that went into the mental hospitals was put there by the British Government before this country achieved its independence and, however forbidding we might think them now, they are monuments to the generosity of a more philanthropic age. They were built at a time when custodial care was the only option for the care of the mentally disabled and they didn't skimp when it came to providing space. Long covered corridors provided places for exercise in bad weather. Like the old voluntary general hospitals they had high ceilings to dissipate the smells which were unavoidable at a time when sanitation had not yet progressed to the levels which we take for granted. Doors and windows were of excellent quality.

Dissipation of Assets

A clear indication of a more equitable attitude towards the mentally disabled at the time when the hospitals were established, was the size of the farms with which they were endowed. These were meant to be used for the benefit of the patients and were designed in part as a buffer against hard times when, for example, the rates might dry up. Of all the injustices imposed on the long-stay patients in our mental hospitals I think the dissipation of these assets was the most reprehensible. It happened in the 1960s when the Department was urging every mental hospital board in the country to get rid of their land, at the same time as they themselves were making grants of land to the voluntary bodies.

St. Ita's, Portrane, had 991 acres of land. The Board *gave away* most of it to the County Council. It would be quite wrong to expect the authorities in the 1960s to have foreseen how useful this land could have been later when the old buildings needed to be replaced or rebuilt in a manner suitable for a modern service. But why were the lands allowed to be given away without the slightest consultation with the people most concerned, or with any of their representatives? The received wisdom was that the land and its working had no therapeutic value for the patients, and that might very well be true. But the donations of land were not intended for therapeutic farming, no more than the land which was vested in Maynooth College or Carysfort College. The Department of Health put huge pressure on the mental hospital boards to get rid of their land in the 1960s. Consequently the mental hospitals, unlike the voluntary organisations which were endowed at very much the same time as the Department was putting pressure on the mental hospital boards, have lost realisable assets which could have been very useful in providing the necessary capital for a new up-dated service. Incidentally it is an interesting fact that a business man who bought some of the land at Santry Court in North Dublin which St. Ita's Hospital owned in addition to the 991 acres near the hospital in Portrane, has held it ever since. Presumably he is patiently waiting for a rezoning of these lands in the future. One is forced to the conclusion that the mental hospital authorities thought it was too much trouble to simply hold the land. They couldn't wait to divest themselves of it.

Notes on Chapter 10

1. In a written answer to a question by Deputy Eamon Gilmore regarding a lien on assets created by capital funding to voluntary agencies in the 1960s, 1970s and 1980s engaged in the provision of residential services for those with mental handicap, Mr. Brian Cowen, Minister for Health and Children, wrote as follows:

   "It was not the practice in the period referred to by the Deputy, to create a lien on assets where the capital funding was provided by the State for the provision of services for mentally handicapped persons and accordingly, the question of exercising any such lien does not arise".

2. Inspector of Mental Hospitals Report.

3. Shaping a healthier future. A strategy for effective healthcare in the 1990s. (Department of Health). Published by the Stationery Office.

11

GRAPPLING WITH THE INTRACTABLE

A working party set up by the Department of Health, to identify and advise the minister on the implementation of the Health Strategy in relation to persons with a mental handicap, entitled *"Enhancing the Partnership"*[1] sees the department relying traditionally on "the Commission/Working group/Task Force model as its favoured method of policy formulation". This claim may very well be entirely true but not in the way the working party intended to convey. Starting with the first Commission - the Commission of Inquiry on Mental Handicap - and continuing with each working party report and policy document since, they were endorsements of policies already in place - policies which had been evolved in private with little or no input from the Department. The Commission of Inquiry into Mental Handicap[2] endorsed residential homes for borderline and mildly handicapped children. It had been going on for years before.

A Fear of Formulating

The working party in 1980[3] agonised about misplacements and set up criteria for matching mental handicap population to appropriate settings but disclaimed the use of these criteria in the introduction to the document. It does, however, warmly endorse the newest policy which was already well under way - the establishment of hostels or houses located in residential areas.

None of these policies was formulated by the Department. The Department was merely a facilitator. No Minister for Health since 1948 and no government has ever been concerned with establishing an equitable policy for the disabled. This is not to say that they have not consistently worked for a larger share of the budget for people with disability, particularly the mentally handicapped. But no Minister has ever tried to change a policy where services for the mentally disabled are uneven in quality and sometimes altogether absent. The composition of these commissions/working groups invariably represented the interests of those with the lion's share of the funding. No Commission and no Working Party/Review Group has ever had a member specifically representing the interests of the excluded.

Nevertheless there have been hints in the most recent policy documents of at least some aspiration to a more just arrangement. For example *"Needs and Abilities"*[4], the report of a Review Group on mental handicap services set up by the Department of Health and which reported in 1990, mentioned "equity and efficiency" and concurred with the view that the services in Ireland "require major re-structuring". The political will to bring this about was another matter.

The idea of a two tier health service where people who are better off are able to buy themselves a better service than what would be available generally, is a familiar one. It is not an idea that we are very comfortable with, especially when a particular service is essential. The Commission on Health Funding[5] gave the income aspect of access to the health services a great deal of attention but the report did not identify the structure of the services for the mentally handicapped or the criteria for their funding nor the pattern of Government investment in services for the mentally disabled as a source of blatant discrimination. Equal access for equal need is not even an aspiration.

Ignoring the Inadequacies

If one doubts this, try examining the life experiences of a mentally handicapped person who also suffers from one of the more difficult conditions such as autism. Thirty years ago there was no support of any kind for the great majority of children with autism and to-day it is not much better. Children with autism had needs but because no agency would touch them, their needs were almost totally unmet. Children with multiple handicaps were similarly excluded for a long time. The disability had to fit into what the agencies wished to provide. If the agency did not wish to cater for that disability, the person with that disability did without. That is what happens when a government cedes control of a service to autonomous agencies. This fundamental flaw has been consistently overlooked by every Working Party and every Commission which attempted to deal with the inadequacies of a service for a group of people who are after all limited in their numbers. A possible exception in these exercises of obfuscation might be the most recent one, the Commission on the Status of People with Disability.

While the Report of the Commission on Health Funding did recognise that there were people with a mental handicap in special homes and psychiatric hospitals who would do much better outside them, their explanation for this misplacement was the tired old excuse of the lack of community services. If the lack of community services were the explanation, why was it that the ones most in need of support were the very ones not selected for residential care in the special homes? In 1990 there were almost 800 people with a mild mental handicap in residential care, the great majority in the care of long established voluntary agencies. The Commission on Health Funding had the benefit of an analysis of the cost effectiveness of alternative levels of care for different groups of mentally handicapped, which had been undertaken by an official at the Department of Finance at the request of the Department of Health in November 1986. Accordingly the Commission was able to recommend "that appropriate costs per place for particular levels of handicap and type of care setting should be established, and agencies providing care funded accordingly by the Executive Authority through its local management structure". This recommendation was similar to one made by Dr. John O'Connell in 1977 when he was the Labour Party spokesman on health. It was ignored then, and twelve years later it was ignored again. The Commission on Health Funding made its report in 1989. Ten years later little has changed. Allocations are not normally related to the numbers and levels of handicap of those served.

Cost Effectiveness

The 1986 study, which was also used as a basis for the report of the Review Group on mental handicap services entitled *"Needs and Abilities 1990"*, was concerned with a comparison of the cost-effectiveness of alternative levels of care for different groups of mentally handicapped. One of the issues examined was whether care in the community was cheaper or dearer than care in the special residential centres, or indeed in the psychiatric hospitals. The analyst concluded that community care was cheaper. Agencies had long ago moved in this direction and had already purchased houses near their centres. Many mildly handicapped people who had come to the residential centres years before were already living in these houses.

It was on this conclusion that the analyst based his strategy for a major restructuring of the mental handicap services in Ireland. He figured that if vacancies were created by the movement of some mentally handicapped out of the centres their places could be taken by a significant number of mentally handicapped people who could now move out of the psychiatric hospital to take up the vacant places. For those who would move from the psychiatric hospitals into community based residences he suggested local authority housing, or rented accommodation while using former psychiatric hospitals as day centres.

The whole plan hinged on the vacating of the special residential centres and the acceptance of the 800 or so people from the psychiatric hospitals. If the mentally handicapped were to be transferred from the centres to a "community setting", as it was described, houses would have to be bought. Capital would have to be found. The analyst discussed various possible sources of capital, ending with the traditional one. "The Department of Health should seek additional capital funding from the Department of Finance". The Department did and eventually got it. The purchase of houses by the voluntary agencies continued. Others had houses built for them on the campus of the original facility.

Once more a policy direction, decided on by the voluntary agencies, was endorsed by a government department. It is probably unlikely that it was intended to use the plight of the mentally handicapped in the mental hospitals to further this development but that is what happened. The voluntary agencies had decided some time before to disperse somewhat the concentrated accommodation in the special homes for the mentally handicapped. Their decision to do so had nothing to do with the situation in the mental hospitals. Any linking of the two was not theirs, but the linking did facilitate the provision of a greatly expanded funding. Needless to say the mentally handicapped in the mental hospitals didn't see a penny of it. The astonishing increase in the costs of these same voluntary agencies in the last decade can hardly be unconnected.

Lack of Co-operation

What seemed like a good plan to the 1986 analyst could not have succeeded without the full cooperation of the voluntary agencies. This cooperation was not forthcoming in 1986 in just the same way as it was not forthcoming in the 1960s when so often during Question Time in the Dáil, an embarrassed Minister would recite the list of Government investment in land and buildings for the provision of extra places for the mentally handicapped.

The policy document *"Needs and Abilities"*, further endorsed the policy of care in the community. The recommendations of the analyst when he recommended fundamental changes in the mental handicap services were adopted.

" This restructuring would require two major elements:
(a) the transfer of people with an intellectual disability from psychiatric hospitals to services for intellectually disabled persons;
(b) the transfer of suitable clients in services for the intellectually disabled from an institutional to a community setting".

Most people took this to mean that in the interests of equity and efficiency the two elements were necessary and that the achievement of (a) depended on the completion of (b). It seemed to make a good deal of sense.

It cannot be said however, that the recommendation received a great deal of prominence in the report. There was little discussion on how such an exercise could be carried out. One is forced to the conclusion that there was no real intention of changing anything. The whole exercise had little or no impact on the mentally handicapped in the psychiatric hospitals.

The Inspector of Mental Hospitals noted that little or no relationship existed between the voluntary services and those providing care for the mentally handicapped in Our Lady's Ennis, apart from an initial assessment undertaken by the Brothers of Charity service at Bawnmore. There had been tentative movement in Castlerea but it had quickly come to an end. The Brothers felt that they were not being given sufficient resources for the transfers. Arrangements to be made by St. Brigid's, Ballinasloe, with the Brothers of Charity at Kilcornan also foundered. On the other side of the country in Wexford the story was much the same. "There were 37 mentally handicapped patients in St. Senan's but there was little integration between the voluntary agencies, the St. John of God service or the health board and St. Senan's itself"[6].

Taken Out of the Picture

It was not because the mentally handicapped had transferred to services for the mentally handicapped that a reduction in the numbers of people with a mental handicap in psychiatric hospitals took place. Ever since the Commission of Inquiry into Mental Illness had completed its report in 1966 the numbers of long-stay patients had steadily decreased. In addition to those who left the psychiatric hospitals through natural causes there were those who didn't go anywhere but were now declared not to be in a psychiatric hospital anymore. This was done by a process known as "de-designation". This term was used by Dr. Browne in 1962 when he recommended that large numbers of mentally handicapped people be shunted to St. Ita's Hospital at Portrane, parts of which could then be "de-designated".

Certain wards would be set aside for the mentally handicapped or the elderly long-stay patients. These wards, which had always been designated as part of the psychiatric hospital, would be de-designated by the stroke of a pen. Large numbers were knocked off the total in this way. It happened in Youghal soon after patients (including long-stay psychiatric patients) had been moved there from Our Lady's in Cork. The psychiatric service continued to be responsible for St. Raphael's, however, but it dropped out the Reports of the Inspector of Mental Hospitals.

In the same way St. Loman's, Mullingar, "lost" up to 90 people with a mental handicap and St. Fintan's in Portlaoise adjusted their figures by 60. Over the whole country almost 300 mentally handicapped people "left" the psychiatric hospitals in this way, not counting the 226 or so in Youghal. The elderly too (if they hadn't died first) found themselves 'magicked' out of the figures by de-designation. The least that can be said about the practice of de-designation was that it was a highly misleading ploy. The de-designated did not change their place of residence nor their nurses. Their conditions did not differ materially from those of any other long-stay patients, except that they lost whatever protection the 1945 Mental Treatment Act afforded. For example, once de-designated they did not feature in any further Reports by the Inspector of Mental Hospitals.

What Happened to Them?

But it was the erosion of the number of long-stay patients of whatever category which made the publication and the composition of the policy document *"Planning for the Future"*[7] not only possible but timely. Since 1966, 18,606 people, mainly long-stay patients, had died in the psychiatric hospitals. It was now possible to talk about closing the hospitals. True there remained approximately 11,741 but there had been a steady decrease in numbers since the peak year of 1959. As ever, the awkward obstacle which stood in the way of cleared, valuable (sometimes very valuable) sites was the long-stay patients. At the time that the report was made about 40 per cent of existing long-stay patients were over 65 years of age which meant that 60 per cent were not. In the fourteen years which have passed since 1984 what kind of a life did these people have? What kind of a state were their hospitals in? What happened to them? We know that in that time many have died, but in what conditions? How did they compare with those of Clonmel in 1959? What effect did "Planning for the Future" have on their lives?

As recommended by the report in paragraph 16.4, a committee established for the purpose at St. Brigid's, Ballinasloe, carried out a survey of long-stay patients in the hospital. The Committee found in its report the startling reality that had been obscured for years. The task of implementing the recommendations of Planning for the Future even in broad outline was overwhelming.

The investment which the Western Health Board would be required to make was enormous. Ballinasloe was a large hospital with a large number of long-stay patients, but the situation there was representative of the situation in many of the hospitals in the country. The implications for the national budget were staggering:

"The re-habilitation and re-training of large numbers of long-term institutional patients will require costly re-training and redeployment of existing staff, leaving aside the costs accruing from the relocation of the patients in the community and the expenditure on recruitment of ancillary staff".

It was impossible.

The years which followed 1984 were years of grave financial stringency. There were two options open to the Health Boards in attempting to implement the plans for the future of the psychiatric hospitals. The first was to make use of well disposed voluntary associations such as the Mental Health Association of Ireland and its branches to help the hospital to procure some houses. This was a slow process and pitifully inadequate despite the very best efforts of the Association. One has only to compare the housing stock which the large directly-funded agencies were able to purchase since the 1980s with that which the Health Boards were able to put together for their long-stay patients during the same period, to realise how inadequate it was.

The second option was to rely on the mortality rates to empty the hospitals for them. This was the option taken. It was quite successful but not so effective as was expected. For example, in appendix 4, the report sets out its predictions for the reduction by death of the long-stay patients in St. Ita's Hospital, Portrane. According to their calculations there should now be 107 long-stay psychiatric patients in St. Ita's. There are in fact 185, not counting the 48 or so in the admission unit which long since, was confidently expected to be located at the new hospital at Beaumont.

In one respect at least the predictions of the Study Group on the Development of the Psychiatric Services was totally accurate:

"It is accepted that many of the mentally handicapped persons at present in psychiatric hospitals will continue to depend on the psychiatric services for care throughout their lives......The general shortage of places for adults within the mental handicap services will also make it difficult to relocate any significant number of mentally handicapped residents from psychiatric hospitals".

Forgotten Places

The study group which had produced *"Planning for the Future"* had warned that "psychiatric hospitals (and their long-stay patients?) should not become forgotten places". The Green Paper on Mental Health[8], was primarily interested in the numbers of long-stay patients who were still alive and in how their numbers might be reduced rather than how those still living at the hospitals were managing. Those people who prepared the Green Paper were mightily impressed by the number of hostels which the psychiatric hospitals had managed to establish. Considering the paucity of capital funding which was made available to the psychiatric hospitals by the Department of Health they were right to be impressed. The total number of patients accommodated in these community based residences in 1992 was 2,441 - well short of the total number of long-stay patients. The total number of psychiatric patients in the public psychiatric hospitals on December 31st 1992, was 6,130, not counting 294 mentally handicapped people who had been de-designated and 578 elderly patients also de-designated. Add in the 200 or so in St. Raphael's, Youghal and the total figure was approximately 7,202 still living out their lives in far from ideal conditions.

And had the Psychiatric Hospitals become forgotten places? A few extracts from the 1992 Report of the Inspector of Mental Hospital's[9]:

".....the absence of laundry facilities at..........had impeded the development of a personal clothing programme for long-stay patients".

".......the overall environment of the long-stay block, Block 1, did little to respect the dignity of individual patients".

".......we were told that it took three to four days to replace a light bulb".

"the lack of curtains around beds was a major problem".

"an activity stimulation programme was urgently needed as many active patients remained all day in their units".

"The poor state of decoration in many wards gave a run down appearance to the hospital".

"We noted there was no psychologist or speech therapist employed in this service".

"The portacabin which had been erected twenty years previously had deteriorated with rotting floors, leaking roofs and leaking windows". (This portacabin was part of a facility into which elderly long-stay patients from the public psychiatric hospitals had been moved.)

"many patients were unoccupied, either sitting in the day rooms or lying on beds".

"overcrowding in the sleeping areas".

"In our view the physical state of four of the male wards......were unacceptable".

"the number of wards which were locked was excessive".

There were, of course, many developments which delighted the Inspector's heart particularly if they were developments which could hasten the day when the old institutions could be pulled down, when all the long-stay patients had departed.

In subsequent reports the Inspector of Mental Hospitals has been unremitting in his criticisms. For example he wrote of St. Ita's, Portrane:

"Units F, G and K..... unsatisfactory..... it was disappointing to note that absolutely no progress had been made to upgrade or relocate patients from these facilities...."

In 1995 he wrote of the same hospital:

"Sixteen of the wards were locked".

In 1996 he wrote:

"....The overall physical standards of decor, furniture, fittings and hygiene at unit K were unsatisfactory....."

The plans revealed in *"Planning for the Future"* have been truly long-term. In the years since 1984 the most significant development has been the relentless decay of the old mental hospitals. Too often they have crumbled away whilst still inhabited by the long-stay patients, whether mentally handicapped, geriatric or mentally ill.

Notes on Chapter 11

1. Enhancing the Partnership. Report of the Working Group on the implementation of the health strategy in relation to persons with a mental handicap.
2. Commission of Inquiry on Mental Handicap Report 1965.
3. Services for the Mentally Handicapped. Report of a Working Party 1980. Stationery Office.
4. Needs and Abilities. A policy for the Intellectually Disabled 1990. Stationery Office.
5. Report of the Commission on Health Funding 1989. Stationery Office.
6. The St John of God service mentioned here refers to the services provided by the Sisters of St. John of God, not those provided by the Brothers of St. John of God in other health board areas.
7. Planning for the Future. Report of a study group on the development of the Psychiatric services. Published in 1984. Stationery Office.
8. Green Paper on Mental Health. Department of Health 1992. Stationery Office.
9. Inspector of Mental Hospitals' Report. 1992.

12

A SAD REFLECTION!

The determination not to repeat the mistakes of the past is one of the most potent forces for improvement in the government of a country. For this force to be effective it is first of all necessary to acknowledge that mistakes were made. There is little evidence, so far as the mentally disabled are concerned, that people in government or out of it have done so in Ireland. The reaction of the general public is not encouraging either. Ireland is not the only country where the mentally disabled have been mistreated, sometimes abominably, and when news of the abuses in other countries reaches us there is often a smugness in the way it is received which is not attractive.

A Political Ritual

In 1977 when Dr. O'Connell put forward his Private Member's Bill (Grants for Mentally Handicapped), Mr. Barry Desmond[1] who joined with his colleague in initiating the debate, reminded the house that it was the first time since 1969 that the Dáil had devoted an exclusive debate to the mental handicap services. In 1977 the debate was something of a novelty. It received little or no media attention. Since that time, every couple of years or so, a member of the opposition proposes a motion deploring the situation of people with a mental handicap. Worthy speeches are made and the process has almost become a ritual. The Minister responds by pointing out the vast amounts of money that are being spent on the services. Promises are made. Two evenings are devoted to the mentally handicapped, watched anxiously by worried parents in the visitors' gallery. The Bill is routinely defeated. Life goes on. Nothing changes. Certainly nothing changes as a result of Parliamentary activity.

This is a profoundly disillusioning fact and should worry us all. Political representatives who are sometimes swamped by the demands made on them by distressed constituents do not seem to see it as part of their function to put together efficient and equitable policies. When approached, they will work very hard to help a particular constituent in a distressing and unjust situation. They will muster as much influence as they can manage to persuade some service provider to come up with a placing. They are, in the main, sympathetic and helpful and usually well informed.

Over the years several public representatives have made valuable contributions to debates on the mental handicap services and services for the mentally ill. Dr. John O'Connell was exceptionally well informed in 1977, as were Mr. Barry Desmond and Dr. Rory O'Hanlon. Mr. John Boland's contribution too was remarkable. His contribution to the debate on the Health (Mental Services) Bill 1980[2] were even more important. What is interesting at this stage is that every one of those named - Mr. Barry Desmond, Mr. John Boland, Dr. Rory O'Hanlon and Dr. John O'Connell - later became Minister for Health. None effected any real change. The political parties to which each belonged made no effort to develop policy either in Government or out of it. Services for the mentally ill receive even less attention from the Dáil. It is nothing less than a scandal that there has been no effective legislation since 1945. The Health (Mental Treatment) Act of 1980 was never implemented.

Failure to Face Up to the Problem

In 1980 when the Health (Mental Services) Bill was in its second stage, Mr. John Boland gave as clear an account of what was wrong with the services at the time as was possible. It was far superior to any that a working party, the preferred option of the Department, could come up with and was a much better contribution than that of the Minister. In the course of his speech he cites the glaring omissions in the Bill, namely the failure to mention the numbers of mentally handicapped in psychiatric hospitals, the absence of any legislation which would give a right to treatment and care for either the psychiatrically ill or the mentally handicapped, the failure to deal with the standards of physical facilities or their provision, and the abolition of the office of the Inspector of Mental Hospitals and the publication of his reports.

139

On the 16th October 1980 Mr. Boland made a claim which should not be overlooked:

"The onus is on the legislature to provide for the rights of the individual, especially in relation to the mentally handicapped, who are least able to ensure their right to treatment and care. This Minister has decided not to face up to that problem".

That Minister did not face up to the problem. Neither did any Minister since. No political party has ever adopted an equitable policy as an aim although some have pushed hard for more funding for all the service providers. But no legislation has ever been presented to the Dail by any Government which would rationalise the whole process of entitlement. This is a pity, for apart from any other benefit the preparatory discussion might clarify our values.

False Perceptions

We are fond of condemning past generations for their hypocrisy particularly the Victorians. This is somewhat ungenerous of us considering that it was the Victorians who left us so many hospitals, not only the mental hospitals but also the large general hospitals such as Jervis Street and the Richmond. When these hospitals, mental and general, needed to be replaced we removed the general hospitals into new purpose-built modern hospital premises. The mental hospitals we leave to decay, sometimes pretending that they are already closed, with several hundred people still living in them. It is possible that members of the Dail think that serious mental illness is a thing of the past. The perception is not accidental. The propagation of the all-embracing virtues of community care through the use of new and improved psychotropic drugs would appear to be a policy decision by administrators. It should not go unquestioned. It is time that every aspect of the welfare of the mentally disabled was debated, preferably in the Dáil.

Outside the psychiatric hospitals, people with a mental handicap who are in residential care are not covered by the Mental Health Act 1945. Outdated and defective as it is, the act affords some safeguards for the welfare of a person with a mental disability. Without it there are no inspectors, no visiting

140

committees, no statutory monitoring. Some of the new institutions, even the smaller community-based residences, are just as closed as the old institutions. By now we should be alert to the dangers of closed institutions particularly for the vulnerable. It is difficult to define what rights people in such a situation are able to exercise.

Discrimination Formalised

In the absence of any real debate on the obligations of the strong towards the weak and on how the state should be involved in these obligations, it is inevitable that a vague confusion of mixed motives should surround the whole area. In this climate Departments of State do odd things.

At the time of writing, the Department of Health is about to implement the transfer of the direct funding of the fourteen voluntary mental handicap agencies to the Health Boards. This change has already begun in two health board areas. This in itself is a very good thing. Direct funding with all its possibilities of cosy relationships is not the way to achieve an equitable service, and most people who are not part of the charmed circle will be glad to see the end of it.

But in order to arrive at an agreement and in order to persuade the voluntary agencies concerned that their priveleged position is in fact unchanged, the discrimination which has always existed is now written into the proposed statutory changes. The voluntary agencies will have first call on any funds. Moreover their input on future development of services out of which their own contracts will arise, is designed to be dominant. In these circumstances the services in the direct control of the health boards are unlikely to develop.

The Commission on the Status of People with Disabilities which published its report at the end of 1996, recommended that every person with a disability should have an Assessment of Needs underpinned by law. It should lead to a Statement of Needs. The person with the disability, be it a physical or mental disability, should have a copy of this statement of needs. The person with the disability or his /her family should then be able to acquire the service and supports he/she needs. If the

141

government were to adopt such a system it should cut out inappropriate placings. Because services would develop on a basis of unmet needs, funding could be redirected towards the meeting of these needs whilst recognising the difference between needs and wants.

It is unlikely that the Commission's recommendations will ever be implemented as regards the mentally handicapped. Instead in every health board region the needs addressed will be the needs (or wants) which the voluntary agencies will be willing to address. The service contracts will be tailored to the wishes of the voluntary agencies. Any negotiations which might take place will be between the voluntary agencies. Once again those people with a mental handicap whom the voluntary agencies don't want will be left out of the loop.

Why This Neglect?

In the first chapter of this book there is an account of how the Reports of the Inspector of Mental Hospitals were not published for thirteen years. Of all the indignities heaped on the mentally disabled by our state this was the most insulting of all. For thirteen years their very existence was forgotten by the highest in the land. The law which was designed to prevent such a thing happening was not effective. Future legislation must be framed in such a way that a repetition of disregard of that kind would be impossible.

But before we prepare such legislation, I think we must face one or two questions. What is in our culture that leads us to place them at the bottom of the heap of the disadvantaged? What is in our culture that makes us decide time after time to keep them there?[3]

The very first time an independent parliament met in January 1919, the Dáil declared its intention of "abolishing the present odious, degrading, and foreign poor law system, substituting therefore a sympathetic native scheme for the care of the nation's aged and infirm"[4]. All in all that is what the new state did. The workhouses which were so distasteful even when the country was famine-stricken are long since gone. Between 1921 and 1925, most of the workhouses were closed. Some were converted into District and County Hospitals and some were converted into

County Homes.

Over the next few decades these hospitals and homes received far more attention than ever the mental hospitals did. In 1949 the Minister visited a number of County Homes and was "greatly shocked by the unsatisfactory state of the buildings and the primitive conditions under which the inmates are in many cases maintained"[5]. He immediately approached the Government for their approval for his application to the Department of Finance for a grant of 70 per cent of the cost of improvements to County Homes. Gradually over the years the County Homes improved mainly by excluding from their care the unmarried mothers, their children, and the mentally handicapped. New arrangements were made for the unmarried mothers and their children which were to involve the Government in extra expenditure. There was no mention of any extra expenditure to enable the mentally handicapped residents to be cared for elsewhere. Presumably they were simply removed to the mental hospitals.

The State invested heavily in the general hospitals during the 1950s and the 1960s, at the same time grant aiding the voluntary system. All this laudable activity was in stark contrast to the treatment which was thought affordable for the long-stay patients in the mental hospitals.

In the late 1950s towns were proud of their hospitals. Every Sunday they were thronged by the visiting relatives of the patients and every day there was constant coming and going. During those same years the mental hospitals stood lonely and unvisited, their isolation reflecting the rejection of their inmates by families and friends. It was a rejection that went deep into our society - as high as the President of the High Court.

Many thousands have died in the mental hospitals since that first year when the Dail and the Senate and the President of the High Court ceased to pay any attention to reports on their conditions. It is right that we should remember them. For those people who died, well within living memory, in Clonmel and Ballinasloe, in Castlebar and Portrane, in Cork and Grangegorman, the only fitting memorial would be the determination that such a state of affairs should never happen again.

Notes on Chapter 12

1. Parliamentary Debates. Dáil Éireann. November 30, 1977. Col 492.
2. Parliamentary Debates. Dáil Éireann. Health (Mental Services) Bill 1980. Cols 169-202.
3. This question was put slightly differently to the representatives of St. Joseph's Association for the Mentally Handicapped when they members of the Economic, Social and Cultural Rights at the pre-sessional hearing in Geneva on December 7, 1998. The question put then was: "What is in Irish culture that makes the country so cruel to the mentally disabled?"
4. Dorothy McArdle. The Irish Republic (page 275).
5. Department of Health. Memorandum for Government. Department of the Taoiseach files S.

INDEX

Nevin, Mr. Donal. 10.

Ó Caoimh, E. 104.
O'Connell, Dr. John. 55. 85. 86. 91. 129. 138. 139.
O'Connell, Mrs Helen. 80.
O'Connor, Dr. Jack. 80.
O'Clerihan, Mr C. 66.
O'Donnell, Dr. Brendan. 76.
O'Donovan, Mr. and Mrs. 76.
Offaly Mentally Handicapped Association. 77.
O'Hanlon, Dr. Rory. 139.
O'Higgins, Mr. T.F. 43. 44.
O'Malley, Mr. Donagh. 33. 52.
O'Reilly, Garda Sergeant Pat. 77.
Our Lady's in Cork. 35. 81. 89. 90. 132.
Our Lady's Ennis. 131.

Peamount. 115.
Planning for the Future. 9. 133. 135 - 137.
Portlaoise. 16. 132.
Portrane.13. 14. 17 - 21. 33. 40. 41. 67. 70. 72. 81.
90 - 100. 103. 104. 106 - 110. 114. 125. 126. 132.
134. 136. 143. 149
Power, Dr. 71.
President of the High Court. 1. 2. 143.

Quinn, Dean. 77.

RTE. 78.
Ramsay, Dr. 24. 26 - 32. 35. 36. 38. 40. 48. 49. 65. 70. 98. 123.
Reeves, Dr. 77.
Religious Orders. 12. 45 -51. 53. 55. 63. 68. 116. 117. 120. 121.
Resident Medical Superintendents. (R. M. S.). 18. 20. 22. 23. 25.
28. 32. 36. 38. 40. 41. 48. 53. 56. 70. 71. 80.
Reynolds, J.F. 104.
Robins, Dr. Joseph. 97.
Roscommon Herald. 50.
Ryan, Dr. Jim. 43. 44.

APPENDIX 1

Showing the area of land associated with each District and Auxiliary Mental Hospital and how it was utilised during the year ended 31st December, 1956.

Mental Hospital	Tilled			In Grass			Occupied by Buildings, Courts, Woods etc.			Total Area		
	A.	R.	P.	A.	R.	P.	A.	R.	P.	A.	R.	P.
Ardee	91	0	32	212	3	8	30	3	0	334	3	0
Ballinasloe	115	0	0	230	0	0	245	0	0	590	0	0
Carlow	181	0	0	255	0	37	46	2	30	482	3	27
Castlebar	54	0	0	199	1	18	16	0	0	269	1	18
Clonmel	98	0	0	219	3	30	30	0	0	347	3	30
Cork	130	0	0	51	0	0	39	0	0	220	0	0
Youghal	42	0	0	61	0	0	9	0	0	112	0	0
Ennis	58	0	0	190	0	0	23	1	21	271	1	21
Enniscorthy	122	0	0	130	0	0	42	0	0	294	0	0
Grangegorman	6	0	0	5	2	0	50	0	21	61	2	21
do. (Portrane)	289	0	0	526	2	31	175	2	35	991	1	26
do (Santry Court)	2	0	0	115	0	0	107	0	0	224	0	0
Kilkenny	121	0	0	195	0	0	34	1	23	350	1	23
Killarney	97	0	0	91	0	0	16	0	0	204	0	0
Letterkenny	* 80	0	0	85	0	0	87	0	0	*252	0	0
Limerick	180	0	0	540	0	0	30	0	0	750	0	0
Monaghan	134	0	0	47	0	0	34	0	0	215	0	0
Mullingar	82	2	0	302	0	4	80	0	0	464	2	4
Portlaoise	141	1	0	216	2	16	9	2	23	367	1	39
Sligo	109	0	0	239	0	0	73	0	26	421	0	26
Waterford	141	2	11	206	2	19	19	2	38.5	367	3	28.5
Gross Totals	2,274	2	3	4,118	3	3	1,198	2	17.5	7,591	3	23.5

* Includes 3 acres rented to Letterkenny Urban District Council

APPENDIX 2

[handwritten annotation: Decision. To note. Canon Buckle already knows all the answers! Mr Kelvin's Letter of thanks]

Parochial House,
Bantry,
Co. Cork.
18th Nov. 1960

A Dune a cara,

I gladly accept your kind invitation to me to act as a member of the Commission of Inquiry which you propose to set up to examine the various questions concerning the care, training and ultimate settlement and socialization of the mentally - handicapped

One very encouraging feature which has emerged during the work of my own Association in Cork is the presence of an almost unlimited fund of good-will, for the solution of the problems, amongst all classes and creeds of the citizens. It seems to me that this good-will can be used most effectively by encouraging Voluntary Institutions and Associations to undertake the work. This will be the most effective way also of keeping at the desired minimum the calls upon Public and State funds.

My own Association too has explored to some extent the question of sheltered employment for the adult mentally-handicapped who have received training. The response of the employers to our enquiries in this matter have been very encouraging also. There is a good deal of simple repetitive work, for example, in the Sunbeam Hosiery factory in Cork and the Directors there are willing to co-operate with my Association to provide a special building in which this work could be done under our supervision. This would involve a considerable amount of preliminary training. It seems to us that that training might be accomplished largely with the aid of the local Vocational Committee.

Once more accept my thanks for your invitation. Both I myself & my Association will do all in our power to help the work of the Commission of Enquiry.

Sincerely Yours

J. Canon Bastible

Seán Uasal MacEntee
Áras Sláinze
Glá Cliat

WALLS OF SILENCE